Council on
Social Work Education

Its Antecedents and First Twenty Years

Katherine A. Kendall

Council on Social Work Education
Alexandria, Virginia

Library of Congress Cataloging-in-Publication Data

Kendall, Katherine A., 1910-
  Council on Social Work Education : its antecedents and first twenty
years / Katherine A. Kendall.
      p. cm.
Includes bibliographical references and index.
  ISBN 0-87293-090-4
  1. Council on Social Work Education—History. 2. Social work
education—United States—History. I. Title.
  HV11.7 .K45 2002
  361.3'071'073—dc21
                                    2002000370

Contents

Foreword

A bit of controversy goes a long way in making a story more interesting or compelling. An author might be tempted to inject a bit of it in a historical work to pique the reader's interest, to stir things up. Fortunately for Katherine Kendall, the Council on Social Work Education's inception and early years came already spiced with confrontation between groups, so no embellishment was necessary. But as we learn in this history of the Council, these protagonists would resolve their differences not through battles but through cooperation.

The confrontation that was catalyst for the Council's formation in 1952 was also its firmest foundation. While opposing camps differed in their views of what defined social work education and what constituted professional preparation, they saw the benefit to themselves and to the profession in uniting. The union behind a commonly held purpose brought the goals of undergraduate and graduate programs of social work education together, but in doing so, neither group's beliefs were ultimately subsumed nor dissipated. It became a union of sometimes competing views, and its decisions were made stronger for having been forged in debate.

These first decades of the Council, as described in the words of many of the people who were there, tell a story of a profession claiming its status and capitalizing on the strength of its varied beliefs. The competition between the National Association of Schools of Social Administration and the American Association of Schools of Social Work for control of accreditation resulted in an organization that could rightfully define the standards for social work education for the entire profession, securing the Council's important role as the sole accrediting body.

Today the profession deals with its own disagreements and struggles between constituencies, some of which touch on the same issues of accreditation control and curriculum the Council's founders faced. These struggles help mirror and maintain the dynamic, evolving environment of our profession.

Our ability to grapple with current interorganizational conflicts can be meliorated by understanding the issues confronting our forebears and how they were resolved. No one is better positioned to provide us with that understanding than Katherine Kendall. Dr. Kendall was not only a participant in much of the history described herein, she has employed her considerable scholarly talents to give us a well-researched and carefully documented account. This book joins a long list of major contributions she has made to the Council since its inception—as staff member; executive director; author of innumerable Council reports, concept papers, articles, and books; consultant; board member; benefactor; advisor; and loyal friend. Her work in curriculum development, for example, was central to the Council's early curriculum policy statements and provides the foundation for much of the current structure and content of social work education. Similarly, her international work helped give social work education in the United States a global perspective and, thereby, enrich and be enriched by social work education throughout the world. The Council's Board of Directors join me in expressing our deep appreciation to Dr. Kendall for making yet another invaluable contribution to the Council in particular and to social work education generally. Her unique insights into the Council's early struggles better equip us and our successors to meet those that confront us today and in the future.

Donald W. Beless
Executive Director
Council on Social Work Education

Acknowledgments

It is not often that one gets a chance to relive twenty rewarding years of a long professional life. Writing this history has made it possible for me, but it could not have happened without a great deal of assistance. The idea of a history of the birth of the Council on Social Work Education grew out of my annual orientation presentations to the Board of Directors. Don Beless urged me to record what I remembered from my years of service in the Council's educational program and as executive director. To lure me out of retirement and bolster my memory with hard facts, he gave me an office at the Council with access to the Master Files, where I experienced again the joys and struggles of the early years. Throughout the production of this chronicle, he has been a major source of both moral and practical support for which I am profoundly grateful. Special thanks must also be extended to Norma Molter of the Council staff for picking me up on her way to work for many months and to Michael Monti for performing a miracle in editing the book and getting it ready in time for the Council's fiftieth anniversary celebration.

The Social Welfare Archives at the University of Minnesota offers the most extensive and detailed records of the Council and its antecedents. From several visits there, I found material not available elsewhere, and I wish to thank Curator David Klaassen for his always gracious assistance. I owe a tremendous debt of gratitude to Joe Schriver of the University of Arkansas at Fayetteville, who made available to me a veritable bonanza of material about the National Association of Schools of Social Administration that he had collected from the Social Welfare Archives for his own research. I couldn't have managed without it.

Finally, I must again express my appreciation to the Library of Congress where I was readmitted to the Scholar's Program to make use of their unmatched collection of material. The journals, books, and articles covering the early history of social work education, together with all that happened in the two decades before and after the formation of the Council, brought to life the events that are described in this historical account. Putting it all together has been a deeply satisfying experience for which I am grateful to all who have helped along the way.

Part One

Council on Social Work Education: Its Antecedents

Chapter One
Setting the Stage

The Council on Social Work Education was launched on January 28, 1952, as a result of a profession-wide effort to resolve an educational conflict. It began operations on July 1 of that same year. In the process of a troubled decade of gestation, confrontation gave way to cooperation around a central, commonly held purpose—the promotion and improvement of social work education as a concern of the total profession. How it all came about presents a fascinating picture of the evolution of social work as a profession and the significance of the internal and external influences that shaped its development. Because the story requires more than a simple recounting of events, the stage will first be set and the actors introduced.

In most accounts of the controversy leading to the formation of the Council, undergraduate programs of social work education are pitted against and seen as victims of oppression by the graduate schools of social work. Kernels of truth to that effect abound in this picture, but it is by no means so simple or that complete. There are other important actors on the stage, including the practice community as represented by the several membership organizations in operation at the time, the voluntary agencies (particularly family welfare societies), the federal agencies (especially the Children's Bureau and the Bureau of Public Assistance), university administrators, and several accrediting bodies.

Sadly missing is an understanding of the inevitability, in the light of their historical beginnings, of the conflict between the undergraduate and graduate proponents of social work education. There is a marked difference in the origin of graduate education as represented by the American Association of Schools of Social Work and undergraduate preparation for social work as represented by the National Association of Schools of Social

Administration. Different purposes were espoused and different paths were followed to reach their specified goals. Within a historical context, it is possible to see that each association was right according to its beliefs and aspirations for the profession.

To come to that understanding, however, it is necessary to look closely at the unfolding of the conflict and its ultimate transformation into shared participation in the launching of the Council on Social Work Education. The words of the people who were there and deeply involved in the process will be used, to the extent possible, to tell the story.

THE MAJOR PLAYERS

The American Association of Schools of Social Work, hereafter referred to as AASSW. Seventeen schools launched the Association of Training Schools for Professional Social Work in July 1919. During this period, most schools were sponsored by private social agencies and located in or near urban areas. In 1937, the association (now known as AASSW) voted to limit membership to graduate schools only, effective in 1939. Until that date, programs were admitted that included undergraduate as well as graduate education.

The National Association of Schools of Social Administration, hereafter referred to as NASSA. Eleven representatives of sociology and social work programs in state universities met in Dallas, Texas, in April 1942 to organize what became NASSA. Motivated by the AASSW decision to require graduate education for social work, the University of Oklahoma began in 1937 to mobilize other state-supported universities in opposition to what it regarded as a misguided action. Under the Social Security Act's burgeoning welfare services there was an urgent need to prepare workers in social work. NASSA saw this as a call for expansion rather than restriction of educational opportunities.

The American Association of Social Workers, hereafter referred to as AASW. As the major, although not the only, organization of social work practitioners, the AASW exerted considerable influence on the development of professional education through its development of standards for membership. Launched in 1921 as an outgrowth of a placement service known as the National Social Workers' Exchange, it was preceded by the American Association of Medical Social Workers in 1918 and the American Association of Visiting Teachers (later the American Association of School Social Workers) in 1919 and followed by the American Association of Psychiatric Social Workers in 1926. All were involved, along with certain other newly organized practitioner groups, in founding the Council on Social Work Education.

The Federal Agencies. The training needs for the public social services that the Social Security Act established or expanded led a number of the federal agencies to become directly involved in the competition between undergraduate and graduate programs of social work education. It fell to the Children's Bureau and the Bureau of Public Assistance, however, to take the leading roles. Katharine Lenroot, chief of the Children's Bureau, emerged as the major player in the beginning scenes, with Jane Hoey, chief of the Bureau of Public Assistance, taking over that role in the final act and outcome of the controversy.

The Accrediting Bodies. The accrediting function loomed large as a bone of contention in the struggle for control of the educational arm of the profession. The AASSW was the acknowledged accrediting body for social work education until 1943 when NASSA was granted recognition as an accrediting body by the National Association of State Universities and the Association of Land-Grant Colleges and State Universities. Their regulatory authority covered undergraduate education plus one year of graduate education leading to an M.A. or M.S. degree. The resulting confusion led to a suspension in 1947 of all accrediting activity in the field of social work education until some accommodation could be reached by the two competing associations.

The National Council on Social Work Education, hereafter referred to as NCSWE. This was the temporary organization that brought together in 1947 all the interested parties involved in working out a solution to the problems related to the academic level of professional education and its accrediting authority. NCSWE undertook as its major charge a comprehensive study of social work education, mobilizing the entire profession in its planning and implementation.

With the major players now on stage, the dramatic ebb and flow of events that took place in the several decades prior to the launching of the Council can be described.

DIFFERENT WORLDS AND DIFFERENT ROOTS

At the heart of the struggle lies a marked difference in the backgrounds and objectives of the two groups. The graduate schools of social work, as represented by AASSW, were descended directly from the training programs for volunteers and salaried workers launched by the Community Organization Society (COS) in London in 1890 and in New York in 1898.[1]

Private Agencies and Casework Practitioners

The first schools in the United States were established not by educational institutions but by practitioners in private social agencies. Their primary interest was to produce practitioners who were better prepared to work with individuals and families, using casework as a special kind of helping relationship. With practice as a central concern, casework in the classroom and supervised practice in the field became, and for many years remained, the hallmark of American social work education.

In the early years, the teachers came from the social agencies, often on a part-time arrangement, and to a large extent the agencies determined the content of the educational programs. In a 1942 report on *Education for the Social Services*, sponsored by the AASSW, it was stated:

> the first schools grew out of the interest of social agencies in securing
> personnel better equipped for agency responsibilities. Thus the focus of
> agency objectives emerged in these programs. As the schools were affili-
> ated with universities, the more general character of the educational pro-
> cess was established. Yet, at intervals, pressure from the agencies for greater
> and greater attention to their specific needs has been intensified.[2]

At the time of the events leading to the formation of the Council, Ben Youngdahl, president of the AASSW in 1948, also noted:

> Even as late as 1935, when the Social Security Act was passed, about two-thirds of all the accredited schools were private. We have built up a system of field work geared to specialized needs and specialized agencies in large cities.[3]

It is understandable, then, that the member schools of AASSW were largely engaged in producing qualified staff skilled in social casework for the private agencies. The faculty members, full-time and part-time, recruited from the private agencies inevitably influenced what was taught in the educational programs. Karl de Schweinitz notes the impact of these factors on the attitude of many qualified social workers:

> The system, the nucleus of the knowledge and skill that later expanded into social casework, not only had its initial identification with the voluntary services but was based on a denial of the efficacy of public efforts to deal with the problem of poverty. In charity organization doctrine, resort to tax funds for relief was evidence of failure to the person who had undertaken to help him. There was something shameful for everybody in public assistance.[4]

It is essential to add that there were notable exceptions: Grace Browning reflected the experience of certain schools when she wrote in 1944:

> Outstanding have been a few farsighted schools which from their inception have fought vigorously for the establishment of public welfare agencies and whose graduates have furbished the shock troops of public service.[5]

She went on to say that, fortunately, there had been a change in the previous decade as schools of social work began to direct their attention to the importance of public welfare as a social work field of practice. Edith Abbott, dean of the School of Social Service Administration at the University of Chicago, emerged early as a champion of public welfare as a basic area of study and practice in social work. Even prior to the passage of the Social Security Act, she declared in no uncertain terms:

> There are no more fundamental or basic subjects of study for our
> profession than public welfare administration, social legislation, in-
> cluding statute law and court decisions bearing upon the major prob-
> lems of social work and methods of research. Must these always be
> referred to, slightingly, as "background courses?"[6]

No matter what the field of practice and despite the development of group
work and community organization, casework along with collateral courses continued to be the preferred area of interest for students. It remained the primary
subject of instruction in both class and field. Social work education, in all its
aspects, however, was becoming more theory-oriented and to a greater extent
research based. Casework, in particular, through incorporation of psychoana-
lytic theory, was becoming more demanding, sophisticated, and professional.
Nevertheless, what was regarded as progress toward ever higher professional
standards by the graduate schools led to what was described by one of the
leaders as "a revolt" by the undergraduate programs in the land-grant colleges
and state universities against the over-emphasis on casework and neglect of
public welfare to the detriment of the profession.

Public Service—Its Responsibilities and Opportunities

The group of university administrators and undergraduate representatives that met in Dallas in April 1942 to launch a new approach to social
work training lost no time in establishing what was designated as NASSA.
The Joint Committee on Accrediting of the Association of Land-Grant
Colleges and Universities, and the National Association of State Universities also moved quickly to give official recognition to the new association.
Chaired by the president of Florida State University, one of the strongest
supporters of the movement, the Accrediting Committee in 1944 formally
recognized NASSA as an accrediting agency in social work. The constitution adopted in that year listed its purpose as training

> persons for service and administration in such fields as the following:
> (1) employment service, unemployment compensation, and old age
> insurance; (2) recreation service [youth services and group work were

later added to this entry]; (3) rural social welfare programs; (4) personnel work and guidance programs to meet current and future needs in
government service, industrial service, and in the guidance programs of
universities, colleges and secondary schools; and (5) public assistance,
to provide trained personnel to administer old age assistance, aid to the
blind, aid to dependent children, and general relief programs. This will
include training in social case work, social group work, community organization, and social statistics and research.[7]

This was a large order for a newly organized association of what, in the
main, were undergraduate courses grouped as a major in a social science
department, most often a department of sociology. A fifth year, with a
social work major and social science minor leading to a master's degree,
was projected, but ultimately offered by relatively few members of NASSA.
As new members were gathered in, separate departments were recommended
and established in some of the colleges and universities in the association.

Commitment to the social sciences as an essential base for professional
education for social work, plus determination to staff large segments of
public service, created its own world of expectations and responsibilities. In
that world, preparation for a broad array of public services called for an
educational pattern different from that of the AASSW. It was their position
that the burgeoning social services offered many positions that could benefit from some training in social work but did not need the highly sophisticated casework skills of graduates of the professional schools.

As stated by Hattie Cal Maxted, a leader in the movement, their mission in
undergraduate education would provide more rather than less training for social work. She said: "The facts are that we may have thought of training for
social workers as graduate training but the greatest percentage of our social
workers have had little or no training and for them training even though undergraduate is an advance."[8]

To their belief in the value of undergraduate preparation for social work,
the founders of NASSA brought a historical background and perspective different from the practice-oriented, agency-sponsored background of the mem-

ber schools of AASSW. The antecedents of undergraduate social work education, like the COS forebears of the graduate schools, date from the turn of the 19th century when social science and sociology were seen as offering great potential for the development of a more scientific philanthropy. E. J. Urwick, the head of the London School of Sociology, the first school of social work in Britain, heralded the new discipline of sociology in these words:

> Within the last decade [1890s] a new science has come to the front—
> the science of social life, or Sociology. Among the teachers and think-
> ers of all civilized nations it has won its place as a separate (although
> not yet clearly defined) subject for study.[9]

THE SOCIAL SCIENCES AND SOCIAL WORK

The relationship of the social sciences to social work emerged early as a difficult and puzzling question in the growth of the profession and figured prominently in the conflict between the undergraduate and graduate educators. NASSA's strong commitment to a broad social science background and criticism of AASSW for what it saw as too narrow an approach to professional education could have been inherited directly from a cantankerous exchange between two of social work's most illustrious forebears. This occurred at the first International Congress of Charities, Correction and Philanthropy held in Chicago in 1893.

Professor Amos Warner, serving as secretary of a section on training objected to the title "Sociology in Institutions of Learning," which had been assigned to it. He regarded philanthropy as a subject in its own right to which he ascribed the name "philanthropology." The Rev. Frederick Wines, presiding officer for the entire Congress, responded sharply to Warner's complaint:

> If we were to consider the teaching of social science in college from
> the narrow point of view of the professional philanthropist, you
> might as well call your section the section on the introduction of
> social therapeutics, etc.; and better, because it is the cure of social
> wrongs which directly interest the philanthropist. A much higher and

larger aim is to correct the narrowness of the philanthropist, by teaching him that the pathological social conditions can not be understood without a complete view, in the first place, of the anatomy and physiology of the social organism, and its normal operation in a condition of health. Much less is the philanthropist (so-called, who is often a mere sentimentalist, whose methods are purely empirical) prepared to administer remedies intelligently without a thorough grounding in the elementary principles of social science.[10]

Professor J. E. Hagerty, a pioneer in undergraduate education for social work, echoed Rev. Wines in simpler language in 1931 when he posed and answered the following questions:

Which fits men and women best to become skilled social workers? Which is most desired, immediate or remote returns? The first class of schools [graduate schools] undoubtedly fits them better for immediate returns. Is this the great desideratum in professional education? I do not believe that it is.

Professional education does not necessarily involve teaching to do specific things. It is very important to give the student in social training the fundamental principles of the social sciences and of psychology and biology, subjects furnishing an excellent discipline in clear thinking on social questions.[11]

With the substitution of social work for philanthropology, Abbott echoes Warner's complaint in asserting that while it would be agreed that social work is not a substitute for social science, "let us not forget that social service is both a cultural and disciplinary subject in its own right."[12] She went on to describe how the Conference of Social Work was originally intertwined with the Social Science Association and regretted their drifting apart as the social sciences developed into separate branches.

Perhaps she had read Wines's portrayal of philanthropists as sentimental because she added: "Again some of these social science friends are afraid that we cannot be scientific because we really care about what we are doing and we are even charged with being sentimental." In rebuttal, she is glad that a social worker cares genuinely about what happens to the unfortunate people for whom she is temporarily responsible and quotes from Flexner: "Humanity and science are not contradictory."[13]

It is noteworthy that even before sociology claimed its place as a separate social science discipline, systematic instruction on philanthropy or charity and correction was given in a number of prestigious universities, including Harvard, Brown, Columbia, Johns Hopkins, Chicago, Stanford, and a few state universities. Warner described these developments in a keynote paper on "Philanthropy in Educational Institutions" at the 1893 International Congress.[14]

Brackett followed up on this subject with a detailed account of a great variety of approaches to academic instruction on philanthropic work at the turn of the century.[15] In most of the examples cited by Brackett, the instruction is sponsored by well-known philanthropically committed academics. In many instances, the courses vanished with the departure of the sponsor.

As separate departments of sociology were established within universities, lectures and discussions on social problems and criminology figured prominently in their educational programs. Many departments also offered instruction on the "social treatment of dependents and defectives" accompanied by visits to social agencies and institutions.[16] Just as the roots of the graduate schools lie within the world of practice and the private agencies, the roots of the undergraduate departments lie within the academic world of social science and, in particular, the departments of sociology.

There is little evidence in the documentary material of recognition of this difference in historical background as a factor to be understood and accepted as legitimate. One may speculate that accommodation to the differing perspectives might have come more quickly and readily if the leaders of NASSA and AASSW had acknowledged the validity of their parallel but separate historical development and were more appreciative of the different worlds from whence they came. As it was, the difference became a barrier to understanding that took more than a decade to overcome.

Chapter Two
The Bones of Contention

The state university presidents and the social work leaders in the National Association of Schools of Social Administration made no secret of the fact that they were embarked on a mission to change the structure, the objectives, and, to a considerable extent, the content of preparation for social work. Harper referred to the movement as a "revolt... of the western and southern colleges and universities against the established system of professional education."[1]

From its beginnings, NASSA received powerful support from the Joint Committee on Accrediting of the Association of Land-Grant Colleges and Universities and the National Association of State Universities. The Joint Committee, at the beginning of the controversy, was chaired by a state university president strongly committed to the mission of the new organization. In granting NASSA responsibility in 1943 for accreditation of their programs of social work education, that Committee brought to a boiling point the struggle between NASSA and AASSW, which had been simmering for almost a decade. The charges by the undergraduate group and the response by the graduate schools clearly reveal NASSA as the contender, with AASSW somewhat belatedly rising to the challenge. Documentation on how the controversy began and the circuitous path to its resolution is replete with high drama, some distortion on both sides, and, finally, a sincere attempt to come to an agreement in the best interests of the profession.

POINT–COUNTERPOINT
The Seven Grievances

Launched as a protest movement, the NASSA group made clear what it did not like about the established association of schools of social work.

W. B. Bizzell, president of the University of Oklahoma, serving as president of the Association of State Universities, listed seven reasons why the Association of Schools of Social Work should be supplanted by a new organization.[2]

Those reasons have been ably summarized by Sheafor and Shank in their historical account of undergraduate education:

(1) AASSW programs were adaptable to large institutions only and failed to be responsive to small schools.

(2) AASSW policies reflected the goals and structure of privately-endowed schools and were unresponsive to publicly-funded universities.

(3) AASSW was urban oriented and failed to recognize rural needs.

(4) AASSW failed to respond to the fact that social workers in public agencies are paid by public funds and that the public schools are charged with the responsibility to train them.

(5) AASSW curriculum requirements were too rigid to accommodate the full scope of social work practice.

(6) AASSW's failure to include undergraduate education left large geographic regions unserved by social work education.

(7) AASSW's emphasis on specialization (i.e., casework) was a too-narrow approach to social work.[3]

NASSA's emphasis on the responsibility of publicly supported universities and colleges to train personnel for service in public agencies can be seen as a logical response to the expansion of the public social services in the 1930s. But even before the initiation of emergency relief programs and the passage of the Social Security Act, voices were heard criticizing the member schools of the AASSW. Among the earlier voices in opposition, James Hagerty, a pioneer in undergraduate education at Ohio State University, spoke the loudest and at the greatest length in his publication on social work training.[4] His opening remarks in a chapter on "Graduate or Undergraduate Schools of Social Work" reflects his view of the graduate schools:

I feel that it would be absurd to discuss the above question were it not for the fact that writers chiefly from the so-called graduate schools of social work have seriously questioned the advisability of giving training in social work to undergraduates.[5]

He points out that the schools were not organized originally as graduate schools and were so identified only because a number of college graduates sought admission along with others who were not college graduates. He reiterates that a graduate student in any university must have completed all the fundamental courses in the subject at the undergraduate level before proceeding for further study.

Another charge on which he and all the later undergraduate critics agreed was the failure of the AASSW schools to produce enough graduates to begin to meet the need for qualified social workers. This, indeed, turned out to be the trump card for the NASSA players. Another high card involved geographical considerations, particularly the lack of training opportunities in the southern and western states and in rural areas.

The curriculum issue also loomed large in the list of grievances. As already noted in Chapter 1, NASSA claimed, in its declarations and in its constitution, to prepare graduates for immediate employment in a number of specific fields. Family welfare, child welfare, and corrections were added to the original list of fields of study, and social insurance replaced employment service and unemployment compensation. Although the curriculum was described as "well-defined and integrated," the emphasis on special training for specific activities in public welfare was seen by AASSW as a vocational rather than a professional approach to social work education.

A major charge was directed at the dominance of casework in the graduate school curriculum. In some respects, this particular criticism was a reflection of disdain for the private agency origins of many of the leading graduate schools and the supremacy of private agency practice, particularly in eastern schools. An unsigned response to a NASSA questionnaire rather strongly expresses frustration:

> I have long been annoyed by the assumption in some Eastern quarters that the typical U.S. social worker is an underdone psychiatrist,

but I find that I am almost equally annoyed with the concept that the
typical U.S. [social] worker is a grossly underpaid, county welfare worker,
with little college work and comparable to a rural school teacher. Both
extremes exist, but isn't the average somewhere in-between?[6]

In other words, NASSA had little patience with the continuing strong
development in theory and practice of casework in the graduate schools as
the technique which, according to Flexner, was one of the essential marks
of a profession.[7]

The AASSW Response

With NASSA leading the charges, AASSW initially found itself on the
defensive, but its rebuttal soon became embellished by its own list of countercharges. The minuscule output of the graduate schools was the charge
most difficult to defend. Sue Spencer, executive secretary of the AASSW,
declared in 1947:

> The great gap between supply and demand is a major threat to our
> whole profession. Unless we can find ways of lessening this gap
> substantially there is real danger that the public recognition of the
> value of professional competence will be lost, that there will be a
> marked decrease in the number of positions for which professional
> training requirements are set, and that a system of pseudo profes-
> sional competence will be adopted to placate public conscience.[8]

Aggressive proposals were put forward to produce more qualified social workers. Programs providing in-service training, educational leave, and
scholarship support did indeed develop under governmental and non-governmental auspices, but it was not until the Council on Social Work Education was well underway that priority programs for both recruitment and
expansion of schools of social work were successfully financed and launched.

The AASSW response to the failure of its members to prepare for the
public social services becomes more complex, colored somewhat by an inherited ancestral attitude toward tax-supported relief. As noted earlier, the
graduate schools came honestly to their commitment to private agency prac-

tice, which concentrated on the social and personal adjustment of clients rather than on provision of relief. Karl de Schweinitz' description of the contrast between the old way and the new way of dealing with the problem of poverty expresses the dilemma facing the traditionally trained social worker in the early days of public welfare. The new way involved entitlement to financial assistance; the old way assumed that the client had a problem the treatment of which might or might not entail economic aid. The new system set down the conditions and requirements for assistance, which, if met, meant the applicant had a right to assistance; the old system left the giving of financial aid to the control of the social worker. De Schweinitz concluded:

> The consequent adjustment was not easy for the older social worker, often an individualist by disposition, who now exchanged the free wheeling of earlier days for the equity and consistency of the new order.[9]

Nevertheless, the need for qualified social workers in the rapidly developing social services could not be denied. With certain schools in the leadership, efforts were made to improve curriculum offerings and to provide at least a modicum of training for the public services. The School of Social Service Administration at the University of Chicago had, from its inception, emphasized the importance of preparing for the public field, and other schools headed by deans or directors with Chicago doctorates fashioned their programs along similar lines. As early as 1928, Abbott put it squarely in an address at a joint session of the AASSW and the American Association of Social Workers:

> There are no more fundamental or basic subjects of study for our profession than public welfare administration, social legislation. . . . Must these always be referred to, slightingly, as "background courses"? They are professional courses, to be enjoyed not by a well-educated few but by the rank and file who are to carry on our social service traditions in the future.[10]

Leighninger, in a graphic description of Abbott and Breckinridge as crusaders for qualified social workers in the public services, notes the Chicago influence and its limits:

> While eastern schools argued about Freud and Rank, social work
> educators in other parts of the country paid more attention to build-
> ing curriculum in public welfare administration and practice. The
> Chicago School played a major role. . . . Gradually, material on pub-
> lic welfare began to be seen as a legitimate part of social work educa-
> tion. . . . Yet, training for public social welfare, while it received greater
> attention during the thirties, never really challenged the dominance of
> the private case work tradition in social work education.[11]

The graduate school defense rested, to a considerable extent, on what
were perceived as unsatisfactory prospects for professional performance in
public welfare offices. They pointed out as valid objections the low salaries,
impossible caseloads, and narrow residence requirements of local or state
residence for staff appointments, often made through a spoils system rather
than a merit system. Many educators with strong connections with private
agencies sensed danger in public welfare practice to the continually evolving high standards of casework practice, a hallmark of the profession. Maurice
Karpf, director of the Jewish School of Social Work and president of the
AASSW, put it this way in 1933 at the height of the Depression:

> Social work received an amount of recognition in the last four years
> which no like period in the past brought to it. But this recognition is
> not an unmixed blessing. The huge tasks and relief burdens which
> social work was called upon to deal with during the last three or four
> years almost wrecked whatever standards social work, and particu-
> larly case work, had developed.[12]

As we shall see in later developments, substantial change in the outlook
and performance of the graduate schools with respect to public welfare
came about with the participation of the federal government in programs of
economic assistance. There was not much to be said about the neglect of
rural areas other than the difficulty of providing quality field work in loca-
tions bereft of agency networks and qualified supervisors. Also, it was thought
unlikely that the colleges serving rural areas would invest the money needed
to establish graduate schools of social work.

No answer was deemed necessary to rebut the undergraduate objection to the emphasis on casework. As previously noted, for the graduate schools casework was the "organized and educationally communicable technique" that Flexner decreed as a key attribute of a profession. No apologies for the casework emphasis in the curriculum were needed or offered. In fact, a major objection to undergraduate social work education, in their view, was the attempt to seem professional by teaching casework. What particularly irked the graduate educators was the audacity of some of the sociology departments in thinking that casework could be taught by faculty members with no social work education or experience.

A similar charge surfaced in relation to field work. The graduate schools valued highly their pattern of field practice under well-qualified supervisors. Commenting diplomatically on the special problem of a "limited form of practice" at the undergraduate level, Gordon Hamilton wrote in the 1945 *Social Work Yearbook*:

> Field work, even more than the other courses, is expensive in terms of supervision and educational controls. Field work is conceded to be a very difficult form of teaching; and unless it is so envisaged and responsibility for making it educational fully assumed, agency practice may easily force students into running errands or else learning a mechanical set of devices and procedures, impeding rather than furthering professional development.[13]

In the same article, Hamilton commented, less diplomatically, on another concern of the graduate schools—the immaturity of undergraduate students. Many of the older schools were established to receive as students persons who had already worked in some form of philanthropic activity. Through the years, social work continued to offer opportunities as a second career or as a profession discovered some years after graduation from college or after employment in a social agency. Sound judgment and ability to deal with complex social problems and dysfunctional individuals were equated with a higher degree of maturity than usually found in undergraduates. Hamilton's comment referred to problems in the growth of a professional self:

The younger the practitioner to be inducted, the less time he is allowed for assimilation of knowledge (difficult enough because of the complexity of social values), the less opportunity given him in educational field work to discover and wrestle with his own childish and prejudiced attitudes, his unreadiness to accept differences in others, the less is it likely that he will acquire those genuinely 'civilized' attitudes on which the profession of social work must ultimately rest.[14]

AASSW RISES TO THE CHALLENGE

How to help staff the rapidly expanding field of the public social services was not a new problem for the leadership of AASSW. Well before the creation of NASSA, John J. Winant, chairman of the Social Security Board, arranged a meeting in 1936 at the request of AASSW to discuss personnel needs for the new programs. Attended by representatives of the Bureau of Public Assistance, the Children's Bureau, and 19 members of AASSW, the initial meeting led to the establishment of an important ongoing committee and the beginning of a strong federal influence on social work education.

The Advisory Committee on Training and Personnel

Appointments to the committee were made by Frances Perkins (U.S. Secretary of Labor) and Winant in consultation with Jane Hoey, Katharine Lenroot, and the Executive Committee of the AASSW.[15] Its members included representatives of the AASSW, the Children's Bureau, the Bureau of Public Assistance, the AASW, and the American Public Welfare Association. The original purpose was rather vaguely stated as cooperating with the Social Security Board in educating lay boards and semi-professional workers. In 1939, upon becoming an official committee of AASSW, the purpose was narrowed to the training needs of the Bureau of Public Assistance and the Children's Bureau. Improvement of personnel standards in the federal and state social service programs to attract qualified social workers emerged as a major concern. Better prospects did seem likely under the merit system established by amendment to the Social Security Act in 1939. Elizabeth

Cosgrove, representing the U.S. Civil Service Commission, reported to the committee on its experience in evaluating professional credentials. She said:

> The Civil Service Commission in evaluating professional education in social work recognizes only the work completed in accredited schools. In evaluating for positions in the case work field, there have been no exceptions; however, a few exceptions have been made for positions in the group work field.[16]

Despite this encouraging word, the merit system did not and, given the shortage of available candidates, probably could not ensure the recruitment and hiring of professionally trained social workers. With the entry of the United States into World War II, other concerns loomed large in committee deliberations. With student enrollment dropping and social workers needed in the defense programs, schools were encouraged to accelerate the two-year programs. Although these multiple pressures might have been expected to lead to greater acceptance of undergraduate education for social work, other influences were also at work to sustain the commitment to graduate education. The most significant was a study, launched by the AASSW and published in 1942.

Education for the Public Social Services

With a special grant from the Rockefeller Foundation, the study proposed:

> to analyze the training needs of the social services established or expanded under the Social Security Act and to evaluate the role of the schools of social work in the preparation of personnel for these services.[17]

The powerful leadership from social work, public service, and related professions involved in the planning and conduct of the research is indeed impressive. On the 25-member Advisory Committee, a 9-member Study Committee, and a 12-member Executive Committee, a veritable galaxy of notables represented major schools of social work, the several practitioner groups, and federal and state agencies concerned with social welfare, along with a bevy of leaders from other disciplines and national agencies in related fields.

The recommendations supported the position of AASSW that preparation for social work requires two years of graduate study, wherever possible. As stated in the report:

> The nature of the jobs established in the services studied demands
> the knowledge and skills of social work and indicates the need for
> professional education at the graduate level.[18]

One year of professional education was recommended if the two-year goal
could not be reached and if that was not possible, college graduation with a
broad social science background was suggested. The report went on to say:

> It is further recommended that no consideration be given to the
> establishment of professional curriculums on an undergraduate ba-
> sis, or to undergraduate specialization in technical courses.[19]

Other recommendations called for modifications in the educational programs of the graduate schools, improvement in personnel practices in the public agencies, expansion of faculty training and field work opportunities in public
welfare, and development of additional graduate programs in universities and
colleges with adequate resources for quality professional education.

With the outbreak of World War II, the report unfortunately did not get
the attention it deserved. What was significant in 1942 was the effort of
AASSW to clarify its responsibilities in the preparation of qualified personnel for the public social services. The graduate schools had already played
an important role in providing brief periods of preparation of staff for the
Federal Emergency Relief Administration established in 1933. That experience along with other forces might in time have influenced the graduate schools
in relation to public welfare, but NASSA's confrontation undoubtedly brought
this challenge to the forefront. Similarly, it took the emergence of NASSA to
really concentrate the attention of AASSW on what was described as
preprofessional education.

PREPROFESSIONAL OR JUNIOR PROFESSIONAL

Finding the proper role for undergraduate education in the preparation
of a social worker remained the major bone of contention for the two com-

peting organizations. NASSA was certainly and understandably more clear than AASSW in its conception of the role, but, for both, considerable cross-fertilization finally came out of the struggle for domination. Unhappily, what could be explained as growth and change has more often been characterized as sly maneuvering—on the part of NASSA with its need to control education for a whole new field of service and on the part of AASSW for its determination to protect professional standards. A look at the positions of both groups in the 1930s and then in the 1940s reveals the changes that occurred as they wrestled with the charges and countercharges. The documentation indicates both believed sincerely that their way would better promote the interests of the profession and the people it serves.

As early as 1935, following a report from its curriculum committee, the AASSW membership accepted recommendations for a statement of policy, which consisted of the following four propositions:

> (1) members of the faculties of schools of social work regard the social sciences and psychology as logical background courses for students who contemplate attending a school of social work;
>
> (2) the subjects of economics, political science, psychology, and sociology are the sciences most closely related to professional courses;
>
> (3) the schools of social work should move toward the adoption of prerequisites, after the manner of medicine and law; and
>
> (4) there is general agreement that introductory courses, other than one on the "field of social work" should not be given to undergraduates.[20]

Although the policy was accepted by the membership, there is little evidence that efforts were made to implement the recommendations. Nevertheless, a principle had been established that graduate education in social work should rest on a background of study in the social sciences. By 1945, it was clear that more than lip service was needed with respect to the role and content of undergraduate education in preparation for social work.

The Consultation Service

A grant from the Field Foundation in 1945 enabled AASSW to offer a consultation service on preprofessional social work education. Sydney Branch, the consultant hired to conduct the one-year project, came from the faculty of the University of Chicago School of Social Service Administration, well-known for its commitment to graduate education, but equally well-known for its commitment to staffing the public social services with qualified social work personnel. The purposes of the consultation project, as described by Branch, incorporated three major efforts:

> (1) to encourage the social scientists to develop preprofessional social
> work sequences, drawn from all of the social sciences and related fields;
> (2) to secure the cooperation of all of the social scientists in devel-
> oping the preprofessional sequence and in interesting students in
> social work; and
> (3) to give AASSW a first hand knowledge of the developments in
> the field of preprofessional social work education.[21]

In the course of the project, the consultant visited colleges in 11 states in the Middle West, the Southwest, the East, and New England. She found great interest among both faculty and students in social work education. She also found a tremendous variety of programs, ranging from no plans for interested students to well-designed sequences of courses. The latter included courses drawn from the social sciences and augmented by orientation to social work and its clientele, to organization of the social services, and to the processes of casework, group work, and community organization.

Her reports included critical views of social work education from both sides of the academic spectrum. She made available to the AASSW a needed measure of information on the strengths and weaknesses of the education offered to future social workers in specific colleges, the problems faced by the colleges together with what she heard as misconceptions and criticism of graduate education. She concluded that a great deal could be accomplished if the undergraduate and graduate colleges, which had much to learn from each other, could cooperate with mutual understanding.

Hathway assessed the result of the consultation service in these words:

> [the] work of Sydney Branch of the University of Chicago has
> brought the whole field of professional education and practice closer
> to a realization that the college graduate who has mastered social
> science within a liberal arts education is really the answer which
> cannot be supplied as yet from the professional schools.[22]

There is no reference to social work courses in this appraisal of the
place of undergraduate education in preparing for employment. Other documentation indicates that social work content of an introductory nature was
entertained, but not to the extent of preparing for what NASSA described
as junior professionals. Harper probably mirrored the views of NASSA when
he referred to the consultation project as just a "counter-reformation."[23]

Along with the consultation service to undergraduate colleges and universities, the AASSW in 1945 also revitalized its Committee on Preprofessional
Education. The recommendations of this committee moved the AASSW
much further along the road to acceptance of undergraduate education as
integral to the education of a social worker.

The Preprofessional Committee

In 1945, the Committee on Preprofessional Education recommended
to AASSW member schools a detailed program for preprofessional education. It called for a specific number of hours (40 to 60) in social science
subjects, identified as anthropology, economics, history, political science,
psychology, and sociology. Ten semester hours in practical or methods courses
were also specified without explanation of what was meant by methods.[24]

In an article prepared in 1945 at the request of the *American Sociological Review* to clarify perceived problems in social work education, the following statement appears:

> when agencies found themselves unable to attract trained workers
> in needed numbers, [the] Schools of Social Work faced the reality
> that their present program made no provisions for meeting the situ-
> ation. . . . The reevaluation of their total plan by the American As-

sociation of Schools of Social Work has led within the past three years to
successive modifications of the program until today it stands as an integrated plan of education, with three recognized stages of preparation.[25]

Those three stages included: (1) instruction at the undergraduate level
where a student would acquire enough knowledge to be useful in a social
service agency as an aide; (2) a first graduate year offering generic professional education leading to a certificate; and (3) a second graduate year
providing full professional preparation with an opportunity for study in an
area of specialization. The AASSW membership, in adopting the committee's
recommendations, had come a long way from the tentative approach of its
first committee on undergraduate education in 1935. The policy still fell
short of preparation for professional practice at the undergraduate level but did
recommend contact with the social services geared to a study of social problems or a survey of current developments in social welfare programs. Fenlason,
chair of the committee, spelled out the significance of the new policy:

> In effect the schools have stated that knowledge of the social sci-
> ences is prerequisite to sound practice in the social services, that, for
> the social worker, specialized knowledge of a given social science
> should be supplemented by at least initial study of the related disci-
> plines and that basic theory should not be sacrificed to technical
> social work courses at the undergraduate level.[26]

She added that unsolved problems and points in need of clarification
remained, but concluded that both sides had begun to believe "an integrated plan of social work education, with designated well formulated content at each level, sponsored by both associations, is not only possible but is
rapidly nearing the blueprint stage."[27]

The Junior Professional

NASSA, too, had come a long way from its original pronouncements.
A committee appointed in 1947 to study its functions, particularly in relation to AASSW, reported consensus that "there is a place at the undergraduate level for both technical and general social work courses." The

NASSA goal remained the preparation of a junior professional social worker but the new position,

> recognized that undergraduate courses and field experience must have a limited content. . . . In general, undergraduate courses should be informative, historical and orientations courses. . . with a limited amount of on-the-job observation and practice.[28]

NASSA's position rested on the conviction that a social work major within the social sciences was a significant new development in education, both legitimate and desirable when taught by competent personnel. Harper, noting what he described as misunderstandings about the NASSA five-year programs, summed up the difference from the AASSW approach:

> Our five-year curriculum does not represent an attempt to crowd the usual six years required for full professional training into five. Instead it is merely another, and we believe an educationally sounder, procedure for arriving at the same point, that is, the completion of the *basic curriculum*. No specialized work is attempted.[29]

He went on to pinpoint, as the major difference, the amount of social science instruction in the NASSA programs. Students not only had a strong undergraduate major in social science and social work, but continued social science instruction at the graduate level. He noted that the social work courses offered in the senior year were substantially the same as those recommended by the AASSW Committee on Preprofessional Education, with perhaps additional semester hours. The fact that a Master of Arts (or Science) degree was awarded rather than a degree in social work seemed to him to clarify the difference between what he clearly saw as AASSW fully qualified professional social workers and the product of NASSA as a junior professional. And that is how he described it:

> Taking stock at this stage [1948], many of NASSA's original objectives would appear to have been attained. First of all, many more students have been graduated annually with at least a minimum of social work education since 1942... they have been introduced to professional education and are under no delusion with respect to

the need for further training if they are to advance in their chosen field. Again, attention has been called to the significance of the undergraduate curriculum, the graduate schools have become "preprofessional conscious," and their association has produced some valuable reports on the subject.[30]

NASSA remained committed to the junior professional model of undergraduate education and AASSW was equally committed to the preprofessional model. Both had come a considerable distance from their early positions. But disagreements remained. The defining issue of accreditation along with intervention by the federal agencies and the profession at large kept the pot boiling. Again, we shall see how the differences in origins and objectives of the two associations, as described in Chapter 1, influence the course of events.

Chapter Three
In Pursuit of Standards

The quest for status as a profession undoubtedly emerged as a significant underlying factor in the way in which undergraduate education for social work was perceived by the American Association of Schools of Social Work, the American Association of Social Workers, the specialized practice groups, and national employing agencies, both public and private. All were committed to graduate education. This unanimity of opinion might be seen, on the one hand, as a stubborn refusal to compromise on qualifications at a time of urgent need for social workers. On the other hand, it could be respected as a justifiable protection of clients and the community against inadequate preparation for the practice of social work as a professional service. Again, as in other aspects of the struggle between NASSA and AASSW, merit may be conceded on both sides, but the sheer weight of support for graduate education by leaders in the field and in the profession appears to favor AASSW.

A HUNGER FOR STATUS

Stanley Davis, an executive of the New York State Charities Aid Association and president of AASW from 1932 to 1934, declared the need for professional standards in 1933:

> I know of no profession in which professional standards sufficiently high to insure adequate preparation for the task to be done are more important than in the field of social work, which deals more vitally than any other with the happiness and well-being of people. . . . Social work cannot develop into a profession of great significance in our national life until our professional standards embrace the public field. This does not mean a leveling down of standards, but a constant, patient process

of leveling up until one professional standard on a common high level
is attained for both public and private social work.[1]

Looking at changes in social work between the two world wars, Kenneth Pray described the slow journey toward professional maturity. He noted the "lack of professional self-conscious and self-confident professional competence" in the World War I years and the lack of a "mechanism through which to join together readily to appraise service and achievement, to compare our differences, and to attain concert of thought and action in behalf of steadily advancing standards of service." He saw as a measure of progress the fact that those gaps had been largely filled in the period between the two world wars.[2]

The advance toward maturity was much on the mind of Sue Spencer, executive secretary of the AASSW during the later years of the conflict with NASSA. Her introduction to the article on social work education in the 1949 *Social Work Yearbook* reflects a view widely shared throughout the field of social welfare:

> Education for social work reflects the uncertainties and conflicts of a young and rapidly growing profession in which demands of the field far out distance resources of the professional schools. These unmet needs are both qualitative and quantitative, and the profession deserves credit for being concerned not only with securing enough workers to man the field but with assuring their competence to assume the grave and ever-increasing responsibilities inherent in professional social work.[3]

On another occasion, she notes the differences in viewpoint of AASSW and NASSA and the hope that the two associations can unite in promoting the best in training for the profession. She goes on to say that social work education properly reflects "the youth of the profession: its sudden enthusiasms, its relatively uncrystallized practice in certain areas, and its unsureness of itself. Youth is a great asset, but maturity is undoubtedly more comfortable."[4]

Graduate education symbolized professional status, not only in the minds of members of AASSW, but in declarations of AASW and other practice groups, the American Public Welfare Association, national private agencies, and at the federal level, the Children's Bureau, the Bureau of Public Assistance, the Veterans Administration, and the Public Health Service. Preprofessional preparation was also universally perceived by these groups as desirable at the undergraduate level and, to some, as a necessary introduction to graduate professional education, but not for professional practice. Their views on the question of standards and academic levels of education are significant as we look later at the role of accreditation in advancing the profession toward the wished-for maturity and the march toward resolution of the internecine conflict.

VOICES FROM THE FIELD

The American Association of Social Workers (AASW)

Stanley Davis, addressing the AASW as its president, declared as the association's primary task the development of a large body of social workers, equipped by aptitude and training for the difficult art of helping people. He continued:

> No one thing, I am persuaded, will so largely determine the future usefulness of social work, the degree of its contribution to human well-being than the Association's success with that primary task. We wish to develop social work as a profession, not for the eclat of professional status but for the assurance that professional equipment gives of a quality of human service that will enable this undertaking for social welfare more and more to fulfill its promise.[5]

Walter West, executive secretary of AASW until 1942, agreed wholeheartedly with this view of the primary function of the organization. The following warning against "the possible widespread development of inadequate professional education" appeared in an unsigned editorial:

> The student who is confronted with announcements from various colleges claiming to give training for social work will need guidance to prevent him from wasting time taking courses that will be of no

vocational advantage to him. The professional schools to which he will wish to give main consideration are the member schools of the American Association of Schools of Social Work.[6]

In articles and editorial comment in *The Compass*, he referred again and again to the responsibility of the practitioner group for the development of standards as a foundation for membership. The first membership requirements, established in the early 1920s, emphasized practice experience rather than education, reflecting perhaps the value placed by private agencies on the skilled practitioner. The requirements specified that applicants could be admitted with a minimum of a high school education, plus not less than four years of social work experience in an agency of recognized standing. Additional education and courses in professional social work were mentioned, but practice experience was the predominant criterion.

James Hagerty, in his excoriation of traditional social work and so-called professional social work education, came down hard on the AASW requirement of social agency experience, rather than educational preparation, as the primary qualification for membership: "It is inconceivable that the educational requirements for admission to a profession could be less."[7]

In 1933, a variety of educational options replaced the emphasis on experience, placing AASW in the position of having to evaluate and approve "technical social work courses." Initially this requirement had been specified as "technical social work courses in an approved school of social work."[8] Comments from chapters and individuals calling for more flexibility led to the change. To assist in the evaluation, specific standards were prepared by a Committee on Training Courses under the chairmanship of Gordon Hamilton, a well-known casework professor at the New York School of Social Work.

A field work requirement of 300 hours under the supervision of AASW members was specified along with a list of professional courses to be taught by AASW members as well as relevant courses to be taught by members of other professions.[9] No problem existed with respect to work taken in schools belonging to AASSW. When it came to evaluating and approving courses in non-member schools or in special training centers, confusion reigned. Recognition of the problems involved led to various proposals for their solution. The only one that survived made available junior membership, which enabled applicants to join with the understanding that additional work in a member school of the AASSW would be necessary for full membership.

Meanwhile, the AASSW, now served by a full-time executive secretary appointed in 1937, had launched a serious accrediting effort. The secretary, Marian Hathway, a highly respected educator and leader in this period, noted the influence of AASSW on the promotion of standards:

> The changes in the requirements for new schools put the Association in the position to force improvements in standards and to assure a measure of uniformity in the understanding of the basic education required for positions in the field of social work. The American Association of Social Workers had provided the Association with much needed support in its efforts to raise standards, when it raised its own membership requirements and prescribed a definite amount of training in a school of social work as a condition of membership.[10]

THE FEDERAL INFLUENCE

In the early stages of the controversy, the federal influence could well be described as the Chicago influence. Commitment to high standards of professional education came easily to the founders and heads of the U.S. Children's Bureau, all of whom had close ties to Abbott and Breckinridge and the University of Chicago School of Social Service Administration. Katharine Lenroot, chief of the Children's Bureau, and Jane Hoey, head of the Bureau of Public Assistance, emerged in this period as leaders in support of professional education at the graduate level. Review of personnel requirements for the study of the public social services concluded:

> The administration of public assistance and child welfare services at the operating, supervisory, and administrative levels requires the application of a body of knowledge and skills, as well as a

discretion and judgment, which can be best attained through professional preparation for the field of social work.[11]

The knowledge and skills needed for the functions of other services established under the Social Security Act were less easily identified, but it was hoped that their ongoing development would justify similar preparation. As the study of the public social services was sponsored by the AASSW, the conclusion with respect to personnel qualifications could perhaps be expected. When one notes, however, the composition of the committees associated with the project, there is every reason to conclude that the views expressed reflected the honest judgment of a wide range of interests. The Advisory Committee, for example, included blue ribbon representation, not only from the graduate schools, the profession, and key federal and state agencies, but other branches of the federal establishment, and other professions and national membership associations.

The full impact of Katharine Lenroot's commitment on the side of graduate professional education cannot be detailed here. Of special significance in the controversy was her promotion of educational leave programs sponsored by state agencies of public welfare, the financing of special training units, and the development of these programs in cooperation with the graduate schools. Her support and that of Jane Hoey were recognized with appreciation by Benjamin Youngdahl in his presidential address at an annual meeting of the AASSW: "Both Katharine Lenroot and Jane Hoey of the Bureau of Public Assistance are giving genuine leadership and have an understanding of the problems of professional education."[12]

NASSA members did not like being left out of the educational plans promoted by the Children's Bureau and its regional representatives. Hattie Cal Maxted, in a letter to Ernest Harper, reported on a meeting of a State Conference that "NASSA and the progress made in undergraduate education was noticeably omitted" in talk on staff preparation by a regional representative of the Children's Bureau. She went on to say:

> Right now it seems to me that the attitude of those regional representatives is a greater handicap than the attitude of the AASSW. The

AASSW members have, for the most part, kept abreast of developments in social work education, at least know something of its aims
and value. These field representatives got out of school several years
ago, and have not kept up with changes in social work education.
They influence more of the practicing social workers in a month
than we do in a year.[13]

Harper responded:

I believe the Children's Bureau is still our worst "enemy". . . . I do
not believe Miss Lenroot has changed her point of view at all. . . .
The Children's Bureau program still specifies AASSW credits for their
child welfare workers attached to the various state departments. We
have found, however, several ways to more or less circumvent their
regulations. . . . Sometime ago, President Tigert wrote and asked if we
were still having trouble with the Federal agencies and I have never
given him any specific report. . . . I might, therefore, write him and
explain that the Children's Bureau particularly needs a little pressure.[14]

While the leadership of the Children's Bureau and the Bureau of Public
Assistance played the most significant role in promoting graduate professional
education for social work, a number of other federal agencies made similar
statements of support. The Veterans Administration and the U.S. Public Health
Service were in complete accord with the AASSW position on the several levels
of education for social work, with an emphasis on liberal arts for preprofessional
preparation and professional degrees for graduate education.

A strong statement by Earl J. McGrath, U.S. Commissioner of Education, left little room for argument. At a meeting of the National Conference
of Social Work, he noted the pressure to prepare all types of social workers
as creating problems of the first magnitude and added that the problem was
not so complicated when social work education was primarily limited to the
preparation of social workers, probably meaning for the private field. With
the coming of the widespread public programs, he recognized that the states
and the public must have an adequate supply of social workers. However,
when he outlined his ideas about long-range planning, he said:

You will have noted that I am assuming that education for social
work will be graduate education; that is, the professional course of
study in social work will be based upon a four-year, undergraduate
program. For several reasons, specialization in social work in the
undergraduate years appears to me to be undesirable. In the first
place, few colleges are prepared to offer such instruction of suitable
quality. It would be many years before any number of colleges could
provide the staff and facilities to offer a major in social work. Only
the rare college of liberal arts can add a professional program such as
social work and maintain it at a level that would produce well-qualified members of the profession. Such programs are likely to be developed on a makeshift basis using such resources of buildings and
people as are at hand.[15]

With the federal agencies concerned with health, welfare, and education behind them and similar support from the profession at large and the
private national employing agencies, the AASSW clearly represented the
prevailing view of the standards necessary for the provision of professional social work education. NASSA, however, also had influential supporters in the presidents of the state colleges and universities, who had
at their command the powerful tool of accreditation, a tool they used
zealously to achieve their ends.

THE ISSUE OF ACCREDITATION

The different objectives of the two organizations come through clearly
in the accreditation controversy. NASSA saw its purpose primarily as preparation for work in a variety of public social service settings. AASSW saw its
purpose as preparation for a lifetime career in a profession. Sheafor and
Shank, in their account of the accreditation issue, have paraphrased comments that sum up the difference:

One analysis of the two organizations suggested that AASSW was
internal to the established profession and sought to develop professional autonomy, raise professional standards, and standardize the

professional base By contrast, the competing organization, NASSA, was external to the established social work profession, was dominated by public universities and welfare agencies, and was focused on responding to the demands for qualified social work personnel throughout the nation.[16]

Leighninger described the contrast rather differently. She wrote:

Founders of the NASSA deliberately chose a loose, informal structure. They sought to keep the association as democratic as possible. They charged no membership fee, and deferred 'until a later time' any stipulation of curriculum content or faculty qualifications for member schools. All this was in marked contrast to the formal structure and standard-setting mission of the AASSW.[17]

Accreditation Background—AASSW

The informal structure of NASSA mirrors exactly what happened when the existing schools of social work came together in 1919 to form the Association of Training Schools for Professional Social Work, later the AASSW. What they had in mind was a loose association of programs with more or less similar aims. As in the case of NASSA some 25 years later, they welcomed any school into their membership to discuss problems and build up a fellowship of common interests. A summary of the first 20 years of the AASSW refers to the loose character of the organization:

No stipulations were made as to the proportions of classroom work and field work. No specified courses were specified as belonging in the curriculum for training a social worker, and the question of qualifications of instructors was not raised. The members were feeling their way. Aside from the fact that courses of instruction were to be provided, the members were agreed on one thing—and that was the necessity of field work as an indispensable part of a student's professional preparation.[18]

Again, like NASSA, new schools were evaluated and recommended for membership by an Executive Committee and admitted by vote of all members at an annual business meeting. Inevitably, the need arose for some form of guidance in making decisions. This led in 1924 to the adoption by AASSW of the following principles:

> 1. That there should be an organic grouping of relevant courses of instruction into a special curriculum for the stated purpose of vocational or professional education for social work.
>
> 2. That there should be a director as the executive head of the school empowered to exercise control over admission requirements and general standards.
>
> 3. That the cooperation of allied professions and the resources of hospital, dispensary, court, school and other social agencies are necessary to develop adequate training for social work.[19]

The principle relating to courses gives more detail, particularly with respect to faculty qualifications. Specialists providing instruction would be expected to be in good standing in their fields; classroom teachers of "technical courses" must be senior members of the AASW; and field work was required to be "under supervision of well qualified social workers who are salaried and voting members of the faculty of the school."[20]

Additional comments by Sydnor Walker, an astute lay observer of social work and social work education, capture this pre-accreditation stage of development, much like the early NASSA stage described by Leighninger. Walker wrote:

> Unless the Association establishes definite standards of membership and sees to their enforcement, there seems small reason for excluding any schools which are interested in becoming members. The value of membership now lies not in the prestige of having met certain requirements, but in the exchange of opinion and in the stimulation which comes from contact with those facing similar situations. . . . Hence, there is now no basis for setting absolute conditions of membership, though the attainment of certain minimum standards of membership is a desirable goal.[21]

That goal was reached by the AASSW in 1932 when a "minimum curriculum" (the first Curriculum Policy Statement) was incorporated in the By-Laws and required of all new members. The purpose was "to find some body of knowledge which may be called basic and which is or should be given by all schools engaged in training for social work."[22] Two years later, following a visit by a part-time executive secretary, all schools were required within a three-year period to meet the requirements imposed upon new schools. Membership was equivalent to accreditation and the result of this first venture into some form of regulation was enthusiastically described as follows:

> The visits of the executive secretary to member schools and appli-
> cant schools furnished the Association with more precise informa-
> tion that it had had at any time in its history. This new experience
> accounts for the growing confidence of the Association and its will-
> ingness to bind its members to the maintenance of higher standards
> of professional education. After 14 years of existence the Association
> had achieved an *esprit de corps* which had for many years been charac-
> teristic of a profession. For some years social workers had been furtively
> speaking of their work as a profession. Now, it appeared, social work
> possessed the features characteristic of a profession.[23]

As noted earlier, a number of the older and thus better established schools were not organized within universities. With the passage of time, the undeniable benefits associated with university affiliation were generally accepted. The increasing effectiveness of AASSW as a standard-setting organization also persuaded the independent schools that their concerns would be protected. By 1935, the AASSW ruled that only those schools established within an institution of higher learning on the approved list of the American Association of Universities were eligible for admission to membership. The New York School of Social Work, the last of the established schools to make the change, became a part of Columbia University in 1940.

In 1939, AASSW took the further step of requiring that the educational programs of schools of social work be offered entirely on the graduate level, leading to the master's degree upon completion of two years of graduate professional study. This was the standard that provoked the state uni-

versities and led to the formation of NASSA. AASSW was not unaware of
possible unintended consequences of its decision. A special committee was
appointed as early as 1936 to consider the special problems that might exist
with respect to developing schools of social work within state universities.
Partial professional study in a one-year graduate program was put forward
as a possible solution. The rationale was described in these words:

> Some universities may find it desirable to establish a school of social
> work in order to assist state public welfare departments and other
> social services in developing trained personnel, but because of lim-
> ited opportunities for field work or limited budgets they may not be
> able to set up a professional curriculum on a two-year basis. The
> Association recognizes that a university might have a first rate one-
> year professional curriculum, whereas it could not maintain a good
> two-year program.[24]

A membership classification for Type II schools offering only the first
year of graduate education was adopted and remained in force until 1952.
Leighninger noted that "the one-year graduate school compromise quieted
the state university protest but left many land grant colleges and other undergraduate institutions out in the cold."[25] And one of the first universities
accepted into membership as a one-year school, much to the dismay of
NASSA leaders, was the University of Oklahoma, which had launched the
NASSA revolt. Until the founding of CSWE, this school straddled both
worlds by maintaining its membership in NASSA.

Accreditation Background—NASSA

In 1943, by unanimous vote, NASSA was recognized as an accrediting
agency for social work education by a Committee on Accrediting, representing
the Association of Land-Grant Colleges and Universities and the National Association of State Universities. John J. Tigert, president of Florida State University and a strong supporter of the new movement, served as chairman of the
Committee on Accreditation. Ernest Harper, NASSA President from 1945–
1947, described the purpose of NASSA's recognition in these terms:

Throughout this period the Joint Committee on Accrediting, as you know from the record, backed the NASSA as its device for bringing about radical modification of the policies of the older association.[26]

To what extent NASSA served as an accrediting agency is not clear. It had no funds or staff. The membership requirements referred to the various fields for which it was preparing personnel and some general specifications about faculty. Few of its members offered one graduate year in addition to a four-year baccalaureate program. The auspices under which the instruction was conducted varied widely from free-standing departments to a collection of courses within a social science framework. NASSA was clearly not ready to take over the responsibility for accrediting social work education. This lack was evidently recognized by the National Association of State Universities, as noted in the following excerpt from a report issued in 1946:

> It is recommended that no action be taken at this time regarding AASSW, but that we continue cooperation with the National Association of Schools of Social Administration and endeavor to assist it to becoming a satisfactory accrediting agency.[27]

In response to this pronouncement, T. W. Cape, president of NASSA, wrote to its members:

> The AASSW would welcome a merger in which the NASSA would be absorbed. Your Committee recommends against such a merger and further recommends that if by January 1,1948, the AASSW does not become more amenable to the objectives which we have been seeking that we ask all of our institutions to contribute a fee of $25.00 which will make it possible for the NASSA to become a functioning accrediting agency.[28]

The Accrediting Ultimatum

It was perhaps unfortunate that the issue of responsibility for the accreditation of social work education occurred at a time of national confusion about accreditation in general. At a Joint Meeting of AASSW and NASSA representatives, Charles E. Friley, representing a new Joint Committee on Accrediting, provided background information, including the development of quantitative and qualitative standards. He stressed the need for accreditation to maintain high educational standards. He said:

> Gradually there grew up attempts not only to accredit institutions
> but divisions and even departments within those institutions... Un-
> fortunately, the accrediting situation became highly complex with
> some two hundred agencies accrediting institutions, divisions and
> departments. Finally, to bring some order out of the confusing and
> chaotic situation, the Joint Committee on Accrediting was formed,
> representing the Association of Land Grant Colleges and Universities,
> the National Association of State Universities, the Association of Urban
> Universities and the Association of American Universities. The Joint
> Committee on Accrediting has worked to simplify accrediting by elimi-
> nating accrediting agencies not needed and consolidating others.[29]

In response to a question from Harper about accrediting an undergraduate curriculum in social work, Friley responded that it might be possible providing the curriculum was offered by a separate division. Further discussion of this question led to this comment, reported in the minutes:

> Mr. Friley thought that the Joint Committee on Accrediting would
> be concerned not only with the accrediting agency but with the
> appropriateness of the accrediting itself. He said that frankly he was
> at a loss to understand exactly what the Joint Committee on Social
> Work Education proposed to accredit.[30]

These various comments were made at a time when the two social work organizations were making a serious effort to find a way to work together toward a mutually satisfactory outcome of the accrediting dilemma. As will be seen in the next chapter, the road to cooperation took many twists and turns, with AASSW, after careful consideration, turning down a proposal for joint responsibility. By this time, however, the two groups had participated with other branches of the profession and the field to organize a third organization, the National Council on Social Work Education, to produce a comprehensive study of social work education. The AASSW regarded as precipitant any final action on accrediting responsibility before the findings and recommendations of the study became available. Nevertheless, the Joint Committee on Accrediting resolved on November 11, 1947:

> That, unless the American Association of Schools of Social Work and the National Association of Schools of Social Administration agree on an accreditation program for Social Work by January 1, 1948, there be no recognized accreditation in this field. When an acceptable program is presented, with the recommendations of both organizations, a new listing will be considered. This action supplants all previous actions in this matter.[31]

As noted above, President Cape of NASSA expressed satisfaction with the action and hoped it would be the means to bring the two associations together. He also felt that "both Dr. Youngdahl, President of AASSW, and Miss Spencer [the executive secretary] are sincerely desirous of a united front in the interest of social work." Observations by Maxted, a pillar of strength for NASSA, portray a sense of bewilderment as to the future of the organization. She wrote:

> I have been doing quite a bit of thinking about NASSA and I'll admit that I am a bit muddled. NASSA has made a real contribution to social work education. . . . There does not seem to be a particular need of accrediting undergraduate departments unless we are to be more professionally minded than we are. Then if we do not accredit departments what is the meaning or purpose of membership in NASSA? On the other hand, undergraduate departments are begging for advice and help and it seems that some kind of an organization is needed for that purpose. What kind should it be?[32]

In a letter to the newly elected president of NASSA, she also saw the need to develop a broader program to help its member schools:

> When all is said and done we organized as a protest group and we did surprisingly effectively but we seem to have difficulty in moving to the next stage of making our organization useful to ourselves.[33]

The ultimatum affected both organizations. Now that the die was cast, something had to be done to preserve an accrediting authority for social work education. Previous attempts had both flourished and floundered, but this time cooperation must be achieved. The long journey toward that end is described in the following chapter.

Chapter Four
The Convoluted Path to Cooperation

The shock of losing responsibility for accreditation of social work education certainly concentrated the minds of both organizations on next steps. Any new listing as an accrediting body would require the recommendation of both the National Association of Schools of Social Administration and the American Association of Schools of Social Work. This was not the first time that AASSW and NASSA faced the challenge of finding common ground. The story of the efforts to build a cooperating relationship reveals that much can be achieved when contenders meet face to face. The road to resolution of the accrediting conflict took many twists and turns, however, before agreement was finally reached.

THE COMMITTEE GAMBIT

Nowhere is the fluctuation between dissension and conciliation more clearly demonstrated than in the deliberations and outcomes of the various committees established to work on the controversy. As early as 1936, AASSW appointed a Committee on Social Work Education in State Universities which asked to be discharged in 1938 because "the problems of membership requirements of State University member schools had been resolved within the year."[1] The nature of the problems and how they presumably were resolved is not explained.

Later that same year, the president of the University of Idaho requested the Associations of Land-Grant Colleges and State Universities to undertake a nationwide study of undergraduate and graduate education for social work. The AASSW offered its assistance and, specifically for that purpose, reinstituted an Advisory Committee on State Universities and Membership Requirements.

45

This led to a first round of discussions in October 1938 between representatives of AASSW, led by Stuart Chapin, chair of its Advisory Committee, and the state universities interested in undergraduate education, led by
John Tigert, president of Florida State University. It was Tigert, later the
chair of the Joint Committee on Accrediting, who promoted and strongly
supported NASSA as an accrediting agency for social work education. Several meetings were held where misunderstandings were discussed and apparently clarified. The shortcomings attributed to AASSW by the land-grant
colleges and state universities were addressed with the anticipation that cor-
rective action would be taken. That this did not happen to the satisfaction
of the land-grant colleges and state universities had much to do with
the emergence of NASSA in 1942.

Leighninger reports on the regret voiced by Chapin on this lost opportunity to prevent the creation of a new organization for social work education. He described the forces behind NASSA as one of the most powerful
combinations of institutions of higher education in the country, involving
"big politics" as well as a threat to established standards of social work
education. He believed the threat could have been deflected if AASSW
had been more disposed to work on the problems presented to the Board
and membership.[2]

A listing of subsequent events, as noted in background information for
a later joint committee, records the following information:

> June 1, 1943—Dr Tigert wrote the president of AASSW, Miss
> Hamilton, stating the seven original complaints that Dr. Bizzell had
> distributed in 1938, and stated that unless the AASSW modified its
> policies, his Committee on Accrediting of State Universities and
> Land Grant Colleges would recognize NASSA.
>
> June 15, 1943—Miss Hamilton replied, offering full cooperation
> and suggesting joint discussion. No answer was received.
>
> December 1943—The AASSW Board considered the report that in
> October, 1943, the Land Grant Colleges meeting in Chicago had
> voted to recognize NASSA as an accrediting association. Result: Miss

Hamilton wrote Dr. Tigert, requesting why his committee had not replied to her suggestion of joint discussion and asking that a copy of her letter of June 15th be sent to all the members of his committee. He agreed and promised to send their comments but AASSW heard nothing further from him.[3]

Tigert's response came one year later in 1944 in the form of a request to Katharine Lenroot of the Children's Bureau to convene a meeting, which brought together 22 representatives of undergraduate and graduate education, the AASW and the specialized practice organizations, higher education, and the federal government. Katharine Lenroot was probably selected as a possible arbiter because of her close association with AASSW in several committees on training and personnel advisory to the Children's Bureau and the Bureau of Public Assistance. The only outcome of any consequence at this meeting was a recommendation for continuing committee work. This took the form of a Joint Committee on Social Work Education, which gave serious consideration to all aspects of the conflict and put forward a series of significant recommendations.

MOVING FORWARD AND CHECKMATE

The two associations, meeting in Cleveland in January 1945, passed the following resolution:

> In order to carry out the interest in the total process of education for social work expressed in this and in previous meetings, it is hereby resolved that a joint committee be established by the AASSW and the NASSA to consist of six (6) members, three from each of the cooperating groups, to study common problems of education for social work. It is also recommended that this committee undertake first the study of the relationship between undergraduate and graduate education and ways in which service for consultation and accrediting may be provided.[4]

The Joint Committee on Social Work Education

The associations were represented by their respective officers or leaders associated with undergraduate education. To ensure evenhanded justice, Esther Lucille Brown, Director of Studies in the Professions, Russell Sage Foundation, was invited to serve as an impartial chairperson. Two meetings were held, one in Chicago in April 1945, and the second, also in Chicago, in December 1945. The detailed minutes reveal a genuine effort by the committee members to arrive at an understanding of their differences and to find common ground on which agreement could be reached. The effort is expressed in these terms:

> Committee members were convinced that an ultimate merger or affiliation of the two associations would be desirable provided the interests of each association could be protected within one organization.[5]

Recognizing, however, that an immediate merger was not possible, they resolved that the committee should be continued to explore the relationship further and should be enlarged to include an additional member from each group to help in the technical aspects of accrediting. They stressed the importance of differentiating introductory courses in casework, group work, and community organization in preprofessional sequences from professional courses in those subjects. They also agreed that agency experience should not exceed a total of one hundred clock hours and should be clearly distinguished from graduate field work. They struggled with the question of the qualification to be conferred upon graduates of the fifth year of a NASSA program. A number of possibilities were considered, but none found unanimous acceptance. In a resolution finally recorded, a majority favored the M.A. degree but a recommendation to that effect was postponed. All were agreed that the graduate schools should recognize undergraduate work, at least to the extent of substituting more advanced courses for course content already covered.

Greatly encouraged by the positive attitudes and outcomes of this meeting, the group recommended further joint meetings. At the second meeting held in Chicago in December 1945, the same positive approach prevailed. Again, with Brown as the impartial chairperson and Sydney Branch as secretary, the group passed as its first resolution its intent to develop the best possible education for social work, its understanding that its recommendations would be subject to reconsideration in the light of ongoing events, and its belief that "eventually one accrediting organization for social work education" would be desirable.[6] Walter Pettit of the New York School of Social Work and Anne Fenlason, chair of the AASSW Committee on Preprofessional Education, told of plans for a comprehensive study on social work education.[7] Ernest Harper suggested that, in addition, a permanent, widely representative Commission on Social Work Education was needed.

These last two areas of discussion may be seen as harbingers of the far-reaching changes soon to occur with the creation of the National Council on Social Work Education as a study group and the initiation of the Hollis-Taylor study that, in turn, launched the present Council on Social Work Education. But those momentous events lie still in the future.

THE CONTENTIOUS ISSUES

Meanwhile, there were knotty questions, particularly with respect to accrediting and degrees, that occupied much of the time of the December meeting. The significance of the resolution dealing with those questions requires its reproduction in its entirety along with an amendment. The following resolution #4, moved by Ernest Harper and seconded by Walter Pettit, was adopted unanimously:

> The Joint Committee recommends to the two Associations that, for the time being, the problem of accrediting be met by an agreement between the two Associations to divide the field, AASSW accrediting schools with a two-year graduate, professional curriculum, and schools with a one-year graduate, professional curriculum; NASSA accrediting schools with a five-year course consisting of a sequence of undergraduate and one-year graduate work in social work and related subjects leading to the Master of Arts in Social Work. The

Joint Committee recognized the need for exchanging experiences and ideas, looking toward greater integration and cooperation between the two Associations.[8]

And the amendment:

Except for present members of the two Associations, any school should belong to and be accredited by only one of the two Associations; in case of any questions as to which Association should issue jurisdiction, the matter should be determined by conference between the school and the two Associations.[9]

Perhaps, in the euphoria of good feeling and the desire to replace contention by cooperation, the representatives of AASSW and NASSA did not fully realize the confusion that would result by having two accrediting agencies for social work education, particularly when both were approving a one-year graduate program with one leading to a certificate and the other to a master's degree. The decision of AASSW to establish one-year graduate programs leading to a certificate as a counter-reform to NASSA's challenge had already roiled the waters. The Joint Committee did attempt to distinguish the two by noting the difference in structure and content. The NASSA program combined social work and social science in the graduate year as it did in the undergraduate years while the content of the one-year graduate program accredited by AASSW was entirely social work.

Of the seven recommendations coming from the committee, most were innocuous and acceptable. The particular question of joint accrediting and the award of a master's degree upon completion of the NASSA graduate year, however, was more than AASSW could accept. As seen in detailed minutes of the Board and the Annual Business Meeting of the membership, the decision to reject this major recommendation was not taken lightly. The Board and the member schools struggled with their need to maintain hard-won standards and a desire, sincerely motivated on the part of many, to put an end to the struggle and come to some kind of agreement with NASSA. The adverse reaction, and the reasons for it, deserves more detailed attention than it has been accorded in previously published accounts.[10]

THE AASSW RESPONSE

Walter Pettit, well-known and admired on both sides of the controversy as a leader in the field of social work education, presented the committee's list of recommendations, first to the AASSW Board of Directors at its meeting in Pittsburgh on January 23–24, 1946, and to the member schools at the Annual Business Meeting immediately following on January 24. In response to action by the membership, additional Board meetings were held on January 25–26 to prepare a resolution that would reflect the position of the membership. An almost verbatim account of the discussion in the minutes of these various sessions indicate the serious consideration given to the question of how best to accommodate the proposal for shared accrediting and, at the same time, to make clear an inability to sanction two decidedly different patterns of social work education.

The Board of Directors

In his presentation to the Board, Pettit commented on the value of the committee's work, giving the two organizations an opportunity to discuss their differing views and philosophy. He stressed that the plan to divide accrediting responsibility was a "temporary expedient" with a view to greater integration at some future time. He pointed out that NASSA had already been granted authority to accredit undergraduate education so it was not a new idea. By finding common ground and working together, he saw a strong likelihood of a later merger into one accrediting agency. He also saw little danger to the position of AASSW as the arbiter for graduate education because NASSA had few members offering a fifth graduate year and was concerned almost entirely with undergraduate education. As there was only one school in the membership of AASSW (the University of Oklahoma) connected with both organizations, the question of conflicting allegiance was not a problem. Should it become a problem, the amendment to the accrediting recommendation covered complications of that nature.

Board members expressed the following concerns: (1) apprehension about officially sanctioning a division of responsibility for accrediting social work education; (2) fears about lowering professional standards by taking on NASSA as an equal partner in accrediting when it had no demonstrable machinery or criteria for that purpose; (3) the possibility that universities and colleges (particularly land-grant institutions) interested in establishing schools of social work would opt to be accredited by NASSA to avoid meeting the higher standards of AASSW; and (4) the difficulty posed for colleges and universities seeking approval of programs that followed the AASSW model of preprofessional education if NASSA had an accrediting monopoly of undergraduate programs.

A strong effort by the AASSW representatives on the Joint Committee to answer the questions raised within the Board led to consideration of a possible merger in the immediate future rather than a division of the accrediting responsibility. Classification of one-year graduate programs had already been accepted as Type II membership, which suggested the possibility of a third classification for NASSA members. Following exploration, the following action was recorded:

> It was the sense of the meeting that the Board of Directors urge that
> AASSW and NASSA explore the possibility of a merger of the two
> associations within the next year or two.[11]

It was further agreed that Pettit would report on the work of the Joint Committee and its recommendations at the Annual Business Meeting and that Gordon Hamilton would present the Board's recommendations of acceptance of the Joint Committee's recommendations *in principle*, with two exceptions. One exception had to do with the award of graduate credit for undergraduate work which, it was decided, was the prerogative of individual universities. The other dealt with recommendation #4 to share accrediting responsibility, for which the following statement was substituted:

> 1. We believe there should be one agency responsible for setting
> and recognizing the standards for social work education.
>
> 2. We believe that preprofessional education is an integral part of a
> total program of social work education.
>
> 3. The AASSW will continue to give consultative service to both

associations in the undergraduate curriculum.

4. It is recommended that a new Joint Continuing Committee explore the possibilities of type of approval or recognition to be given to these curricula, looking forward to eventual establishment of other classes of membership in the AASSW.[12]

The Member Schools

AASSW counted 46 graduate programs in its total membership, as of January 1946, and all but two of the member schools were represented at the Annual Business Meeting. As expected, the proposal for shared accrediting responsibility dominated the discussion. Several delegates joined Pettit in pushing the idea of a merger, not as a future possibility but as an immediate step. A more definite statement, it was said, would let NASSA know exactly what AASSW wanted. Pettit added that this would also let the Joint Committee on Accrediting know that AASSW was making a positive suggestion while turning down resolution #4 because it felt it could not recognize as an equal accrediting agency a "group about which it knows very little and which actually knows very little about itself."[13] A motion, proposed by Arthur Dunham, one of the AASSW representatives on the Joint Committee on Social Work Education, recommended that the suggested new Joint Continuing Committee "explore the possibilities of affecting, in a year or two, a substantial measure of integration of the two associations."[14] When put to a vote following further discussion, the motion was narrowly lost by one vote (18 to 19).

As a final action, the Board's report was referred back with instructions to edit or reword what it wished to present to the membership, along with a concrete recommendation for acceptance or rejection. In compliance with this request, the Board, on January 25, prepared the following resolution for presentation at a second business meeting on January 26, where it was approved:

> Although accrediting for social work is in the first instance the immediate concern of the schools of social work, other groups, nota-

bly those organizations employing the graduates of the schools, have an eventual and very practical concern with this problem and the solution which is found. It is with no wish to temporize, but with the earnest hope that the final solution may be a sound one that the Board recommends that:

The present Joint Committee on Social Work Education be disbanded in accordance with its own request, with expression of appreciation for both the care with which the work has been done and the more precise definition which it has evolved of the problem.

An interim committee be appointed to continue collaboration on the common problems involved in the presence of two organizations in the field of education for social work, in view of the inherent necessity of there being but one accrediting agency in a professional field. In addition to representation from AASSW and NASSA, representation from the following organizations should be included: Bureau of Public Assistance of the Social Security Board, Children's Bureau, APWA, AASW.

The Board be authorized to study the creation of a broadly constituted commission on education for social work. . . [15]

This outcome did not sit well with the Joint Committee on Accrediting of the State Universities. At a meeting held soon after in April 1946, they reported on the high hopes they had held for a clearing up of the problems in social work education and declared:

These hopes were dashed with the important parts of the recommendations adopted by the Joint Committee on Social Work of the two Associations, rejected in the annual meeting of AASSW which was held in Pittsburgh on January 26–28, 1946. We are now back where we started with the AASSW. For two or three years they have apparently been stalling. We now have no agreements with them.[16]

THE NASSA REACTION

The NASSA leaders reacted with dismay, touched with bitterness, at the final outcome of the joint efforts of the two associations to put forward proposals agreeable to both sides. Evidently, Maxted was sufficiently convinced the accrediting recommendation would be accepted that, in December 1945, she answered an inquiry about membership in these terms:

> It was agreed [by the Joint Committee on Social Work Education] that for the time being the American Association of Schools will accredit full and one year graduate professional curricula while the National Association will be responsible for undergraduate or 'junior professional,' and five-year master's degree programs.[17]

Unfortunately the mistake carried over into the term of T. C. Cape, elected president of NASSA in 1947, who complained irritably to Benjamin Youngdahl, president of the AASSW, that an agreement to divide the field had been violated. Youngdahl responded:

> I have just checked the minutes of our Annual Business Meeting held in Pittsburgh on January 24, 1946, and I find that Resolution #4 of the Joint Committee of the two Associations (this provided for a division of the field) was never adopted by our Association. A substitute was adopted which emphasized the fact that preprofessional education is an integral part of a total program of social work education. . . . So far as I am able to interpret the AASSW, there is no desire on the part of the membership other than to improve the standards and to forward the development of professional education for social work to meet more effectively the needs of the field.[18]

In a membership poll conducted in August 1945, the NASSA schools, now consisting of 29 programs, had approved all seven recommendations. An additional question asking for their views on merging immediately with AASSW met, however, with strong disapproval.[19] Yet, in the next two years, this was the road they hoped to travel.

The letdown at the disappointing action of the AASSW is palpable, as seen in letters written by Harper and Maxted, the two stalwart members of the

NASSA Executive Committee. President Harper wrote to Joseph Anderson, executive secretary, about the possibility of some form of membership in AASW:

> In view of the fact that the AASSW recently turned down most of the recommendations of the Joint Committee [on Social Work Education] it would appear that from now on the two associations will drift further apart instead of closer together.[20]

Maxted wrote to Harper in June 1945:

> I think the NASSA is an extremely shaky organization, as evidenced by some of the replies and lack of replies which I received from some of our schools. There are only a handful of us who are really interested. . . . If the NASSA goes under now any hope of really getting order or sense into the whole field of social work education is sunk for some time to come.[21]

Harper replied:

> I have been aware almost from the start that the NASSA is indeed a very shaky organization and as president I have been doing a lot of bluffing. I only hope I won't be "called" before we can make good. I am convinced furthermore that we need to become stronger whether we merge or not.[22]

While the rejection of the recommendation for shared accrediting seemed to be a breaking point, it turned out to be the lever that moved the profession toward agreement and consolidation. The future was by no means as bleak as it must have seemed to NASSA at the time. In entering the scene, the American Association of Social Workers had picked up the ideas, previously expressed on both sides of the conflict, that something more than an educator-based joint committee should work on the problem and, beyond that, a comprehensive study was needed to arrive at a solution.

AASW AS *DEUS EX MACHINA*

Represented by Sue Spencer, at that time a member of the AASW staff, and Joseph Anderson, executive secretary, the AASW brought to the Board and the Annual Business Meeting of AASSW a noteworthy alternative to the recommendations of the Joint Committee on Social Work Education. Along with the specialized practitioner groups, AASW had, from the beginning of the controversy, made known its support of AASSW standards and its conception of professional social work education as graduate education. It also had a Committee on Professional Education, which now offered a suggestion with far-reaching consequences. It asked for the immediate establishment of a council on social work education, which would include representatives from AASSW and NASSA, from the several specialized practice organizations, and the national agencies. They thought the field of practice rather than the two educational associations should decide whether or not there should be two accrediting agencies. A major task of the council would be to develop plans for a comprehensive study of social work education and to seek funds to conduct it. It recommended that any action on dividing the field with two accrediting bodies be held in abeyance pending completion of the study.

AASW offered to underwrite the expenses and provide the staff for the proposed council. It also suggested that AASW participate in any plans for an expanded consultation service that might be provided by a council to both AASSW and NASSA member programs. Spencer saw this as gradually leading to a merger of the two organizations. The Board agreed that the professional organizations and the field of practice, as represented by the employing agencies, could and should be brought together in such a council, but that the leadership and direction should come from AASSW.

Anderson, in a final word to the AASSW member schools, expressed the strong interest of the AASW in all matters bearing upon the development and improvement of the social work profession. That inescapably included, he said, not only social work education, but personnel practices, salaries, and appraisals of competence. He noted that the several professional organizations had been working separately on their objectives, but, in the face of what was perceived as a problem for the whole field, the concerted efforts of all the involved organizations and employing agencies was needed to work in cooperation with the educational associations. Thus, we get a glimpse of what was yet to come in the form of a National Council on Social Work Education, a comprehensive study, and the establishment of the present Council on Social Work Education. How it all evolved is the subject of the next chapter.

Chapter 5
The Curtain Falls on AASSW and NASSA

By 1946, the combination of suspended accrediting and a spreading uneasiness with the standoff in the NASSA–AASSW negotiations led to renewed efforts to bring the struggle to an end. Finding a way out of the difficulties that the controversy posed not only for the educators but also for the profession and the field as a whole introduces a whole new cast of characters in the continuing drama. The American Association of Social Workers, along with the several specialized practice groups,[1] the many employing agencies, both public and private, as well as other professional groups, all became intimately involved. As already noted, suggestions for a study and some form of a broad commission on social work education had come from both the graduate and undergraduate educators. How those hazy ideas coalesced into definite plans for a new strategy marks the beginning of the end of the decade-long struggle.

With both associations having endorsed continuing negotiations under a more broadly based Interim Committee, the threatened stalemate became, in fact, a last chance to put an end to the battle of wills for the future of the profession. The new committee included members from the Children's Bureau, the Bureau of Public Assistance, and the American Public Welfare Association in addition to representatives of the American Association of Schools of Social Work and the National Association of Schools of Social Administration. They met twice in 1946 and recommended the establishment of a National Council on Social Work Education, outlining the conditions of its membership and its major functions. They further proposed that AASW should convene the first meeting of the Council, if approved by AASSW and NASSA. Both educational associations accepted the recommendations of the Interim Committee, which then declared itself discharged.[2] The stage is now set for the last act.

THE NATIONAL COUNCIL ON SOCIAL WORK EDUCATION

At the first meeting of the NCSWE held in New York on August 26–27, 1946, officers were elected, with Irene Farnham Conrad, executive director of the Nashville Council of Social Agencies and a former president of AASW, as chair; Arlien Johnson, for AASSW, and Ernest Harper, for NASSA, as first and second vice-chairs; and Joe Anderson, of AASW, as secretary. In addition to representatives of the various social work organizations and the public social services, the membership included representatives of the Associations of American Colleges and American Universities, and Joint Committee of Accrediting of Association of Land-Grant Colleges and Universities, the National Association of State Universities, and the Association of Urban Universities. This was indeed a broad-based combination of interests, all targeted on social work education. The membership became even more comprehensive when it was further broadened to include members at large from the social sciences and other related fields.

While delighted to accept staff service from AASW, the membership agreed that the National Council should become incorporated as a separate organization. The Certificate of Incorporation, issued in 1947, listed two purposes:

1. To bring together organizations interested in social work education for discussion of their common problems, to serve as a clearing house and to provide machinery for cooperative activities related to social work education.

2. To engage in research, including the continuous collection of data on personnel needs and educational problems in social work and sponsorship of special studies on such personnel needs and such educational problems as the need arises.[3]

There was no question as to the major activity to be undertaken by the new organization. It was clear to all involved that a study was needed to find a solution to the problems relating to the AASSW–NASSA conflict and particularly to accreditation. At its first meeting, therefore, a comprehensive study of social work education was authorized. This involved planning and staffing the study, appointing a study committee to carry major responsibility for oversight and assistance to the staff, and organizing a national advisory committee composed of university presidents and corresponding luminaries from a variety of fields and occupations.

Planning the Study

The objectives, content, and methods of social work education were to be examined in the light of the actual and potential needs of social work practice in a time of rapid social change. A parallel proposal for a collection of statistical data, also accepted at this meeting, became the basis of a study by the U.S. Bureau of Labor Statistics. The following statement reveals the strong support accorded the National Council for its prompt and decisive action:

> The whole profession of social work is mobilized around this study through the NCSWE. Both Associations of Schools are participating fully in planning for the study and believe this to be absolutely essential to the resolution of differences, the strengthening of professional education, and the establishment of a single accrediting body for social work education. The membership associations are in urgent need of the findings of groups in the fields fundamental to the advancement of social work practice.[4]

A highly effective study committee, under the leadership first of Kenneth Pray and, later upon his death, of Harriett Bartlett, included Jane Hoey, Ernest Harper, Donald Howard, and Wilbur Newstetter. In a personal memoir, Alice Taylor Davis, assistant director of the study, recorded this observation:

> The devoted work of the members of the study committee was a central force that contributed to the eventual completion of the study by stimulating, informing, guiding, and calming the profession as the study moved along.[5]

Sue Spencer, now executive secretary of AASSW, and Joseph Anderson, executive director of AASW, provided staff service and, with Ernest Harper of NASSA, maintained liaison with the participating organizations. Davis said of their participation:

The study required from these three professionals, devotion, great
patience, reams of time, and often considerable negotiating skills to
keep the interaction among the associations, the schools, and the
staff moving forward.[6]

Questions of Money and Staff

Financing the National Council as well as the study posed the usual
problem in social work of large ambitions and small resources. Profession-
wide belief in NCSWE and the need for a study, however, produced donations
from across the country and across the range of interests in social work education and practice. NCSWE also benefited from contributed professional and
clerical services, reducing the need for money in the bank. An initial budget of
$500 covered the cost of four meetings of the study committee. A budget of
$250,000, put forward to finance an organizational survey along with a study
of social work practice and education, found limited financial support.

The Carnegie Foundation, which had earlier expressed interest in providing financial help, awarded a grant of $31,000 to launch the study, stipu-
lating that: (1) it should be more limited, in light of the funds available,
than contemplated in the proposal and (2) the director should come from
outside the profession. The two requirements gave rise to questions about
the reduced scope of the study and some apprehension about a director
with no experience in social work or social work education. Nevertheless,
the National Council accepted the conditions and, from a long list of candidates, appointed Ernest V. Hollis as the director.

This turned out to be a fortunate choice. Hollis, as Chief of College
Administration for the U.S. Office of Education, had participated in studies
of a number of other professions. Better still, he was given a leave of absence on full salary to direct the study, thus removing a significant salary
item from the budget. The National Education Association, which had
handled the funds for an earlier study in which Hollis was involved, agreed
to do the same for the study of social work education. Alice Taylor Davis,[7]
a respected social worker with wide experience in social work practice and

education, administration and research, was selected as the assistant director. She was recruited from the Bureau of Public Assistance, which provided office space. The study was launched on October 1, 1948.

Process and Progress

Reactions to the study plans ranged from delighted acceptance to reluctant relief that at last something specific was being done to settle the
questions posed by the AASSW–NASSA conflict. Harper was particularly
enthusiastic about the choice of an "outsider" for the director. His support
was evidently of tremendous help to the staff as the study progressed. Davis
described Harper as a faithful and able committee member whose cooperation with Hollis did much to achieve "the final acceptance of the study's
recommendations by both groups of schools and the NCSWE."[8]

Kenneth Pray, dean of the Pennsylvania School of Social Work, served
until his untimely death as the first chair of NCSWE. Well-known and highly
respected in the profession, he spoke for many in the graduate schools
when he described the study in these terms:

> It is a truly momentous adventure, in which the stakes for all of us
> are enormous. The potential gains are great beyond calculation. But
> the risks, too, are by no means negligible. We are initially taking our
> lives in our hands. We are throwing open to question, and subject-
> ing to critical reevaluation, all that we have built by patient, labori-
> ous work over a whole generation.[9]

He went on to note that it was a sign of maturity, courage, and vision
that the profession of social work was willing, out of a sense of responsibility, to undergo a searching, impartial inquiry upon the foundations of its
professionalism. Harriett Bartlett, an equally well-known and respected
educator and medical social worker, replaced Pray as chair of the study
committee. Davis described her as "a leader par excellence—wise, patient,
well organized, and analytical. She used her extensive knowledge of education, research, and practice with utmost diplomatic skill in relations with
staff, the study committee members, and the profession."[10]

Differing expectations as to what should be studied and the methods to
be employed in the collection of material led to periods of high tension in
the initial phase of the research. At meetings of the AASSW, there seemed
to be a misunderstanding of what was being attempted. Bartlett wrote:

> A great deal of confusion seems to center about the expectation that
> this is to be a fact-finding study or survey. Dr. Hollis said he under-
> stood from the beginning that it was neither practical nor desirable
> to attempt statistical studies which would convince by weight of
> evidence. We sought his help as a person outside our field who
> could bring to bear on our problems a body of principles from higher
> education and broad practical experience.[11]

Davis described the change in attitudes as the study committee, the
director, faculties, deans, and practitioners throughout the country worked
together. They developed, she said, "a mutual respect and trust and responded enthusiastically to the stimulus of involvement and eager anticipation of the findings and recommendations."[12]

A problem expressed by Bartlett reflected, however, what seemed to be
a universal concern. Could a study of education for social work proceed
without a clear understanding of the knowledge, skills, and attitudes necessary for professional practice? The need for a study of practice along with a
study of education had been emphasized in the initial discussions within the
National Council, but insufficient financing effectively eliminated any such
possibility. Bartlett put it bluntly when she said:

> we must do this type of study sometime and the sooner we get
> started, the better. In fact, from my viewpoint, we should have
> begun twenty years ago.[13]

Following three years of field visits, analysis of reams of material, and
countless sessions, not only with professional groups but, also, with university and college administrators and members of the public, the report was
approved by the study committee in February 1951, officially accepted in
April, and published by Columbia University Press in December. These
words of praise were wired to Hollis upon its approval:

Congratulations and warm appreciation. Study Committee finds report creative, fresh, exciting, provocative, statesmanlike and objective. What more can you ask?[14]

THE HOLLIS-TAYLOR REPORT

When the report made its public appearance as *Social Work Education in the United States*, it held no surprises. The chapters, in draft, had been widely distributed and discussed. Hollis, in speeches and journal articles, had given advance notice of his views on general and professional education and the positions he was likely to take on the problems at issue. He held no brief for accreditation of what might be offered as undergraduate education and made clear his position on the level of education for professional social work. His early pronouncements, such as the following on the role of the undergraduate college, troubled the leaders of NASSA:

> In the chapter dealing with professional education, I will deal with and describe and justify the giving of this form of education in a separate graduate professional school whose program and procedures are controlled by social work educators working in cooperation with all other elements of the social work profession.
>
> In keeping with a similar line of reasoning, it will be my position that the people who are now charged with the responsibility of operating undergraduate colleges for the purposes of general and liberal education should have as clear-cut a responsibility for the social welfare concepts taught at this level as they have for concepts basic to law, medicine, public health, business administration, and similar fields. In proposing concepts I shall follow the clearly discernible trend among most professions of modifying or eliminating specific pre-professional requirements in favor of sound liberal education.[15]

Writing to Harold E. Wetzel, NASSA President from 1949 to 1952, Ernest Harper stated his agreement with Hollis in opposing any form of approval of undergraduate curricula, but added:

Try setting down Hollis proposals in one column and our own philosophy of social work education in another and study the result. I've
found it rather disconcerting. I favor his accreditation recommendation but on nearly everything else our position has been the reverse! . . .
If he is right we must revise our philosophy and get busy on the task.[16]

Role of Undergraduate Education

Following the decade of contention about graduate and undergraduate
education in social work, the final recommendations were eagerly awaited.
Hollis referred to the decision taken by AASSW in 1937 to require graduate
education in these words:

> While the decision regarding graduate study may have been prema-
> ture at the time, the present level of developments in general educa-
> tion and in professional social work indicates that it is a sound policy
> for the future.[17]

In the final recommendations, the commitment to graduate education
is clear, but with a highly significant proviso. Professional preparation does
not stand alone, but begins with an undergraduate concentration and pro-
ceeds through graduate study and ongoing professional development. The
nature of the undergraduate concentration, as outlined in the report, is
hard to follow in terms of the content to be included, but not in what should
be excluded, as here recorded:

> It should not include concepts and experiences that require the intel-
> lectual and social maturation associated with later stages of graduate
> professional development. For example, it should not include the teach-
> ing of professional skills or require students to engage in casework and
> other professional practice as a learning experience prior to their under-
> going a series of graduated learning experiences that include both a
> knowledge and feeling component. At the other extreme, an under-
> graduate concentration should not include learning of a technical and
> vocational nature that can be secured more quickly and effectively as
> on-the-job training in a social work agency or as outcomes of especially

designed semi-professional courses of a terminal character for which
credit toward college graduation ordinarily is not given.[18]

The content suggested for inclusion is described as embedded in prac-
tically every field or department in the college, with particular mention of
anthropology, philosophy, biology, literature, statistics, psychology, genet-
ics, sociology, ethics, home economics, religion, economics, and government. The impossibility of taking the usual credit courses in each or all of
those fields was said to require the "unglamorous and even painful task of
identifying key concepts and selecting teaching materials for a composite
course or courses. . ."[19] In discussing the concepts to be communicated not
only to future social workers but also to all undergraduate students in arts
and sciences, Hollis laid particular stress on the need of every educated
citizen to understand the philosophy and purposes of social welfare.

The authors recognized that reorganization of undergraduate education in this regard would not be easy. They put the burden of working out
the concepts and teaching materials on whatever organization emerged to
represent a unified social work profession. However, the administration of
the concentration along with responsibility for organization of the content
into courses and sequences was left to the undergraduate college. The report, as noted here, counted on talented teaching to bridge the gap between professional content and undergraduate course offerings:

> What is needed are teachers who, in addition to having an intellectual
> command of their fields, know the contexts in which prospective social
> workers use the learning outcomes of their fields. Professionalizing arts
> and sciences concepts is a matter of giving the emotional tone or colora-
> tion and valuation associated with professional application. . .[20]

Mixed Reactions

Arlien Johnson, an influential graduate educator, noted a problem with
this particular recommendation that was widely shared. She accepted the
proposed objectives of undergraduate education as excellent and even as stir-
ring the imagination, but questioned the proposed method of achievement:

But how? . . . They ostensibly leave control to the liberal arts college but they "professionalize" the content of the instruction. Every profession yearns for such a happy solution—and the liberal arts
college is very jealous of its own prerogatives. Where will lie the
balance of power? No, in spite of the desirability of the authors'
'concentration,' it seems to me it could be rarely achieved. . .[21]

Helen Wright, the founding president of the Council on Social Work
Education, was critical of some of the recommendations, but was ready to
move on the "unglamorous" task of identifying key concepts to be taught
at the undergraduate level of social work education:

As Dr. Hollis has well pointed out, the professional school has an obligation to work with the undergraduate college to let them know the
needs of students who enter graduate schools of social work. In other
words, we can do the job of professional education which is demanded
of us only if we can get students who are prepared for education which
is wholly professional—not the mixture of general and professional
that is given today in the name of professional education.[22]

She recognized the difficulty of predicting when the suggested changes
could take place but emphasized an obligation on the part of the profession
to move in that direction. She identified benefits beyond those applicable to
social work education:

The effect of the changes that are needed here to prepare students
for a professional curriculum would not be limited to the profession
of social work. They would facilitate communication with other
professional groups and would do much to make possible the achievement of the broad aims of social work. It cannot be stated too often
that the goals of social work cannot be attained by social workers
alone; they must be understood and accepted by others.[23]

How undergraduate educators reacted can be sensed in an article by
Ernest Harper. He described the changes that took place in attitudes and
views on undergraduate education as a result of the many sources of interaction before and during the study process. He granted that the recom-

mended concentration was somewhat less professional than favored by many undergraduate colleges, particularly with respect to skills teaching and practice. He regarded the report and accepted its findings as "bench marks" for future development, not as "blue prints for immediate action." He understood Hollis to be "quite conscious of the temporary need and justification for a more vocationally oriented undergraduate curriculum than the proposed concentration recommended as a long-time function of the college." Working on that long-time function was welcomed by Harper as a major task for the newly created Council on Social Work Education, specifically its Division of Undergraduate Departments. He wrote:

> It will be the job of this division, in cooperation with that on graduate schools to assist the colleges in discovering and defining the social welfare concepts which the authors hope can be made to infiltrate general education, as well as those which may properly be allocated to the junior-senior concentration. . . . Undergraduate social work courses in the future, as Dr. Hollis sees them, will not only be interdisciplinary and comprehensive in nature but will also be constructed on the assumption that 'knowing, doing, and being,' on the part of the student should proceed hand in hand.[24]

Proposals for Graduate Education

The authors clearly state, in the Preface, that the study hoped to produce benchmarks for use in charting for the profession and universities a course of action for the next two or three decades. Emphasis is placed on what the study did not try to do: it was not a survey, not a treatise on organization and administration, not a manual on accreditation, and definitely it was not a curriculum study. The recommendations were designed to deal with broad fundamentals, which would set forth principles and policies for use by the profession in developing curriculum content and establishing organizational and administrative procedures.[25]

The recommendations for graduate education developed within this broad framework produced another set of mixed reactions. The member schools of AASSW were gratified by the resolution of the two major conflicts: (1) the role of undergraduate education in the preparation of social workers and (2) the recommendation that only graduate education for social work should be accredited. A repetitive reference throughout the study to basic (generic) education was welcomed by the Curriculum Committee of the AASSW and several of the leading schools, all of whom were working on curriculum reform in that direction. Hollis recommended what he called basic professional education for an array of social work functions far beyond those traditionally associated with the profession. He saw this as the most fundamental need of the profession and called attention to an address delivered by Edith Abbott in 1928, in which she called for a basic curriculum with an integrated class and field program to prepare social workers for a profession, not for narrowly conceived practice based on "casework methods and such phenomena as the ego libido and various psychiatric diagnoses, and such exigencies as community chest fund campaigns."[26] The strong support in the study for generic preparation was stated, as follows:

> The assumption is that a social worker employs or should employ similar professional skills under defined circumstances regardless of whether he is engaged in a private group work or casework agency or is employed by the courts, an industrial corporation, a labor union, a federal agency, or a county welfare department.[27]

This broadening of the scope of social work education, although appreciated by many, was perceived by some as an attack on casework. Indeed, the pronouncements on casework and field work became the most widely discussed and debated part of the final report. The study took the position that while casework was the profession's greatest strength, it also was an important handicap to improvement of the curriculum.

Casework was described as the "matrix out of which most social work principles, content, and processes have emerged,"[28] thus becoming synonymous with social work itself and limiting its influence.

To achieve a broader vision for social work education, the study called for the identification of concepts, which would then be arranged into sequences providing continuity and progression in learning, which in turn would be organized into comprehensive areas of instruction. In a later assessment of this recommendation, Grace Coyle wrote:

> Some of us remember the shock of the Hollis-Taylor report on Social Work Education. The report stated that social work education lacked adequate conceptual thinking and could not develop to its true professional level until it had grown its own consistent set of concepts. After some initial resentment at this attack, real movement has been made in recent years in this direction.[29]

The recommendations on field work generated the greatest shock to the graduate schools. Field work, along with casework, had from the beginnings in the charity organization movement given social work its distinctive character as an emerging profession. Hollis questioned the disproportionate amount of time allocated to field work, the costs involved, and the qualifications of agency supervisors to teach graduate students. He argued, further, that first-year students were not ready to assume responsibility for working with a case or group. He proposed a different method of achieving the "learning 'to do' and 'to be' associated with field teaching while bringing it into line with graduate education."[30] The instruction in the first year would be conducted in the classroom with a panel of school and agency field teachers. Teaching units were to be organized with objectives identical to those of classroom work. This would enable the student to progress from observation and group participation to the assumption of individual responsibility for direct service to individuals or groups. He urged research and experimentation to clarify methods of field instruction and concluded:

> the paramount principle to be observed in revising the field teaching aspects of the basic curriculum is to have the same broad content of social work taught in the classroom and in the field and to relate the field assignments given students to their background and knowledge and experience.[31]

This call for better-organized and more conceptual teaching in both class and field had a dubious reception at the time. In the 1950s and 1960s, however, curriculum reform, including research and experimentation with new approaches to teaching and learning in the field, became key program activities for the present Council on Social Work Education.

CLOSING THE CURTAIN

A major principle, forcefully underlined throughout the Hollis-Taylor report, asserted that education for social work is a responsibility not only of educators but equally of organized practitioners, employing agencies, and the interested public. Widely accepted by the profession, this assertion became the cornerstone of all subsequent developments. The authors declared:

> It is the position of this report that all organized segments of the social work profession should join in the development and equitable support of an organization through which they and the public can have an effective voice in shaping and maintaining educational and accrediting policies and procedures.[32]

With the study close to completion, the National Council, in October 1949, established a Special Committee on Structure for a Social Work Education Organization. Following two meetings, the Special Committee presented a report in March 1950 that included a statement of assumptions, a statement of functions, and suggested by-laws for what would emerge in 1952 as the Council on Social Work Education. The Special Committee introduced its report with this account of its assignment:

> It was agreed [by NCSWE] that plans should be made immediately for implementation of the findings and recommendations of the study. Specifically, it was suggested that consideration be given by the [National] Council to the kind of organizational structure which would be necessary for the development of programs of social work education to replace the existing organizations in the field. There was general acceptance of the principle that the responsibility for developing sound programs of social work education must be shared

by the educational institutions, the professional membership organizations, the employing agencies and the general public. The recommendations in the study stress the importance of having a single
unified and adequately financed social work education organization
in which the above groups share their appropriate roles.[33]

The Beginning of the End

The inevitability of their passage from the scene as separate organizations
prompted the leaders of AASSW and NASSA to express their thoughts in
farewell speeches. The supporting cast from the field and the profession also
had words to say about the advent of a new force in social work education.

AASSW

Helen Wright, the last president of AASSW and the first president of
CSWE, addressed the graduate schools at the final annual meeting of the
association in January 1951. By the following January, she expected the
new Council on Social Work Education to have taken over many of the
tasks formerly the responsibility of AASSW. She introduced her speech with
the following remarks:

> The schools which are represented here today have varying feelings
> about what this will mean for the advancement of social work edu-
> cation to which we in the schools are devoting our lives. A few, I
> fear, believe we are selling our birthright for a mess of pottage; a few
> may look on the new organization as the Moses that will quickly
> lead us to the promised land; probably most have some questions
> about the step we are taking—even though the step seems inevi-
> table and in the right direction.[34]

NASSA

Hattie Cal Maxted, then serving as president of NASSA, addressed the
membership at their final meeting in May 1952. She referred to the path
they had followed for 10 years and concluded:

It does not appear to be bragging if we claim that NASSA should be given credit for providing the motivating force for the formation of the Council. It seems almost fantastic what a small group with no prestige and no money to speak of has accomplished. [35]

She went on to express high hopes for undergraduate education within the new organization and said:

NASSA as a protest group will disappear and, we hope, that persons interested in social work education will consider both undergraduate and graduate education to have an equally important, if different, place in the field of social work and that we can all work together to improve both types of education.[36]

Ernest Harper had worked closely with Hollis and Taylor to bring about the merger. His final words, in a critique of the report, consisted of a tribute to all who had contributed to the outcome along with a plaintive personal remark: "It has been a long road and the human cost has been great."[37] Anticipating the merger, he had applied for AASSW membership, which was granted early in 1952. The Universities of Oklahoma and Florida had earlier taken the same step, much to the chagrin of both Harper and Maxted. Notwithstanding his newly minted membership in AASSW, Harper's allegiance remained with NASSA, as seen in a letter to Maxted:

As you know, I waited until the last possible moment and can face the prospect of being within the AASSW with equanimity only with the knowledge that its days are limited and after July first, if all goes well, we will all be together.[38]

Maxted was brief in her acknowledgement of the news:

Congratulations on being admitted to AASSW. . . . I am wondering if AASSW is gradually taking our members or if we are setting up a fifth column within their ranks.[39]

The Practitioners

AASW welcomed the news that the National Council had established a committee to develop plans for a single unified organization for social work education. Much was said at a meeting of its Board of Directors in January 1950 about the stake of the total profession in the educational preparation of its members. The following excerpt expresses support for a broadly based new organization:

> There is a growing conviction in the field, as represented in the NCSWE, that the responsibility for the development and advancement of educational institutions and programs must be shared by all the members of the social work community, educational institutions, the professional membership and the general public.[40]

They expressed gratification at the action of the National Council in moving quickly to produce a constitution for a single unified organization and urged financial support from all the interests involved. The AASW was already moving in that direction through a special assessment on its members to assist the AASSW in meeting its obligations and winding up its affairs in the transition to a new entity. In addition, a committee was established to explore the feasibility of a plan for ongoing support of social work education through an appropriate contribution from the AASW membership.[41]

Employing Agencies

The employing agencies were represented on the National Council by the American Public Welfare Association for the public field and the National Social Welfare Assembly for the major private agencies. Two questions were raised in their examination of the Structure Report and the proposed by-laws: (1) how to ensure participation of the various non-academic groups through appropriate representation in governance and program activities, and (2) how to meet the urgent need for adequate financing and identification of possible sources of support. They recognized, as seen in the following account, a difference in the degree of interest in education among those groups and the consequences for financial support:

> Representatives of the voluntary agencies indicated that acceptance of the plan by the individual agencies would depend on the degree to which there was understanding on the part of the professional

and lay leadership regarding their stake in social work education. The opinion was expressed also that as this understanding increased there would be a greater acceptance of financial responsibility on the part of employing agencies.[42]

Questions of representation and financing remained to be answered. How it was done will be described in the story of the creation of the Council on Social Work Education, as told in Part Two of this historical account. Meanwhile, let the curtain fall on the story of its antecedents with these words of wisdom from Harriett Bartlett, which may still provide thoughts to ponder:

> As we consider the implications of the study we can see that in the past, social workers have been too concerned with segmental, specific, and immediate interests. We have done too much acting and not enough thinking. To attain our full growth we must not only be able to grasp the intellectual concept of a united profession but also go through a change of feeling which will place togetherness ahead of separateness. We must learn to think and act together in a sustained way toward common objectives.[43]

Part Two

**Council on Social Work Education:
First Twenty Years**

Chapter Six
New Beginnings

On a brisk sunny day in January 1952, representatives of the graduate schools, the undergraduate departments, the seven membership organizations, and the social work and social welfare employing agencies came together at the Roosevelt Hotel in New York City to launch a new organization—the present Council on Social Work Education. At last, major differences had been resolved, making possible the adoption of by-laws at a constitutional convention attended by a veritable galaxy of dignitaries. The atmosphere exuded feelings of achievement, excitement, and relief. As in all new beginnings, faith and hope conquered reservations about what would happen next. The superseded National Council had paved the way for this culminating event through the excellent work over a two-year period of its Special Committee on Structure, which drafted a constitution that served as a model for the final version.[1]

ERECTING THE FRAMEWORK

The unifying concept of social work education as the concern of the total profession had to find expression in the way in which the new organization was governed and financed. Questions of representation and voting rights were discussed and resolved through the provision of two classes of membership, constituent and associate. The constituent members, which included the graduate schools, undergraduate departments, the several membership associations, and the national employing agencies, were represented, all with voting rights, on the Council of Delegates, the chief legislative body. Associate membership was available to individuals and organizations not entitled to constituent membership but interested in social work education and willing to support the activities of the newfound Council. Associate members were entitled to all rights and privileges of membership except for the right to vote and representation on the Council of Delegates.

With agreement that the Council would begin operations on July 1, 1952, the founders lost no time in preparing for that memorable event. Nathan Cohen, the able chair of the terminating National Council on Social Work Education, convened the first meeting of the new Council of Delegates on May 27, 1952, in Chicago. A previously appointed Nominating Committee with Fedele Fauri, now a dean but formerly with the Social Security Administration, as the chair presented a single slate for officers and Board members. Harold Wetzel, a former president of NASSA, moved its acceptance and the following officers were elected:

President	Helen Wright, University of Chicago
First Vice-President	Benjamin Youngdahl, Washington University
Second Vice-President	Ernest Harper, Michigan State University
Third Vice-President	Jane Hoey, Bureau of Public Assistance
Secretary	Nathan Cohen, New York School of Social Work
Treasurer	Wilbur Newstetter, University of Pittsburgh

The Council also elected 15 of the 18-member Board of Directors, leaving for later election the three delegates-at-large representing other professions and the general public. The Board of Directors immediately came to order on that same day to elect an Executive Committee, retain for one year the staff of the AASSW, accept an invitation from Washington University to hold its first Annual Program Meeting in St. Louis in January 1953, and to plan for the organization of the four standing commissions authorized in the by-laws. Administrative questions involving office space, tax exemption, and finances were also dealt with, clearing the way to begin operations on July 1, 1952.

THE TASKS OF TRANSITION

For several years the American Association of Schools of Social Work had shared an office with the American Association of Social Work at One

Park Avenue, New York, with the executive secretaries and their respective assistants anchoring each end. The relations were cordial and mutually supportive. The vision for the new Council, however, demanded more ample and independent housing, yet no other location could be considered until there was enough money in the budget to cover a much higher rent. Thus, the doors that opened on July 1 for the Council on Social Work Education were exactly the same as the doors that closed on the AASSW. The Council took over the furniture, the files, essential program activities, the remaining assets, and the staff of the AASSW.

The transfer of staff and all equipment from the association of graduate schools could perhaps have raised questions. That this did not happen was due to rather special circumstances. NASSA had no employed staff and no office space or equipment to offer and no money was available to provide furnished quarters for the new organization. Katherine Kendall, hired as educational secretary, had joined AASSW as executive secretary in January 1951 with responsibility for moving the association into the Council on Social Work Education. Her employment in the previous decade as assistant director of the Latin American and International Unit of the Children's Bureau and as a social affairs officer in the Secretariat of the United Nations had removed her from involvement in the troubles of social work education in the United States. Elizabeth (Betty) Neely, hired as secretary for commissions, was also a new employee with no direct involvement in the graduate–undergraduate controversy. She had come to the staff of AASSW as associate executive secretary from an executive position with the Young Women's Christian Association and 18 years of experience in developing leaders among young women in business and industry. Both, from their previous professional experience, welcomed the breadth of vision implicit in the mission of the new Council and the wide representation of interests in its organization and governance. When Mildred Sikkema, who had served as executive secretary of the National Association of School Social Workers, joined the staff in June 1954, the core team working for many years with Ernest Witte was complete.

To find the right executive director was clearly the first order of business for the Board of Directors. A search begun under the direction of President Helen Wright led to the selection of Witte, who was unanimously and enthusiastically approved by the Board at its second meeting in November 1952, with the appointment to become effective in January 1953. Witte was exactly what the Council on Social Work Education needed to become a new and guiding force in social work education. His background as a social work dean at the University of Washington and the University of Nebraska combined with his experience as a senior official in the Bureau of Public Assistance provided much needed leadership to bring together former warring factions and move the Council forward in new directions. As president of the AASW, he had already deeply involved the field of practice with the new organization of educators through his success in sponsoring a dues supplement of $1 on each AASW member in support of social work education.

His views on what needed to be done to make the Council succeed are worth recording. This is some of what he said in his official unveiling at the first Annual Program Meeting in St. Louis in January 1953:

> We are not at all clear as to just what we are. Are we a service agency, are we a coordinating agency, or do we see ourselves as an operating agency? Or, do we combine all those functions? . . . While we have many friends, . . . I think that also there are many who are hostile, indifferent or just don't understand us at all. . . . There is need for some definitive long-range planning. We need to determine for ourselves the directions in which we are proceeding and the milestones that need to be created along the way.[2]

He noted there had been a good deal of talk about problems in relationships. Wouldn't it be wiser, he asked, instead of indulging in rumors and more and more talk that only made some people more and more defensive, to concentrate on working together to get a sense of direction and to develop a true team spirit? The extent to which he was being regarded as a messiah bothered him. He sensed that his emergence on the scene was encouraging a "messianic complex" in both staff and Board, which expected him to solve overnight all the Council's problems. He made it clear that he thought the problems could be solved but that the accomplishments would come from everyone working together over the long pull.

UNIFYING THE CONSTITUENCY

The working together of a wide array of interests had clearly emerged as the central idea underlying the Council on Social Work Education. This called for close cooperation of the educational programs, undergraduate and graduate, with the membership organizations, the employing agencies, and the general public. It was easy enough to provide for cooperative relationships in the by-laws and organizational structure. How to overcome lingering doubts and vested interests occupied the minds of the founding leaders. Helen Wright, the newly elected president, noted in her inaugural address at the first Annual Program Meeting in 1953:

> We have brought together in a single organization a number of organizations, each of which has been concerned in its own way with education for social work or some phase of such education. We have done this because we believe that together we may march more surely toward the promised land. But as we have all been marching separately we have inevitably become accustomed to certain ways of doing things, certain roles that we have defined as ours. If we are to march together successfully each organization must think through anew what is now its proper role in relation to education, what that it has done before can now appropriately be done by the Council. The Council is new and untried; can we trust it to carry us forward?. . . Unless the organizations that make up the Council can have. . . faith and accept some discomfort, the Council will be but another organization among many and will but add to the previous confusion, not move us toward our goal. We have come together because we believe in a united effort; our first task is to see that the effort is really united.[3]

For each constituent member of the new organization, there were problems of relationship to be overcome and hopes to be fulfilled.

The Educational Institutions

Wright, in that same inaugural address, said with respect to the under-graduate–graduate relationships,

> we have come together at a pretty high level of abstraction, and old
> differences will undoubtedly raise their heads as we move forward
> toward more specific thinking. I believe, however, that we can get
> the agreement that is necessary; we have learned something about
> give and take in the first part of our journey; we have gained some
> trust in each other's good faith, some respect for each other's point
> of view. I believe that we shall not forget what we have learned as
> we try to move forward.[4]

Problems arose with respect to the functions of the four standing commissions charged with programmatic responsibilities.[5] This was particularly true in the relationship of the Commission on Schools and Departments, with its Undergraduate and Graduate Divisions, to the rest of the Council. At first, the commission anticipated that it would be assigned major educational services provided by former AASSW committees concerned with the advanced curriculum, teaching materials, admissions, and socio-cultural content. It was also thought the commission should carry responsibility for the educational aspects of the Annual Program Meeting.[6] The possible perception that the Graduate Division of the Commission was resuscitating the AASSW revealed the need to clarify the role and function of each of the commissions.

The chair of the Commission on Schools and Departments reported several significant initiatives involving cooperative work on the nature and content of undergraduate education by graduate and undergraduate faculty members. Excellent rapport between the two groups was reported after the first meeting of the commission in 1953.[7] Harold Wetzel, a former president of NASSA and now chair of the Undergraduate Division, spoke to the differences that existed in the strength of the supporting social science departments offering undergraduate education and the need for sharing and pooling information on the content of undergraduate sequences. He said that much more was needed as a unifying process than calling all introductory courses by the same name and added "this first annual meeting of the Council on Social Work Education is a happy beginning."[8]

Membership Organizations

The specialized membership organizations with long-term experience in developing curriculum content and accrediting of psychiatric and medical social work sequences in graduate education naturally wondered about their continuing educational responsibility in the new united structure. In this connection and as a general statement of policy, Nathan Cohen, as a member of the Board of Directors, summarized the philosophy that should guide the Council in its relationships:

> The coming into being of the Council on Social Work Education represents a recognition of the importance of interdependence, which concept, in relation to the Council, might include the following:
>
> 1. Schools, programs, and agencies are a means to an end and not an end in themselves, that the end set by all of those groups making up the Council is the furtherance of social work education.
>
> 2. That the efforts of the various groups which make up the Council are inextricably interwoven in the achievement of the overall goal of furthering social work education. Therefore, all the constituent groups in their participation in the Council must be concerned with the goals of social work education as a whole rather than limit themselves to specialized interests or the specialized approach of the particular group.
>
> 3. Different groups may utilize different byways and highways to reach those goals and there should be encouragement of their contribution. At the same time, it should be realized that without a sufficient emphasis on the overall goals as well as difference, the very fabric that makes difference possible can be destroyed.[9]

By their inclusion on the Commission on Accreditation and direct involvement in the various committees concerned with education, the several membership organizations with educational responsibilities soon found their rightful place within the new structure.

Employing Agencies

The wide range of public and voluntary agencies related or potentially related to the Council called for individualized consideration of the extent of their interest and involvement. Again in her inaugural address, Wright spoke forcefully on the need for definition of the relationship between the schools of social work and the agencies in which students were placed and later employed. She asserted that agencies and schools should do much more joint thinking of which little had been done locally and none nationally. She concluded: "It is my firm conviction that unless this Council can promote joint thinking between schools and agencies on school curricula and agency in-service training, it will fail in one of its major opportunities to improve education for social work."[10]

A similar plea came from the American Public Welfare Association. As a major participant in the preceding National Council, APWA continued with the new Council to call attention to the personnel shortages in the public social services. Emphasis was also placed on the need for a study of the vast array of public jobs to discover the knowledge and skills they required so that better decisions could be made about suitable training. The idea that not all positions required graduates of the two-year professional curriculum continued to be voiced. Maurice O. Hunt, speaking for APWA, said this at the first Annual Program Meeting of the new Council:

> we might as well face the fact that for many years to come the principle source of new, young workers coming into the public social services is likely to be the undergraduate school. The sheer volume of the number of workers needed points to this conclusion.[11]

He went on to point out the necessity to improve and expand undergraduate training in order to produce public service employees with a foundation for staff training and progression into graduate programs for full qualification as social workers. The Council was expected to give leadership in clarifying the goals and content of undergraduate education along with the provision of assistance in the development of in-service training. Remarking on the progress of cooperative work done nationally to encourage joint thinking and planning between schools and agencies, he now recommended similar activity at the state level. Representation on statewide committees from public and private agencies, the professional membership organizations, and the schools would offer a great opportunity for constructive work on an urgent problem.

A representative voice of leading private agencies came from Jeanette Regensburg, a member of the staff of the Community Service Society of New York. She described current needs in the private field as requiring highly skilled practitioners, with competence to work with other professions from a position of firm self-identification as a social worker. It was a tribute to the new constellation of forces within CSWE to hear, from this bastion of casework at the peak of its psychodynamic development, strong support for a broader curriculum. The desirability was stressed for an undergraduate underpinning to include knowledge from the social and biological sciences and understanding of the effect of political, economic, and cultural factors on the social welfare system. An increased knowledge of group process, better understanding of community organization and administration, and a plea for knowledge of the history of social work in the United States all reflected expectations of an enlarged vision for the educational task. The closing sentence expresses an optimistic view of the future:

> Consistent opportunity, such as is offered by this morning's meeting [Annual Program Meeting], and hopefully also will be possible in working committees, for joint consideration of professional education, its objectives and its content, cannot fail to result in the production of social workers with increasing competence to fulfill the obligations entrusted to them.[12]

A more forceful view of what was needed in social work education was taken by a representative of community chests and councils, Chester Bower. In a hard-hitting account of the dangers of social work isolation from the larger community, he emphasized the need for the Council to get a community viewpoint into the faculty, the curriculum, and field work. With illustrations such as the following, he asserted that more than a course in community organization was needed:

> I asked nearly a hundred people the question, 'If you had an opportunity to influence the professional education of social workers, what would you wish done differently than is now being done?' . . . there was a remarkable unanimity of opinion around one concept. It is this: Social workers should be more 'community conscious' than they are.
>
> We are all painfully aware of the need to have the general public understand welfare, health, and recreation programs, and the role of the professional worker in them. But how is the public going to get that knowledge and understanding if he never meets a social worker? . . . Apparently only the select few in social work have enough contact with board members, Chamber of Commerce committees, service clubs, and budget committee members to feel at home with them and able to talk their language. This is an unhealthy situation for both social workers and the community.[13]

The founders of the Council, aware of what Bower called social work isolation, hoped to make the profession more community-conscious through the inclusion of the general public in its brave new approach to social work education.

The General Public

While Council members, in the main, were not unaware of the desirability of citizen support of social service, they faced a completely new development in finding productive ways to share their problems and all aspects of their work with representatives of the general public. To some extent, the way had been paved by the participation of persons from outside the field in the forerunner National Council, but a more telling influence came from the Hollis-Taylor report. Hollis was particularly keen to broaden the sights of social work educators through their identification of social welfare concepts for use in liberal arts programs. He saw this as necessary to the education of future citizens who, as legislators, businesspeople, lawyers, doctors, educators, etc., would be in a position to influence social policies and the need for qualified personnel for social welfare programs.

> On its part, the social work profession should face squarely up to the fact that it cannot have a milieu favorable to the development of social work, comparable to that now enjoyed by the education and health professions, until each community and state has a substantial contingent of citizens who are informed and in sympathy with the purpose of social welfare programs.[14]

An early representative of the general public on the Council board outlined in detail the significance of lay participation in the professional preparation of social workers. She wrote:

> Social work education *ought to be* everybody's concern—as much that of volunteers and board members as of deans and agency executives. Unfortunately, it isn't. As a volunteer and board member in medical and social welfare agencies, I have found that there is an abysmal lack of awareness of the values, processes, and problems of social work education, not only in the community at large but on the boards of directors of welfare agencies. It seems a thing apart from the agency's direct services with which the board member has become familiar. . . . If this form of education is really to become a vital concern of laymen, then there is a large gap yet to be bridged. The Council has taken a significant step in helping to bridge this gap, by asking laymen to serve on its board, council, and commissions.[15]

Determining what was meant by the general public and who should serve as delegates-at-large emerged as one of the first tasks of the newly formed Council. The Executive Committee, meeting shortly after the be-

ginning of operations in July 1952, established the following categories and
quotas to be used in the election of 12 delegates-at-large for the Council on
Delegates of 78 members: 5 from the laymen category; 4 from higher
education; 2 from other professions; and 1 from labor. The necessity of
obtaining urgently needed financial support had much to do with the pre-
dominance of lay members as representatives from outside the profession
in the governance of the Council. This was indeed an important consideration, but in the first 20 years of CSWE it is clear that citizen participation not
only produced substantial contributions in terms of money but, more significantly, in community understanding and support of social work education.

THE FINANCIAL FACTOR

Inevitably, discussion of these many hopes and expectations raised the
question of how the complicated structure and ambitious program proposals for the new organization would be financed. The following sources of
income, presented by a Committee on Personnel and Finance in July 1952,
showed optimistic and conservative estimates:[16]

Source of Funds	Optimistic	In Sight
Membership Dues		
Graduate Schools	14,000	14,000
Undergraduate Departments	1,250	475
Membership Associations	13,000	13,000
Employing Agencies	5,000	2,450
Associate Members	2,000	—
Contributions		
AASSW (carried over)	3,000	2,850
NASSA (carried over)	300	300
Individuals	2,000	—
Annual Meeting Registrations	1,200	1,200
Publications	3,000	3,000
USPHS Grant	16,480	16,480
TOTAL	**61,230**	**53,605**

General Fund Only

Income	45,230	37,605
Expenditures	42,312	42,312
Plus or Minus	+2,918	-4,707

Even taking into account differences in cost of living and inflation, the estimated income was seriously inadequate to support the Council. Fundraising became a priority activity that awaited the arrival of an executive director. It is obvious, however, that without the grant from the National Institute of Mental Health and the membership dues from the practitioner associations, the survival of the new organization would have been problematic. As in several previous crises for the AASSW, the AASW along with the specialized membership groups came to the rescue with a levy of $1 per member in support of social work education. The story of how this came about deserves recognition.

Practitioner Support[17]

In 1947, the prospect of its early demise as an independent organization faced the AASSW with a severe financial crisis. Membership dues had been doubled, thus raised to the maximum possible limit. Outside funds from foundations could no longer be solicited or obtained because of the uncertainty about the future of the association. To meet the emergency, the AASSW Board of Directors appealed to the AASW for an initial grant of $2,000. The response, while strongly affirming responsibility for quality social work education, voiced regret that its own uncertain financial position required a negative answer. The AASW did, however, appoint a committee, with representation from both organizations, to consider cooperation on joint projects. For several years thereafter, the AASW agreed to carry for the AASSW responsibility for the collection and publication of enrollment statistics, the preparation and distribution of recruitment material, and the provision of professional and clerical service of a general nature in the field of social work education. While serious consideration was given at that time to a merger of the two organizations, the establishment of the National Council and launching of the Hollis-Taylor study promised a new and different solution to the problems in social work education.

In 1949, the need for financial support of the AASSW surfaced again. This time the Executive Committee of AASW was much more receptive. To assist in the development of a single unified educational association, it tentatively proposed a special levy on its membership in support of social work education. Subsequently in 1950, the AASW Board of Directors adopted a resolution recommending that, beginning July 1, 1950, an assessment of $1 be levied on both full and junior members of the association, with the $10,000 thus raised made available to AASSW.

The Delegate Conference approved the proposed assessment later that year. While the intent of the resolution seemed to cover a one-year contribution, there was a clear implication that support of social work education would be a continuing responsibility. Only one vote was cast against the action recommended by the Board of Directors (the name of the lone dissenter and the reasons for the action are not recorded). The AASW stood committed to financial support of the Council on Social Work Education and the other practitioner groups followed suit.

Many voices were raised in support of the $1 assessment, but there was none more eloquent than the voice of Ernest Witte, at that time the president of AASW, and later the executive director of the Council. His ringing endorsement of the resolutions in support of social work education had much to do with the overwhelming acceptance of a new financial responsibility. An excerpt follows:

> The only possibility of financing the Council on Social Work Education, which is going to bring unity in the whole field of education between two different organizations which were both claiming accrediting functions, has now been resolved. . . . we are also getting a wider across the board representation of the profession, along with some of the general citizenry. . . .
>
> Through the Council, we are going to have a service to the schools

of social work in the improvement of their educational standard, in a more uniform educational standard, in strengthening some of the weaker schools, in helping schools develop curricula, in doing research in the field of social work education, in developing literature for that field of education, and all the other things that go into an educational program and a standard setting organization.

Now, who are the groups that are likely to finance social work education: They are the practitioners in the field and that is us. Then there are the schools of social work in the educational field. They have been carrying most of the burden heretofore, and they will continue to help the financing. And for the first time, we are going to have the national membership organizations. . . . We are bringing all of those interests together in trying to get finances to do a better job than has even been done before in the field of education of social work.[18]

Kendall, at that time executive secretary of AASSW, reported at the final business meeting of the association in January 1952, that all the practitioner groups had joined the AASW in contributing $1 per member:

I do want to call particular attention to one financial fact that carries special significance at this time. In recent years, several of the membership organizations have made a financial contribution to the work of the Association. This year, for the first time, every membership organization—the medical social workers, the psychiatric social workers, the group workers, the school social workers—so contributed and I should add that the contributions were gladly made despite the straightened financial circumstances of everyone of those organizations. The money itself is, of course, a welcome addition to our meager resources, but more important than the money is the evidence thus presented of support by the profession of social work education. This is indeed a happy augury for the future success of the Council on Social Work Education.[19]

THE CANADIAN CONNECTION

No mention has been made of the participation of Canadian schools of social work, first as members accredited by the AASSW and in 1952 as charter members of the Council on Social Work Education. While not internally affected by the AASSW–NASSA controversy, the Canadian representatives on the AASSW Board of Directors and major committees played an important role in the development of educational policy and services, both before and after the founding of the Council on Social Work Education.

The University of Toronto had the longest tenure, beginning in 1919 as a founding member of AASSW. The University of British Columbia, McGill University, and the University of Manitoba, as a one-year school, later joined the AASSW prior to the formation of the Council. At the last moment, just in time to become charter members, the Canadian contingent was enlarged to include the University of Ottawa, Laval University, and the University of Montreal.

Until 1970, the Canadian schools were accredited by the Council and entitled to the same services as their counterparts in the United States. Any services supported by U.S. Government grants were made available to the Canadian schools from the general fund. With the birth of the Council, however, questions arose in Canada as to the proper place of their schools in the new organization.

A paper presented in 1955 reported on a Canadian study that dealt with this question.[20] The Canadian schools said they wanted the advantages of CSWE accreditation as they were not yet ready to establish their own accrediting system. Faculty members also very much wanted to continue to participate in the educational activities as they had leaned heavily on the wider contacts, the availability of teaching materials and other aids, and the opportunities for an exchange of problems and experience. Nevertheless, there was concern that the few Canadian schools would get lost in the broadened CSWE constituency. Despite the similarities, the differences in size, auspices, and in language for several of the schools pointed to the need for the Canadian schools to study their own problems, using the Hollis-Taylor report as a guide.

A new Canadian Association for Education in the Social Services, somewhat patterned on the U.S. model, was established in 1967. It included a Committee of Schools, the Canadian Association of Social Workers (CASW), and the Canadian Welfare Council. The Canadian schools continued their connection with CSWE and CASW became a constituent national agency member of the Council in 1968. By 1970, with the establishment of a number of new schools across Canada, the Committee of Schools became the Canadian Association of Schools of Social Work. The development of its own accrediting policies and procedures led, in 1970, to termination of the relationship with CSWE. Two or three of the original eight schools, while joining the new Canadian membership association, also maintained for a few years their accredited status as CSWE graduate school members. The parting was sad but not unfriendly. As elected officers and committee chairs and members of important educational and program services, Canadian leaders had done outstanding work, to the benefit of both countries. The end of what was a family as well as a formal relationship marked the beginning of a new kind of cooperation between the United States and Canada across national borders.

MARCHING FORWARD

The launching of the Council in 1952 laid bare problems of governance and resources to be solved as well as opportunities to be seized. On July 1, 1952, the constituent membership included 59 accredited graduate schools, 19 undergraduate departments, 7 practitioner organizations, and 18 employing agencies, of which 16 came from the private and 2 from the public field.[21] Ten years later, the number of employing agencies had increased to 46, the undergraduate departments had mushroomed to 115, and the accredited graduate schools had gained only 4 additional members for a count of 63.[22] Federal agencies not formally represented because of restrictions on their payment of dues later participated with the understanding that financial support would be available through service contracts. Representatives of the general public had not yet been identified.

With the arrival of Ernest Witte as executive director in January 1953, the snug office arrangement with AASW, while inexpensive, was no longer viable. It was a stroke of luck and a happy omen for the future that the Carnegie Corporation had decided to finance a building across from the United Nations for the sole purpose of housing non-governmental organizations (NGOs). The Council moved into a small suite of offices which, in the 20-year period under review, were traded time and again for constantly larger space to accommodate the ever-expanding activities.

In moving forward, emphasis will be placed on a straightforward account of how the Council was governed and financed, its manifold responsibilities, and how they were discharged. With the scores of people providing leadership and service as staff and as officers and as members of multitudinous administrative units and committees, specific individuals will not be singled out unless there is a special reason for so doing. What follows, therefore, are just the relevant facts and viewpoints on what went on in the first 20 years when the author was directly involved.

Chapter Seven
Trial and Error in Governing

The ink was barely dry on the new by-laws before problems became apparent. Following the precedent set by the American Association of Schools of Social Work and the National Council on Social Work Education, the new Council on Social Work Education (CSWE)[1] was incorporated in New York State. As early as September 1953, a question arose as to the legality under New York corporation law of the powers assigned to the Council of Delegates and to the Commission on Accreditation.

THE ORGANIZATIONAL STRUCTURE[2]

To give all major organizational groups with a stake in social work education a role in governing CSWE, the by-laws established a Council of Delegates of 78 members. There were two classes of membership: (1) constituent with the right to vote and representation on the Council of Delegates and (2) associate with all rights and privileges except the right to vote and representation. The voting power in the Council of Delegates was distributed as follows:

- 30 from education, with 20 initially designated by AASSW and 10 by NASSA. Subsequently, the Commission on Schools and Departments carried this responsibility, with the same proportion from the graduate schools and undergraduate departments.
- 18 from the 7 practitioner organizations.
- 18 from employing agencies, with 9 designated by the American Public Welfare Association and 9 from private agencies designated by the National Social Welfare Assembly.
- 12 delegates-at-large, drawn from higher education, other professions, labor, and the general public.

Voting was by individuals, not organizations. The associate category of members included individuals, state and local agencies, and other organizations interested in social work education.

The Council of Delegates was designated as the major legislative body with power to determine policies and to act on all matters referred to it. At the same time, the Board of Directors was described as the governing body of CSWE, limited, however, to actions taken by the Council of Delegates.

Four standing commissions were appointed to discharge the functions and carry forward the program of the new organization: Accreditation; Program, Planning and Services, and Publications; Research; and Schools and Departments of Social Work. The Commission on Accreditation had sole responsibility for formulating standards and for the approval or disapproval of educational programs. Standards were referred to the Council of Delegates for approval, bypassing the Board of Directors, which was given the minor responsibility of appointing a three-member committee to act on appeals from commission decisions.

The legal question raised in 1953 concerned the powers given to the Council of Delegates and the Commission on Accreditation and also the limitations imposed on the Board of Directors. An officer of CSWE, troubled by the ambiguity as well as the legality of the distribution of power, sought an opinion from the dean of the law school at the University of Pittsburgh. The reply indicated that Section 27 of the New York Corporation Law specified as a basic principle: "The business of a corporation shall be managed by its board of directors."[3] The question of how to deal with this problem was not immediately answered, but became part of a general concern about the viability of the administrative structure.

Within little more than one year, it became evident that the structure was so complex as to impede effective administration and program planning. This led in 1953 to the appointment of a Committee to Study the Function and Purpose of the Council of Delegates with instructions not to change the fundamental structure of CSWE or the balance of representation. The first report to the Board late in 1954 declared:

The experience with the present structure of the Council of Delegates has not been a satisfactory one. Attendance has been only fair and there has been constant criticism from delegates around a lack of clarity about the role and function of the Council of Delegates.[4]

The committee emphasized that the structure, in theory, did carry out the desired objective to reflect in the new organization the concern of the total profession for the promotion of sound programs of social work education. However, the large size of the Council of Delegates, the infrequency and brevity of its meetings, with no provision for payment of expenses, made implementation of a policy-making function extremely difficult. The apparent contradiction in the by-laws giving some responsibility for policy-making to the Board of Directors compounded the problem. Upon review of the policy decisions that had been made by the Board, the committee declared "that such decisions could not have been postponed or handled within the present Council of Delegates operation."[5] Something had to be done.

By-Law Revisions, 1958

For almost six years, a process of revision occupied a series of committees, involved the Council of Delegates in continuing discussions, and produced four drafts of suggested new provisions. The staff responded to a request for their views with a seven-page document outlining and documenting the problems faced in the administration of the CSWE program. In this sample of what they said, the difficulty of carrying out an effective program is clearly stated:

The present structure was created to fulfill the laudable purpose of insuring profession-wide participation in the achievement of the Council's objectives. It is no reflection on this purpose that the machinery has shown itself as so involved and cumbersome as to be almost unworkable in the light of current and prospective personnel and funds available to the Council. The complexity of the structure may be deduced from the fact that the pattern of organization seems to require that the staff work with two policy-making bodies, three

executive committees, three nominating committees, a restrictive
and time-consuming nominations and appointment procedure, and
divisions and commissions (one excepted) with unclear functions
and confused relationships.[6]

A final draft of the by-laws was approved by the Council of Delegates in 1958. The two categories of membership, constituent and
associate, were continued with a slight change in wording. The Council
of Delegates was renamed the House of Delegates with a significant
change in its composition and a new charge to serve as an advisory and
consultative body to the Board of Directors. The composition of the
House of Delegates was spelled out, as follows:

- 24 members of the Board of Directors.

- 55 delegates from U.S. graduate schools.

- 7 delegates from Canadian graduate schools.

- 107 delegates from undergraduate departments.

- 40 delegates from national employing agencies.

- 18 delegates from the National Association of Social Workers.

- 18 delegates-at-large, consisting as before of representatives from higher
  education, other professions, and the general public.[7]

A major change took place with respect to the commissions. Accreditation remained the same in composition and mandate, but the Board of
Directors, not the House of Delegates, was given the responsibility of approving standards. The commissions dealing with program areas and with
research were found to have spent endless time in unsuccessful attempts to
define their functions. The revision abolished those commissions, replacing
them with standing and ad hoc committees, to be appointed by the Board
of Directors as needed to carry out specific tasks.

The Commission on Schools and Departments with its Divisions of
Graduate Schools and Undergraduate Departments had posed a particularly ticklish problem, as suggested by the staff in their description of the
commission as all form with no substance.[8] The divisions were set up as
miniature management units with all the paraphernalia of conducting busi-

ness as they had before the merger. Most of the activities of the Council called for broad representation from the entire constituency, not just the educators. Also, the uncertainty and conflicting claims as to where certain activities (curriculum development was a key example) should be carried out led to an impasse, to the detriment of the Council's program. Nevertheless, it was clearly recognized and accepted that the graduate and undergraduate educators needed a place where they could talk among themselves and share with each other.

In the revision, the commission was converted into a Conference of Schools and Departments composed, as before, of two divisions, and governed by an Executive Committee of three persons on which each division had a representative. The Executive Committee was charged with responsibility for arranging, in connection with the Annual Program Meeting, joint and separate program meetings of the divisions for discussion of matters of internal interest to the graduate and undergraduate educators. The changes removed the suggestion that AASSW and NASSA were continuing their existence as a *sub rosa* operation within the embrace of the Council on Social Work Education. The AASSW had not, at the beginning, discontinued its legal identity as a corporation. It was about this time that it severed that connection. (It is instructive to observe that the need of the two groups to establish separate identities resurged in the 1980s when the deans of the graduate schools established the National Association of Deans and Directors of Schools of Social Work and the directors of undergraduate programs followed suit with the Association of Baccalaureate Social Work Program Directors.)

CHANGES IN THE 1960s
By-Law Revisions, 1964

From its inception, the Council actively supported an international perspective as an essential ingredient of professional education for social work. Many social work faculty members were involved in relief and rehabilitation activities and international consultation assignments following World War II. This fostered, in the 1950s and early 1960s, a commitment to a world-view of social work responsibilities. This was reflected in a variety of international activities under Council sponsorship, which took the form of committee work, active engagement with the U.S. Department of State and the United Nations on advisory services, international exchange of students, a special relationship with the International Association of Schools of Social Work, and, through contracts, direct technical assistance to schools in India and Africa.

Through contractual arrangements with the International Cooperation Administration (later the Agency for International Development), the Council from 1956 to 1962 administered, under Ernest Witte's direction, a project involving advisory service and student exchange with selected schools in India. This was followed by a similar project in Africa that resulted in the organization of a School of Social Service in the first integrated institution of higher education in Zambia (then Northern Rhodesia).

With Katherine Kendall's election as Honorary Secretary of the International Association of Schools on Social Work in 1954, the Council served in effect as a volunteer secretariat, but with no commitment to funds for that purpose. This led to involvement in high-priority programs of the Social Commission of the United Nations and cooperative work on programs dealing with social work training and advisory services to the new nations emerging in the post-War period.

Those activities, together with active committee work and sponsorship with other organizations of significant regional and international seminars and conferences, underlined the need for recognition of such activities in the by-laws as well as in the work program. As a result the following amendment was added to the statement of purpose and adopted in 1964:

> . . . and to cooperate with appropriate national, regional, and international organizations in international activities designed to promote and improve social work education.[9]

By-Law Revisions, 1968

An additional change, minor in nature but highly significant in its implications, was made in 1968 to alter the organizational structure. How this came about involved a rethinking of the program of the Council in the light of new forces at work within the field of social welfare and within the profession. A document titled "Time for Decision," presented to the Board of Directors in 1965, described the impact of the social movements of the times and the Great Society programs as having "a sledgehammer effect on staff thinking about the future of social work education and the CSWE program."[10]

Far-reaching changes in the welfare structure and the national concern with poverty highlighted new concepts of helping that involved the poor in working out their own destiny. Different patterns of working with other helping professions were foreseen in the passage of legislation supporting new programs for medical care, mental health, and education. The emergence of action-oriented, service-minded young people headed for the Peace Corps, Vista, Project Head Start, and community action projects introduced new considerations in planning for the future in social work education. Inner-city and minority group concerns combined with the introduction of student involvement in committee activity acted as a powerful force for change.

In analyzing the Council program in preparation for adoption by the Board of Directors, the staff looked at ways in which educational capacity could be increased to meet new manpower needs, and how recruitment and curriculum planning could be more effectively organized to capture and absorb into social work more of the service-minded generation. Core activities were identified and grouped as divisions within a new commission structure, identified as Accreditation, Educational Services, Educational Research, and International Education.

The creation of a Commission of International Education on par with other major commissions with key functions came about in response to President Johnson's initiation and strong support of the International Education Act of 1966. The prospect of cooperative, interdisciplinary work and expanded international services in a nationwide program, projected by John W. Gardner, U.S. Secretary of Health, Education and Welfare, prompted Kendall to move from the position of executive director to become director of international education. Arnulf M. Pins, associate director, succeeded her as executive director in 1966. Congress passed the International Education Act but failed to appropriate funds for its implementation. Grants for special projects kept the International Commission and Division afloat for several years but both disappeared from the by-laws and the program when Kendall left the Council in 1971 to become the salaried secretary-general of the International Association of Schools of Social Work.

A significant but short-lived addition to the by-laws established a National Committee for Social Work Education to serve as liaison between the Council and the business and corporate leadership of the nation.[11] Considerable committee work bearing on inner-city concerns and recruitment of students and faculty from ethnic minorities was beginning to have a major influence, but had not yet surfaced for by-law consideration. The revisions were adopted at the Annual Business Meeting of the Council in January 1968.[12]

CHANGES IN THE 1970s

Toward the end of the 1960s, community activism, client empowerment, student confrontation of authority, and a heightened awareness of inadequate representation of minorities led to more profound structural alteration. The Board of Directors, in the fall of 1968, appointed a committee to further revise and update the by-laws. The intention was to reflect new objectives and functions of the Council as well as new membership and policy decisions of the Board of Directors.

Student Participation

A Committee on Students was formed in 1967 as an outgrowth of a Committee on Admissions. At the first meeting, the Committee chair, declared:

> that the tasks before this new Committee were some of the most
> difficult problems facing social work education today: students' de-
> sires for greater participation; the challenge of the educationally dis-
> advantaged and the problems of admissions collaboration.[13]

In the beginning, the committee membership did not include students. At a later meeting in October 1968, two students from the National Federation of Student Social Workers were invited to attend as observers. A recommendation that students be involved in other CSWE commissions and committees had brought a response from the Commission on Educational Services that participation should begin and be limited to the Committee on Students. The Board of Directors, however, accepted the idea in principle, but asked for more information on the criteria and method of selection of student members. The Committee responded immediately with proposed criteria and outlined a workable method of selection through a newly organized National Federation of Student Social Workers. The Board, in November 1969, accepted an application for constituent membership from the Student Federation, which at that time counted in its membership 50 graduate schools and two undergraduate programs.[14]

From its new position as a constituent member soon to be admitted to the House of Delegates, the committee made a number of activist recommendations, including the need for priority attention to the recruitment, admission, and training of students from ethnic minorities.[15] The influence of those recommendations from the Committee on Students on the governance of the Council became strongly apparent in the discussion of by-law changes in 1970 and with the adoption of radically changed by-laws in 1972.

A NEW PATTERN OF GOVERNANCE

The original by-laws, with the revisions already noted, had served the Council well during its embryonic stage of growth and development. The philosophical foundation of profession-wide participation and citizen involvement remained intact, as envisioned at its creation in 1952. The vast differences in the societal context of the early 1970s from that of the early 1950s inevitably led to a major reform in the governance of the Council.

By-Law Revisions, 1970

Revisions prepared by a committee were presented by a prominent citizen member of the Board of Directors to the House of Delegates at its annual business meeting in Williamsburg, Virginia, in January 1970. The

major changes included a new statement of purpose and provision for expanded membership and representation from diverse groups on the Nominating Committee and the Board of Directors. A motion to accept the
revisions gave rise to heated and acrimonious debate, sparked to a considerable extent by a sizeable student delegation. A counter-motion to reject
all the proposed revisions and to appoint a new group to consider even
broader reform was immediately put forward by the chair of the Committee on Students.

Following spirited discussion, a number of proposals were accepted
and several, including the transformation of the Council into an individual
membership organization and the addition of clients at every level of deci-
sion-making within the Council, were defeated. The House of Delegates
finally voted to accept the proposed new statement of purpose along with
provisions for increasing the membership on the Board and Nominating
Committee. The new statement of purpose reflected major new directions
put in motion in the mid-1960s to extend the Council's mission "to assure
an adequate supply of appropriately educated professional, paraprofessional
and technical social work personnel to plan, administer, provide and improve social services and other related human services."[16]

By-Law Revisions, 1972

A Structure and Review Committee was appointed by the president to
revise the by-laws in accordance with the mandate issuing from the 1970
meeting of the House of Delegates for a more sweeping reform of structure
and governance. Significant issues for consideration included the distribution of power between the House of Delegates and the Board of Directors;
reassessment of the composition of the Council as an organization of institutions, agencies, and other collective entities; and the possibility of direct
selection and involvement of special interest groups in decision making. The
recommendations of the Committee touched on all those points, leading to a
major modification of structure and governance that continued, with some
additions and deletions, to 1989 when the House of Delegates was abolished.

The functions of the House of Delegates were enlarged to include the power to establish rather than simply recommend the goals and policy of the Council and to review activities and recommend program priorities. The composition of the House was completely altered to allow for a more democratically selected and representative governing body. The delegates would now consist of individuals selected from and responsible to specific constituencies. The by-laws called for a total of 140 delegates from 10 constituencies plus whatever number of Board members not already in the House as representatives of another constituent group.

Graduate deans and undergraduate directors led the list with equal representation of 15 members each. This classification paved the way for their later separation and incorporation as separate entities—the National Association of Deans and Directors of Schools of Social Work and the Association of Baccalaureate Social Work Program Directors. Graduate and undergraduate faculty were also each represented by 18 members. American Indian, Asian American, Black, Chicano, and Puerto Rican ethnic minority groups were each allotted three delegates. A new voting structure entitled these representatives to a double vote, once as minority group and once as graduate or undergraduate representatives. This was apparently an unintended consequence that became difficult to correct. Student involvement was authorized through the participation of nine graduate and nine undergraduate representatives to be elected by the National Federation of Student Social Workers. The practitioner category represented by NASW disappeared for reasons related to finances, but delegates at large were still allotted 12 places.[17]

The Board of Directors was enlarged from 24 to 32 members. In addition to 5 officers and, for one year, the immediate past president, 6 of the 32 members could represent any interest and 26 must be chosen from the categories listed for the House of Delegates. The new House of Delegates continued the practice of electing the members of the Board of Directors from nominations provided by the elected Nominating Committee. The new by-laws were adopted by an overwhelming vote of 157 to 12 at a meeting of the House of Delegates on April 18, 1972.[18]

The changes embodied in the 1972 by-laws ushered in a new era for the Council on Social Work Education. Much that was good and useful in the first 20 years no longer seemed relevant. While lip service continued in references to non-academic members and citizen participation, attention was focused elsewhere with the inevitable result that both disappeared from the scene. The students disappeared with the demise of the Federation of Students. The educators were left in complete control, thus overturning the original assumption that professional education for social work was too important to the profession as a whole and to the community at large to be seen as the monopoly of the educational institutions.

Chapter Eight
Purpose, Functions, and Priorities

Before the advent of mission statements and strategic plans, statements of purpose and functions served as the compass for the Council on Social Work Education in outlining its functions and determining its priorities. The original purpose, as noted below, was brief and to the point—*the development of sound programs of social work education*. A substantial change in length and content surfaced in the 1970 revision of the by-laws. Later revisions, however, eliminating much of the detail in the 1970 version, returned, in essence, to the purpose as originally stated at the creation of the Council.

STATEMENTS OF PURPOSE

The by-laws adopted at the constitutional convention in January 1952 stated:

> The purpose of the corporation shall be to promote the development of sound programs of social work education in the United States, its territories and possessions, and Canada through accreditation, consultation, interpretation, research, publications and through such other services as may be necessary.[1]

Significant by-law changes in 1958 changed the structure and governance, but left the purpose untouched. An amendment in 1964 added international activities to the list of functions, validating the extensive ongoing work in that program area.[2] A later by-law revision in 1968 again altered the structure, but there was no change in the statement of purpose until 1970 when the following expanded version was adopted:

> The purpose of the Council shall be to give leadership and service to social work education in the United States and Canada in order to ensure an adequate supply of appropriately educated professional,

paraprofessional and technical social work personnel needed to plan, administer, provide and improve social services and other related human services. The Council shall be concerned with the quantity and quality of social work education at all levels and its continuing relevance to human well being.

The Council shall provide leadership in relation to national issues and legislation affecting social work education and in furthering under-standing and support of social work education, and shall cooperate with other groups in activities affecting the social and human services, and in strengthening international social work education.

The Council shall carry out its purpose through accreditation as well as through other standard-setting activities, consultation, confer-ences and workshops, research, publications, special projects, and through other means.[3]

The spelling out in such detail of functions and activities served to highlight the Council's commitment to both quantity and quality. It was no accident, as we shall see in the section dealing with priorities, that the activi-ties heading the list dealt with the questions of an adequate supply and appropriate levels of preparation of professional, paraprofessional, and tech-nical personnel for the social and other human services. The shift from a simple statement of an educational purpose to a broader listing of desirable functions was a delayed expression of decisions reached in the mid-1960s to give priority to expansion and excellence. In 1970, however, the social forces at work in this period exerted a more immediate influence. Among the most significant were demands for new approaches in social work education and practice from both faculty and students caught up in movements away from traditional to less conventional ways of righting wrongs, fighting poverty, supporting civil rights, and promoting social justice. For most of the 20-year period, however, the functions and priorities were related to the pro-motion and improvement of programs of social work education, regarded until the early 1970s as preparation in graduate schools of social work.

FUNCTIONS AND PRIORITIES

Program activities and priorities, as suggested by staff, commissions, and committees, were reviewed and approved annually by the Board of Directors. The 1971 article on social work education in the NASW *Encyclopedia of Social Work* accurately summed up the situation in the first 20 years:

> There is virtually no activity of interest and importance to education
> or social work that is not in some way touched by CSWE through
> consultation, committee activities, workshops, conferences, publica-
> tions, research, publicity, action programs, and the like.[4]

Assessing the Work Program

Review and discussion of the Work Program prepared by the staff constituted the major item of business for the Board of Directors at its first meeting in the fall of each year. This responsibility, taken very seriously by both staff and the Board, was reflected in a document, weighty in content as well as in number of pages. The entire professional and administrative staff allocated one week each year at a retreat in May or June to prepare a comprehensive list of activities for discussion and approval by the Board.

In the early years, when only six or seven people were involved, this became a delight as well as a work session because the week was spent in a commodious summer home belonging to Betty Neely on the beach in Ocean City, Maryland. Later, to accommodate the rapidly growing number of professional and management support staff, the retreat was held in New York in whatever borrowed space could be found large enough for the purpose. The important feature was to get away from the office and the daily grind. This practice continued well into the 20-year period, but finally disappeared as the staff continued to expand. Other means were found to involve the Board of Directors in the assessment of activities and determination of priorities.

The procedure at the retreat involved examination of the work accomplished in the previous year against established goals, review of all recommendations and suggestions submitted for new or revised activities, and projection of short-range and long-range goals for the future. The end product emerged as a suggested Work Program, with all activities briefly described and classified within accepted major functions and under the following four categories:

A. Current program activities which are ongoing to which the Council is committed and gives staff service.

B. Proposed program activities which have been approved by the Board but which are dependent upon receipt of special funds.

C. Program activities which have been suggested to the Board but which have not yet been accepted as a Council responsibility.

D. Program activities completed during the previous year.

The following examples from the 1956–57 Work Program give a flavor of Council operations in the early years. Under the functional classification of Educational Standards and the category of ongoing activities, the following item heads the list:

Continuous review, formulation and reformulation of accrediting standards for programs of professional education and for special programs within the basic program. The Commission on Accreditation is currently redrafting procedural sections of the Manual of Accrediting Standards pertaining to "Objectives," "Qualifications of Deans and Directors," and is elaborating and is reformulating the Curriculum section. A new section on "Complaint Procedures" is in preparation. Guides are also being developed on "Adequate Budgets and Size of Faculty." Standards and procedures affected by the changed policy with respect to approval of specializations will be examined, and appropriate new or revised sections of the Manual will be prepared.

Other items include information on scheduled reviews, site visits with regional accrediting bodies, and cooperative work with the National Commission on Accrediting.

There are 15 items under the Educational Services function, with the ongoing activities leaning heavily on curriculum consultation and development, teaching records, and special projects, and all related to the graduate programs. Limited work is noted, as follows, with the undergraduate constituency:

Advisory correspondence and limited consultation to colleges and uni-versities with departments related to social welfare and limited par-ticipation in state conferences on undergraduate education related to social work. Consultation by correspondence continues and some increase in on-the-spot consultation has been possible though the latter remains far too limited to serve the need adequately. Partici-pation in undergraduate state conferences is also affected by the limitations of staff time.[5]

Consultation service to undergraduate departments on a regular and planned basis appears as the leading item under educational activities ap-proved by the Board with implementation dependent upon funding. The item also indicates that an application had been submitted to the National Institute of Mental Health for support of this activity as a special project.

Under the functional classification of Program Services, the impor-tance of recruitment in this period stands out with a listing of items that covers three pages of activities to which the Council was committed. Under the Research function, a similar situation can be seen with respect to a newly launched curriculum study that dominated all other accepted activities.

Board review included discussion of the different activities with major attention to the listing under proposed activities, approved and not yet ap-proved, that could be undertaken only if funds became available for their support. Needless to say, the discussion inevitably underlined the responsi-bility of the Board to assist in finding the necessary funds. The program that finally emerged tended, in the early years, to develop by the gradual addi-tion of new activities along with expansion of functions dating back to the earlier days of the American Association of Schools of Social Work. Every effort was made, however, by the Board and staff to avoid the dislocations that could result from the mere accretion of activities. The Board also carefully monitored restricted fund activities, a significant source of program support throughout the 20-year period, to be sure they fell within accepted functions.

Establishing Priorities

Establishing priorities often led to a struggle between the desire for financial support and the need to remain within the boundaries of the accepted functions. Quality and quantity, excellence and expansion—in whatever form the goal was stated, the production of more and better social workers dictated the priorities and primary functions of the Council in the first 20 years. While accreditation as a means of maintaining quality has from the beginning been accorded top priority, noticeable differences emerge in the relative weights given to quality and quantity.

From 1953 to 1963, recruitment for the profession took precedence over all other activities except accreditation. The long struggle with NASSA, centered to a large extent around the meager production of graduates from the professional schools, was a constant reminder of the need for the Council to do better. The continuing critical and apparently chronic shortage of qualified social workers confronted the Council almost immediately as an urgent problem requiring priority attention. The wisdom of this decision to give recruitment highest priority after accreditation was borne out when, about 10 years later, the Council gave high priority to the establishment of additional schools of social work in order to accommodate the great increase in the number of applicants for admission. Recruitment also was the major activity that deeply involved each and every one of the constituent member groups, easily validating what, at times, seemed to be a cumbersome organizational structure for the support of social work education.

RECRUITMENT AS A HIGH PRIORITY

Recruitment was by no means a new activity. In the early 1940s, both AASSW and AASW had recruitment committees. They were particularly active during the years of World War II and the Korean War, working with the U.S. Department of Defense through a Committee on Social Work in Defense Mobilization. The National Social Welfare Assembly, composed of the major public and private national employing agencies, had also selected recruitment as an area of special concern. These early efforts were modest compared to the program developed by the Council in the next decade.

Launching the Priority Program

Recruitment as a top priority was announced at the Council's first Annual Program Meeting held in January 1953. A disturbing drop in enrollment from its peak in 1950 confronted the graduate schools and the profession with what was regarded as the most immediate and pressing problem to be addressed by the Council. The possible causes for the decrease were attributed in part to the low birthrate in the Depression years combined with the high level of employment in the early 1950s. It was clearly evident to many, however, that the uncertain status of social work as a profession and lack of public knowledge of what it could offer as a career could not be ignored as contributing factors.

A broadly representative Recruiting Committee immediately took on the challenge of marketing social work as a highly desirable career. The perennial question of how to determine the educational requirements for different social work positions without a study of practice persisted but, as on previous occasions, was left unanswered. Barring such a study, it was decided that recruitment for the field could profitably be based on past experience and current practice. Although the Recruiting Committee included faculty from undergraduate colleges and vocational guidance personnel, current experience meant, in effect, that efforts were limited to recruitment for the graduate schools.

With the Social Welfare Assembly and the several practitioner groups now united as the National Association of Social Workers (NASW) also involved with recruitment, it became necessary to sort out the respective responsibilities. The Council emerged as the major operating agency, with the Social Welfare Assembly performing general coordinating functions and NASW handling inquiries and providing recruitment materials. Joint meetings were held to avoid duplication and promote close cooperation. It is to the credit of the participating organizations that a decision was soon reached to consolidate all these efforts into one consolidated program. Commitment to the activity took precedence over protection of turf. This resulted in 1961 in the establishment of a National Commission for Social Work Careers, jointly sponsored by NASW and CSWE, but housed and administered by the Council. Basic financing provided by the two sponsors was augmented by support from many additional sources. The National Commission operated almost as a semi-autonomous unit within the Council with its own staff and budget and a field service to communities throughout the country.

An incredible amount of nationwide activity is recorded throughout the 1950s and 1960s. The Council's committee had early in the program established pilot centers to test the steadily increasing volume of recruitment materials it was soon distributing. Copies of *Social Work Fellowships and Scholarships in the United States and Canada,* an annual publication, were distributed by the thousands along with articles in popular magazines extolling social work as a career, reprints of favorable publicity in newspapers (Figure 1), and even blurbs by well-known cartoonists (Figure 2). Special issues on recruitment, appearing regularly in *Social Work Education,* the CSWE bimonthly news publication, carried articles on all phases of the program. Local committees and offices with paid or volunteer staff shot up across the land to promote community-wide career programs served and coordinated by the National Commission for Social Work Careers. Reports on the different approaches and events sponsored by the growing number of such programs throughout the country appeared in special issues of *Social Work Education* devoted to recruitment. More than once, the sentiment was expressed that, with money and staff, everything was possible, even a refurbishing of the social work image from the dowdy do-gooder to the enthusiastic and charismatic practitioner of an exciting and rewarding profession.

The new image was effectively projected in a recruitment film called "Summer of Decision," which was produced and directed professionally with rising young stage and screen actors as the performers. James A. Linen, publisher of *Time* magazine, chaired an 80-member Film Sponsoring Committee, composed of civic and social service leaders from across the coun-

FIGURE 1. Recruitment Efforts Chronicled in CSWE Newsletter

FIGURE 2. Cartoon for Cover of Special Recruitment Issue of *Social Work Education* 2, no. 1 (February 1954)

The cartoon by Milton Caniff on the cover of this issue is Mr. Caniff's contribution to our recruitment effort. Drawn at our request for display purposes in connection with recruitment for social work in defense mobilization, we believe it warrants a wide audience.

try. He served as master of ceremonies at a national premiere held in New York on October 15, 1959, where a talk by Russell Ballard of Hull House on "Should You Be a Social Worker?" was published as a double-page spread in *Life* magazine and *The Saturday Evening Post*. The film, which was a smashing success and widely used, described the summer work experience in a social agency of an undergraduate who had some interest in social work but needed to know more about it. This type of experience, organized by the community recruitment offices, proved highly successful as a form of recruitment for the profession.

The recruitment program could not have achieved success without the interest and financial support of the broad CSWE constituency. In 1957, the Council organized a National Citizens Committee on Careers to assist in finding the resources to carry out its increasingly effective national program. The National Commission on Social Work Careers also had its own citizens advisory committee. As we shall see, in the section on Finances, this widespread involvement of interested citizens in recruitment opened up major opportunities for the financial support of the Council and many of its activities.

BROADENING THE VISION

The next significant review of functions began in 1963 with the appointment of a Board committee to undertake a complete analysis of Council activities and to produce a statement of functions with a new listing of priorities. At its fall meeting in 1964, the Board reviewed and accepted a "Statement of Primary Functions" as outlined under the following five major objectives:[6]

> *Objective A: To improve the quality of social work education.* This
> went beyond accreditation to stimulate curriculum change and ex-
> perimentation, to study of learning theory and method, to promote
> research and theory development, to enhance the competence of
> graduate and undergraduate faculty and increase their numbers.
> Particular attention was given to study and development of under-
> graduate social welfare programs, including curriculum and faculty

development and their relationship to various levels of practice and to graduate education.

Objective B: To expand resources for social work education of high quality through expansion of opportunities for preparation in both graduate and undergraduate programs, planned development of new graduate schools and new undergraduate programs and assistance in development of programs at various levels of social welfare training.

Objective C: To increase the number of people of high quality interested in social work careers. This objective would continue to be achieved through the activities of the National Commission for Social Work Careers.

Objective D: To establish and maintain relationships with relevant groups in the interest of interpreting, developing, and improving social work education and insuring an adequate supply of social welfare personnel. As an objective of a different order from the others, it was not subject to program operations or to a priority position.

Objective E: To learn from and to contribute to social work education in other countries through participation in the work of relevant international organizations, continuing work on the education of foreign students and preparation of American students for service abroad, and cooperation in initiation programs of social work education in other countries.

What emerged clearly from this review and acceptance of a new statement of functions and priorities was a call for quality along with quantity, more and better social workers, excellence with expansion. Recruitment remained important, but with the successful operation of the National Commission on Careers, it was now ranked in third place as a priority function.

EXPANSION OF RESPONSIBILITIES

The staff, at its annual retreats in 1964 and 1965 saw a need for further examination of the core, the scope, and outer limits of the Council's responsibilities in carrying out the Board mandate to give attention to quality as well as quantity. A document titled "Time for Decision," prepared by the executive director, had the primary purpose of bringing out differences of opinion so that program plans would not be developed within basically different and hidden frames of reference.[7] It was pointed out it could no longer be assumed that the same perception of professional social work education as graduate education was shared by all constituent members of the Council. Nevertheless, differences, if known and open to discussion, could move the profession forward in a time of challenge and almost unlimited opportunities for social work education.

The promotion of sound programs of social work education, as mandated in the by-laws, presumably served as the central purpose of the Council. What brought the several constituencies together around that central purpose was a particular relationship to professional social work. The graduate schools were in the business of producing professional social workers; NASW was made up of professional social workers; and the national agencies sought to staff their services with professional social workers. Preparation for professional social work could thus be perceived as the purpose uniting all members of the Council. But as professional social work was seen as the product of graduate education, this left in question the central purpose as perceived for and by the undergraduate departments.

Beginning in 1952 and continuing in the early years, there was recognition and sufficient acceptance to produce consensus among the different constituencies that professional education was graduate education. However, the consensus was based on an assumption and a promise that graduate education had its roots in the two upper years of undergraduate education. The central purpose, therefore, was perceived as a continuum of education beginning with an undergraduate concentration in the arts and sciences as basic to a more advanced study of social work. This promise was not redeemed in full, in large part because of failure, as expressed in "Time for Decision," to take responsibility for the problem in a *positive* way. Much of the responsibility that was taken was of a *negative* sort, more concerned with preventing possible encroachments on professional education rather than promoting the kind of development that would gain the support of all the CSWE constituencies. The document advocated that the Council move outward forcefully from a defined base of graduate professional education to embrace a broader mission of training and education to meet all social work manpower needs.

Exploration of the proposal exposed a wide range of views, both within the staff and the Board, not so much on the wisdom of outward movement but rather on the nature and extent of that movement.[8] Much of the discussion centered on what CSWE should or should not do in the area of undergraduate education. Questions raised by the staff speculated on possible new roles for CSWE in defining undergraduate education as required preparation for graduate study with initiation of work on prerequisites, in defining undergraduate preparation for positions not requiring professional education, and in modifying professional education through model-building activities. There was also a question as to the role, if any, for the Council with respect to staff development.

To those questions, the Board of Directors added its own queries about expanding the responsibilities of the Council beyond its major concern with graduate professional education. Issues such as the following were explored:

- Whether the responsibility of CSWE is for undergraduate education as preparation for graduate study or for employment or both.

- Whether the whole gamut of education beginning with technical education in the junior and community colleges and extending to progress in doctoral education should fall within the expanded purview of CSWE.

- Whether, and how, in the absence of accrediting authority or legal control, CSWE could exert sufficient influence or provide the leadership necessary to ensure quality in the undergraduate education for which it assumed responsibility.

- Whether, and to what extent, the individual schools of social work should sponsor all educational programs to meet the full range of social work manpower needs.

Recognizing that acceptance of a broader vision and new functions would have far-reaching consequences yet to be determined, the Board, at its meeting in October 1965, nevertheless adopted unanimously the following resolution:

> The Council on Social Work Education recognizes its obligation to extend the range of its concerns more vigorously, both in principle and in practice, beyond the core responsibility for the advancement of professional education to the broader scope of training and education to meet all social work manpower needs. We recognize that this direction of the Council may require reorganization of its structure and a change in deployment of its staff and resources. We also recognize that as the Council on Social Work Education moves more directly into the area of undergraduate education and other levels below or different from graduate education, it will have to rely not on authority or rights formally delegated to it but on its capacity for educational leadership and cooperative work with many other interested bodies.[9]

At a special session convened at the annual meeting of the House of Delegates in January 1966, the resolution and a document summarizing staff and Board proposals on "Meeting Social Welfare Manpower Needs" were discussed under the chairmanship of Herman D. Stein, the incoming president of the Council. Reactions ranged widely, as expected, to the broader responsibilities and possible changes in the deployment of resources and staff. The call for change to meet the needs of the times was readily endorsed by some and found reluctant acceptance by others. With respect to undergraduate education, the most contentious issue, opinions varied, as seen in the following comment, from,

> apprehension lest the profession alter its present position, shared by many other professions, that liberal arts education is a desirable prerequisite for entry into graduate schools of social work.[10]

To the final comment by one delegate,

> that professional education is already being taught at the undergraduate level; the question is then whether the Council should take responsibility for it.[11]

The three recorders of the discussion, noting the many points of view, voiced the following summary opinion of the outcome:

Since no consensus was sought, the influence and weight of each view-point cannot be recorded. However, it is the unanimous opinion of the recorders that the weight of the discussion was favorable to:

1. The resolution of the Board

2. An integrated program approach to social work education at all levels.

3. The importance of increased Council leadership in undergradu-ate social welfare education.[12]

The Board of Directors responded to the discussion in the House of Delegates by immediately appointing a broadly representative Special Com-mittee to review and report on the questions and issues raised in all previous considerations of a broader mission for the Council. The Special Commit-tee posed additional questions with their answers, which are here summarized:

1. *What does the Board mean by professional education?* Consensus was reached that professional education at this point in time was perceived as graduate education at the master's level, but there were differences in the degree of commitment to this position.

2. *On what basis does the Council rest its claim to responsibility for a broader scope of training and education to meet all social welfare manpower needs?* It was agreed that this obligation . . . derives from the position of the CSWE as the spokesman for education for the profession.

3. *How does the Council conceive its responsibility at the under-graduate level?* The views expressed in the House of Delegates seemed to several members to underline a more active involve-ment by the Council in building a vocational route at the un-dergraduate level to social work employment. The content of this vocational route was not discussed, but there was consen-sus that persons with a bachelor's degree who enter social work employment should receive a general social welfare preparation (not specific training for public assistance, corrections, etc.) fol-lowed by in-service training under professional direction.

4. *What should be the relationship of the CSWE to staff development*

and in-service training? The members agreed that the Council's concern with formal education precludes active involvement in agency programs of continuing education. There was consensus, however, that the Council should be related to all those forms of continuing education that emerge as a function, of schools of social work.

5. *What is the position of the CSWE on the question of authority and formal rights in the area of undergraduate education?* Whether or not the CSWE should in the future attempt to move in this direction [accreditation], it appeared to the Committee clearly not a direction in which it should now move, if for no other reason than that it could not realistically exercise any significant surveillance. . . . . The CSWE, however, as the spokesman for the highest level of social work education, can and does now move into the undergraduate arena essentially because of the respect accorded to it by undergraduate educators.[13]

The Board of Directors slightly amended and unanimously accepted the report of the Committee at its meeting in March 1966. The new priorities now clearly called for *expansion* of facilities for the adulation of social workers and *excellence* in their preparation. The challenge of carrying forward a program to support the newly underlined priorities and their implementation now fell on Arnulf M. Pins, who had joined the staff as associate director in 1963 and was named executive director in September 1966, upon Katherine Kendall's transfer to full-time assignment as Director of International Education and secretary-general of the International Association of Schools of Social Work.

Two years later, the Board further underlined the new dimensions of the Council's purpose and functions. A listing of priorities prepared by the staff carry forward the emphasis on quality and quantity, but introduce new initiatives sparked by the turbulence of the times and the commitment of social work as a profession to social justice. The new priorities required the Council to:

1. Broaden, deepen, and change the curriculum to make it more relevant.

2. Increase social work manpower at all levels to man the nation's health and welfare services.

3. Clarify and strengthen the rights and roles of students in schools of social work.

4. Initiate and take action on federal legislation affecting social welfare and social work education.

5. Increase involvement and effectiveness of social work with inner-city problems, minority group concerns, and anti-poverty activities.[14]

As already noted in the description of by-law changes, student activism within the schools of social work and at Council meetings demanded attention to student rights and responsibilities. The need for more significant participation of minorities in social work education as teachers and students led to the appointment of a Special Committee on Minority Groups in 1967 and its replacement by a permanent Commission on Minority Groups in 1970.

The previously limited role of speaking out on legislation only if related to social work education was broadened to encompass all legislative developments affecting social welfare. The social work curriculum, teaching materials, and research to be relevant would now need to include content on poverty, race relations, inner-city problems, and the advocacy role of social workers. And, finally, concern with manpower shortages was enlarged to include not only new goals for undergraduate education but also responsibility for continuing education and program development at the community college level.

The 1970s can thus be seen to mark the end of the first cycle of growth and development of the Council on Social Work Education. The functions and priorities of 1969 reflected a readiness to deal responsibly with changing needs and opportunities for social work education. For the radical changes soon to come, initiating a new cycle of growth and development, the first 20 years had laid a solid foundation.

Chapter Nine

Finances—The Dollar Chase

Throughout the 20 years of this historical account, CSWE was poor in relation to its needs and aspirations, but was by no means impoverished. Ernest Witte, in describing what he had learned from his experience as executive director, summed up the financial situation in these words:

> The first lesson has to do with the spiraling costs of a dynamic program and the seeming impossibility of acquiring sufficient funds to finance its essential needs, particularly in the light of the expectations of the Council by the field. Although our general budget has quadrupled in these ten years, we seem almost as far as ever from meeting the insistent pressures for funds. . . . Everyone is seemingly interested in program activities which call for increased expenditures, but fewer are interested in or willing to help raise the necessary funds. . . . It is perhaps unnecessary to indicate that the Council has a program underway which is beyond its current financial resources to support.[1]

The budget for 1962, with its general fund income of $207,000 and an additional $134,00 in project funds,[2] was a far cry from the budget of $54,000 in income actually available to launch the Council in 1952.[3] As we shall see, an incredible amount of support was coming from special grants and contracts, thanks to the indefatigable fundraising efforts of the executive director and a series of dedicated Finance Committee members. Fortunately, too, the first 20 years coincided with a positive climate for action by the federal government to promote a more equitable and caring society, along with support from fellow social workers as advocates in important positions in all the major agencies and bureaus concerned with health and welfare programs. This was also a period when foundations actively supported social welfare initiatives, and corporations, feeling an onrush of social responsibility, seemed eager to fund activities of benefit to their communities. Against this background, it is instructive to see how the money was raised and the sources from whence it came.

THE CSWE CONSTITUENCY

Basic support through the two decades continued to come from the fees levied on constituent members, particularly dues income from the educational institutions and the accreditation fees paid by the graduate schools. In the report of income and expenditures for 1952–1953, the graduate schools carried the major burden, contributing $13,150 as against $325 from the undergraduate departments, represented at that time by only 19 members. Ten years later, the graduate school dues accounted for $23,000 and undergraduate departments now contributed $3,000, reflecting a substantial increase in the number of undergraduate members.

The establishment of a category of associate members for individuals, local agencies, and organizations not eligible for voting membership brought in a steadily growing amount of dues income. Witte was particularly keen on recruiting associate members. He stated clearly that, in his opinion, the work of the Council was for the good of all in the field and he saw no reason why there should be any embarrassment in asking colleagues to join the Council as associate members. Needless to say, the staff felt obliged to enlist as associate members all the colleagues they encountered in their field trips, meetings, and consultations. This actually did not prove to be a problem because the experience of receiving helpful services from the Council created a climate of appreciation and support.

The initial dues scale for the national employing agencies ranged from $100 to $1,000, with a decision on the amount to be paid left to the agencies. This resulted in too many agencies selecting an amount that the Board regarded as much less than their fair share of Council dues. On the second anniversary in 1954, 24 national agencies contributed approximately $3,000 in dues income.[4] Ten years later, the number of agencies had increased to

46, with dues payments in the amount of $18,500.[5] A number of the national offices of the various agencies assisted in fundraising by asking their local affiliates across the country to join as associate members, which led to a considerable increase in income from that source in the 20-year period.

CSWE could not have been established and probably could not have survived without the support of the American Association of Social Workers and other practitioner associations. The AASW dues assessment of $1 per member for social work education reflected a genuine belief in the importance of a high level of preparation for social work practice. When the assessment was made originally for the benefit of the American Association of Schools of Social Work in 1950 and continued for CSWE in 1952, the annual payment constituted an assured amount of support ranging upward from an initial $10,000 to $27,000 in 1964. This contribution came to an end in 1969 when NASW no longer remained as a dues-paying constituent member of the Council. The events leading up to this unhappy outcome portray a somewhat characteristic pattern in CSWE–NASW relationships. Through the years, before and after the launching of the Council, the educators and practitioners in their respective associations have been on the whole mutually supportive. There have been periods, however, of strong collegial cooperation as well as episodes of troublesome confrontation. In the early 1960s, questions raised about the financial relationship were answered in a spirit of strong collegial cooperation. In the late 1960s, on the other hand, the financial relationship was ended without discussion in an atmosphere of antagonism and rivalry.

THE PRACTITIONERS WITHDRAW

The NASW Board of Directors and its Delegate Assembly began to question in 1960 the $1 per member assessment paid to CSWE in support of social work education. The National Office of NASW and several of the larger chapters, hard pressed for funds to finance their own programs, looked at their steadily increasing membership with alarm at the amount of money being funneled to the Council. Concern was also expressed at the loss of participation by the practitioners as a result of the change in the function of the House of Delegates. Not all big city chapters shared this concern.

The New York City Chapter objected strenuously to any suggestion of change in the financial relationship with CSWE. Indeed, the chapter voted against any reduction in the contribution, and instead, requested permission from NASW to raise chapter dues to meet its own expanding needs. The president of the chapter, Mitchell Ginsberg, is recorded to have said: "The New York City Chapter endorses wholeheartedly the responsibility of every professional worker to support professional education and believes that the contribution should be no less than one dollar per member and it might be even higher."[6]

After review of developments within the programs of the two organizations, an ad hoc committee of the NASW Board recommended the appointment of a joint board committee to review and clarify the respective functions of the two associations on educational matters, with a view to establishing a proper rationale for NASW financial support of the Council. The recommendation was accepted by both boards.[7]

The Joint Committee, composed of recognized leaders in education and practice, met twice a year over a period of three years from 1961–1964. Everything in the relationship came under review. All problems were identified and various solutions were explored, including two extremes: (1) merger of the two organizations, and (2) complete separation, with no financial or program relationship. Both extremes were discarded as untenable in the light of philosophical, practical, and historical considerations basic to the relationship between practice and education in social work. In arriving at a middle ground, the committee highlighted the distinctive and common concerns of CSWE and NASW in education for the profession.

For NASW, social work education was recognized as the route through which social workers become qualified as professional social workers and thus qualified for membership in the professional association. The competence of the professional and the strength and influence of the profession derived in large part from the quality of education provided by the schools of social work. CSWE activities designed to establish, maintain, and strengthen professional schools in all their activities were seen, therefore, as necessarily of concern to the professional membership association and to its individual members.

For CSWE, professional practice was recognized as a primary source of educational objectives, a major source of learning opportunities for students in field instruction, and the ultimate test of the effectiveness of programs of professional education. NASW activities designed to improve, extend, and interpret social work as a professional practice, to certify competence, and to delineate and develop practice areas and knowledge were likewise seen as necessarily of concern to the educational organization and its membership.

The committee accepted as a guiding philosophical consideration the desirable interdependence of social work education and social work practice, with each organization contributing, separately and together, to excellence and effectiveness of social work personnel and professional service. For effective collaboration, however, the committee recognized the need for greater clarity in the respective roles and responsibilities of the two organizations along with cooperative planning around program activities in which both had an interest. The continuing productive participation of practitioners in the work of CSWE commissions and committees together with the success of the recruitment program under the sponsorship of the National Commission on Social Work Careers exemplified the value of shared responsibility.

At its final meeting, the committee acted on the assumption that NASW had a basic obligation to support activities designed to strengthen and extend social work education. How to discharge that obligation to the satisfaction of both organizations became the question to answer. The simplicity of $1 per member as the method of payment appealed strongly to the CSWE members of the committee, but they accepted NASW objections to a compulsory check-off on annual dues and the understandable concern, as the membership increased, about the limitless nature of the formula. They recommended a substantial annual contribution to the general fund of the Council through a financial agreement for a specific period of time.

The CSWE Board requested the advice of the House of Delegates before taking final action. A document setting forth all the questions at issue, circulated to the House well in advance of its meeting, aroused great interest.[8] The 18 delegates representing NASW, and many of the delegates representing agencies and schools, held preparatory meetings to become informed and discuss possible courses of action. At the meeting itself, constructive suggestions to strengthen the relationship were made to the two organizations which, it was agreed, should continue their separate existence. It was also agreed, unanimously by the NASW delegates and overwhelmingly by the House as a whole, that financial support should be continued. The need to make NASW participation in the work of the Council more visible to its members was underlined.

The final outcome, fully approved by both organizations, committed the NASW to an annual payment of a lump sum of $27,000, the amount based on NASW membership statistics and budgeted by the Council for the fiscal year 1964–1965. The same amount was assured for a period of five years, with the proviso that it be renegotiated at the end of the third year. In addition, the House strongly supported a series of proposals suggested for more effective means of communication, representation on the respective boards as well as on commissions and committees, periodic joint staff meetings, and joint review of program priorities and activities. The proposals were, on the whole, faithfully implemented in the ensuing five years.

This period of close collegial cooperation came to an end in 1970. Joseph Anderson, who had served for 26 years as the executive director, first of the AASW and then of NASW, resigned in April of that year. Throughout much of the period of dissension between NASSA and AASSW and in the planning and creation of CSWE, he had been a pillar of support. The sharing of office space at the formation of the Council and continuing close relationships among the staff members of the two organizations contributed to a feeling of participatory involvement in promoting the goals and living the values of both organizations. While other factors were involved, the discussions that came later between colleagues who had not been part of the historical development of the two organization made a difference in the quality of communication.

At its meeting in the spring of 1970, the CSWE Board reviewed the agreement reached with NASW regarding the financial contribution and cooperative relationships. Concern was expressed at a number of events where NASW had acted unilaterally in ways contrary to the agreement. The following examples were given:

> NASW delegates at the CSWE House of Delegates took action to revise the structure of CSWE without ever raising their concern at a Joint Board Committee meeting; NASW changed its membership requirements and in so doing, assigned a role to CSWE (standard-setting for undergraduate programs) without prior discussion with CSWE; NASW announced in its News that CSWE would determine equivalency for undergraduate programs without ever asking CSWE if we could or were ready to do this.[9]

At the request of CSWE, a meeting of the Joint CSWE–NASW Board Committee was held to discuss these matters as well as the financial agreement. When the agreement was reviewed at the end of the first three-year period, a recommendation by the Joint Committee that the NASW increase the amount to $35,000 in 1969 was not acted upon. The NASW members confirmed, however, that the agreement reached in 1964 was still in effect, until revised. They stated further they would recommend to their Board of Directors that the annual contribution of $27,000 continue for one more year to allow time to develop a new and more rational basis for the contribution. In July 1970, the new executive director of NASW informed CSWE of the following action by its Board of Directors:

> As we had previously indicated, the NASW considers it has an obligation for $27,000 for the period July 1, 1970 through June 30, 1971.

> I must advise you that by action of the NASW Board of Directors we cannot commit ourselves to any financial obligations beyond June 30, 1971.[10]

When further negotiations failed to produce a satisfactory outcome, NASW, in April 1972, formally notified the Council that it wished to discontinue the present relationship between the two organizations and would prefer not to have representation on the Council Board, commissions, and committees. At the annual meeting of the CSWE House of Delegates later that month, a delegate representing NASW indicated that the association did not wish to become part of the proposed new structure for the Council. It was stated further that the decision to discontinue what NASW described as an interlocking relationship did not, however, reflect a diminished interest on the part of the organized practitioners in social work education. Nor did it rule out the possibility of future financial support. The hope was expressed that the new relationship between two independent organizations would encourage continued cooperation. The House of Delegates passed a motion, with majority but not unanimous support, to delete all reference to NASW wherever it appeared in the amended by-laws.[11] The period of close collegial cooperation throughout much of the first 20 years in the life of the Council came to an end with the departure of NASW as a constituent member representing the field of practice. Cooperation did continue, but renewed financial support remained a dead issue.

FEDERAL SUPPORT

The Council on Social Work Education in its early years had a great and generous friend in the federal government, particularly in the 1960s when legislation was passed that had a profound effect on social work education. This was not accidental. A Deans Advisory Committee to the Secretary of Health, Education, and Welfare (HEW) played an active role in promoting the need for federal support of schools of social work. Even more significant, perhaps, was the establishment by HEW of a Departmental Task Force on Social Work Education and Manpower which produced a

report in 1965 titled *Closing the Gap in Social Work Manpower*.[12] A prestigious committee, chaired by Milton Wittman, chief of the Social Work Branch
of the Manpower and Training Division of the National Institute of Mental
Health, worked with Dorothy Byrd Daly, the project director, to outline
every aspect of the staffing problems in the social services and to document
the need for organized and financial support from the federal government
to find solutions. Concentrated and vigorous lobbying by all elements of the
profession also had its effect. The call for action found a gratifying response
within HEW and within the Congress. This led, as noted below, to land-
mark legislation in 1967 for non-categorical support of preparation for
social work at the undergraduate as well as graduate level. However, the most
widespread and lasting support from the federal government was provided,
beginning at a much earlier date, by the National Institute of Mental Health.

The National Institute of Mental Health (NIMH)

NIMH, established in 1946, headed the list of federal agencies as a
major resource for programs of social work education in the schools and
for the Council on Social Work Education throughout these first 20 years.
A constant stream of well-funded projects resulted, in large part, from the
commitment and advocacy of Wittman. While the initial grants to the graduate
schools of social work were limited to psychiatric social work, it was not
long before the scope of NIMH support was greatly expanded. With social
work seen as a primary mental health discipline plus the requirement of the
generic curriculum to ground all social work students in mental health concepts, almost all aspects of social work education became of interest to
NIMH and were therefore eligible for NIMH support.

The initial grant to the Council was a carryover from the AASSW which
received a grant from NIMH in 1950 for committee work and staff service
on advanced education, including terminal third-year programs with a clinical orientation. The purpose was to produce researchers, faculty, and skilled
clinical practitioners comparable to professionals in related mental health
disciplines. The adoption of the 1952 curriculum policy statement with its

emphasis on a generic two-year program did not immediately do away with psychiatric and other specializations, but it was only a matter of a few years before they disappeared and NIMH sought to strengthen all of social work education through a variety of special projects. The most important in the 1950s included a five-year curriculum consultation project and a successor five-year field work consultation project, both of which turned out to be among the Council's most successful and effective programs for curriculum change and development. Another important grant in the 1950s supported the research on human growth and behavior and publication of a volume of that name in the Council's comprehensive Curriculum Study.

In the 1960s, NIMH moved with the Council into a number of new program areas, extending support to projects on faculty development, social work manpower, undergraduate education, community work, continuing education, minority concerns, and drug abuse. As will be noted later, staff service and consultation for undergraduate education funded by NIMH played a significant role in the inauguration of professional programs at the BSW level of social work education. NIMH grants also supported the development of new schools of social work to meet the greatly increased demand for social work education. Thus, in the 1950s and 1960s, it can be said that the social work branch of NIMH seemed to be there for CSWE whenever a new and urgent need arose to improve the quality and increase the quantity of professionally qualified social work personnel.

The Welfare Administration, HEW

A number of other branches of HEW were well-represented from 1952 onward with grants and service contracts in various aspects of Council activities, but the Welfare Administration, under its several different titles, did not enter the picture financially in a significant way until the 1960s. A message to Congress in 1966 by President Lyndon B. Johnson on "Domestic Health and Education" set in motion a powerful series of events. He said:

> There are more than 12,000 unfilled vacancies for qualified social
> workers, at a time when we need their skills more than ever. These

workers are important to the success of our poverty, health, and education programs. A Task Force on Social Work Manpower and Education has just completed an extensive study of the problem. I have asked the Secretary of Health, Education and Welfare to consult with educational leaders and other specialists and to submit recommendations to me to overcome this shortage.[13]

Legislation authorizing non-categorical support for social work education was introduced to the House of Representatives in February 1967 by Wilbur Mills, chairman of the House Ways and Means Committee. Described as the "Social Work Manpower and Training Legislation" (Title IV of H.R. 12080), it was passed in the House in August 1967 and in the Senate in November 1967. Attached as Section 707 to the Social Security Act Amendments of 1967, it was known thenceforth as the 707 program. The legislation made possible support of social work education through grants for the expansion and improvement of undergraduate as well as graduate preparation for social work. In 1969, with the arrival of the Nixon Administration, the program began to be questioned and was ultimately phased out in 1974. In its short life, it made an incalculable impact on social work education in general and in a number of important respects on the structure and program of the Council.

Other Branches of HEW

The War on Poverty and recognition of community organization as a direct service concentration in the new 1962 curriculum policy statement brought in substantial funding from the Office of Juvenile Delinquency and Youth Development on various aspects of curriculum development for community work. Other projects funded by that office included the production of new kinds of teaching materials for the field of corrections.

During this period of expanding financial aid to advance social programs, the Council was sometimes given funds to take on projects. On one occasion, a sizable grant to undertake research in the field of child welfare came from the Children's Bureau of HEW. Upon examination of what was needed to carry out the proposed project, the grant was returned with the explanation that the proposed activity required expertise that could more effectively be provided by a practice organization. It was a disconcerting experience for the Council to return money that could have been of great help in increasing staff and it was equally disconcerting for the Bureau to have its offer refused.

Contracts with the different branches of HEW for institutes, seminars, conferences, and the production of educational materials provided considerable support in the early years. Contracts also served as a substitute for the payment of dues, which was not permitted for the federal offices, to enable participation in Council membership as representatives of employing agencies. The Office of Vocational Rehabilitation supported a number of significant meetings and contributed to the study of rehabilitation and publication of the report on that subject in the Curriculum Study. The Welfare Administration, the Veterans Administration, and the U.S. Public Health Service also made possible institutes and conferences that produced valuable reports. From 1954 to 1971, the strong international component of the Council program was supported in the main through government contracts with the U.S. International Cooperation Administration and its successor, the Agency for International Development.

CITIZEN AND CORPORATE SUPPORT

In 1952, financial support for the Council, with the exception of an NIMH grant, came from sources integral to the profession or closely related to it. Ten years later, the financial report for 1962–1963 showed $39,000 in the general fund from community chests, corporations, individual citizens, and foundations. Foundations were also represented in project support, which added up to $257,000 in 1962.[14] This considerable increase in income resulted from the tireless efforts of Ernest Witte, who started fundraising from the moment he accepted the position of executive director, as well as from the help of committed Board members, who often tapped their own inside sources of funds and influence to gain support for the Council. With the exception of low-key but creative work by Samuel Hyman, a development consultant who was also a social worker, several attempts to use professional fundraisers were not successful. Finding money for the general fund to supplement membership dues constituted the most difficult task, as Witte discovered in his first year in office. The many foundations he visited had little or no interest in providing support for ongoing operations, but an encouraging number kept the door open for specific projects. It was through the special projects funded by a number of foundations, large and small, that the Council managed to finance the multifaceted program described in Chapter 11.

One of the first grants Witte obtained for the Council came from the Field Foundation to initiate a study on the content of the social work curriculum, an area of concern to both undergraduate and graduate educators that was not covered by the Hollis-Taylor report. Individual subject areas within the overall curriculum study were supported by the Ittleson Family Foundation, the National Tuberculosis Association, the New York Fund for Children, and the Rockefeller Brothers. The Ford Foundation was particularly helpful in the 1960s with substantial grants for faculty training, curriculum development, and teaching materials in the fields of corrections and aging. When undergraduate education surfaced as a means of alleviating the continuing shortage of social workers, funds for a variety of program activities became available from the Doris Duke Foundation, the Heinz Endowment, the New York Community Trust, and the Esso Grant Foundation.

From 1964 onwards, the Lois and Samuel Silberman Fund, with social work education as its central concern, was unstinting in its support of CSWE studies and projects. It was also a powerful influence for support from a number of other sources, particularly the corporate world. The Council's emphasis on expansion in numbers as well as excellence in the quality of the personnel needed to staff social welfare programs appeared to be the magnet that pulled in funds from civic leaders and the world of business.

Increasing the general fund beyond what was available from membership dues and miscellaneous sources of income posed problems throughout the entire period of this historical account. There were limits beyond which dues could not be raised. Tapping corporate funds and inclusion in United Funds for unrestricted grants offered attractive opportunities that the Council actively pursued. The participation of lay leaders in the work of the Council as members of the Board and the House of Delegates was a significant factor in obtaining support from United Funds, corporations, and family foundations. The rationale for support, as indicated, rested on the need for social work personnel of high quality and in sufficient numbers to provide the professional services required to fulfill the objectives of the nation's public and private social programs, in which millions of dollars were being invested. The National Commission on Careers in Social Work already had an active citizen's committee providing money for recruitment. General support for a wider range of program activities was urgently needed. To obtain that kind of support, the Council looked to community chests and United Funds.

A breakthrough with chests and funds came in 1958 when the National Budget Committee on Health and Welfare Agencies, having approved the budget adopted by the Council for that year, notified all the community chests and councils throughout the nation of the need for financial support of social work education. In its report, the committee listed the statistics on the staffing crisis and then said:

> It is the Council's responsibility to arouse the nation, and curiously enough, the social welfare field itself, to this perilous situation, and to challenge us to the effort and expenditure necessary for its solution...
> A budget of $180,708, the amount asked by the Council for 1959 is not large enough, considering the magnitude and urgency of the problem. It is approved by the Committee, but only as a minimum and with the earnest hope that much greater financial support will be forthcoming.[15]

Support did come, slowly at first but with growing momentum as influential deans and directors worked with civic leaders in their communities to get an annual allocation for the Council. Arthur Kruse, CSWE Treasurer, reporting on income in 1966, noted with satisfaction:

> In 1962, total income from Community Chests and Funds in the
> form of annual allocations was $33,142. In 1966–67 the Council
> expects to receive allocations of $55,000, representing an increase
> of almost 65 percent. This substantial rise reflects community recog-
> nition of the pressing demands for more and better educated social
> workers. Total gifts from corporations, foundations, labor organiza-
> tions, and individuals are almost seven times greater than they were
> five years ago, an indication of the growing visibility and awareness
> of social work education among business and industry.[16]

Two citizen members of the Board of Directors, Henry Sachs and
Samuel Silberman, vigorously promoted the involvement of business and
industry in recognizing the importance of social work education in qualify-
ing social welfare personnel. Leo Perlis, an equally committed Board member, tried to do the same for labor organizations. In 1959, Sachs proposed
the development of a "Fund for the Advancement of Social Work Education." With Board approval, a financial campaign was launched to achieve
the following purposes:

> (1) extensive public interpretation of social work; (2) expansion of
> scholarships and fellowships; (3) legislative action to increase gov-
> ernmental support for social work education and scholarships; (4)
> expansion of the capacity of schools of social work, including field
> instruction opportunities, faculty, and facilities; and (5) recruitment
> of more social work students.[17]

The plan was endorsed by the national agency membership, which
pledged continuing contributions over a period of five years. The most
important outcome was the formal organization of a National Committee
for Social Work Education composed of 16 business, industrial, and community leaders. The chair, William Treuhaft, a leading business executive
and civic leader in Cleveland, Ohio, was well-known as one of the founders
of a national program in which corporations were asked to donate one
percent of their profits, before taxes, to colleges and universities.

The membership included presidents and directors of a variety of corporations and industries, including such notables as General Lucius Clay, Commander-in-Chief of the U.S. Forces in Europe during World War II, and Marion Folsom, Secretary of HEW in the mid 1950s. The major functions included the interpretation of social work to the general public and the involvement of leading citizens, including corporate, business, professional, and community leaders, in support of social work education. Anticipating that this would be an ongoing activity, the by-laws were amended in 1968 to place the committee within the administrative structure of the Council.

A number of successful luncheon meetings were held that resulted in increased financial support. As we have seen, however, the growing unrest within the CSWE constituency led to major changes in its structure and governance. A perception of corporate support as paternalism contributed to the deletion of the National Citizen's Committee from the amended by-laws. That and other factors having to do with the changing social and political climate under the Nixon Administration put a brake on this effort to make productive use of interested and socially responsive citizens in interpreting social work favorably and more widely to the general public and to augment financial resources for social work education.

Chapter Ten
The Path to Excellence

Accreditation, rooted to a large extent in approved curriculum policy state-ments, has been seen from an early stage in the development of social work education as a means of defining and delineating educational standards. The problems arising from the competition between National Association of Schools of Social Administration and American Association of Schools of Social Work for recognition as accrediting agencies were presumably settled with the establishment of the Council on Social Work Education. Agree-ment was reached on two issues: (1) only graduate schools should be ac-credited; and (2) sole responsibility for all social work accrediting rested with the Council. While recruitment may have been more visible in the early years as a Council priority, the highest priority given to accreditation was never questioned.

A question that immediately arose concerned how to involve the broader constituency in a function that previously had been assigned exclusively to educators. The answer came in this description of the composition of the Commission on Accreditation as set forth in the by-laws:

> The Commission on Accreditation shall be composed of 15 mem-bers, each of whom shall have a responsible relationship to the edu-cational process; 9 of whom shall be full-time members in accredited graduate schools of social work; 3 of whom shall be in a responsible and official relationship to the professional education work of the social work membership associations; and the remaining 3 to be individuals selected from any of the four membership groups com-prising the Council of Delegates. . .[1]

Faculty members previously involved in accrediting the medical, psy-chiatric, and school social work specializations served as NASW representatives. Throughout the period that Canadian schools participated as constituent members of the Council, one member of the commission always came from that country. The three unspecified members included representatives from, respectively, the Council of Social Agencies and the federal Bureau of Public Assistance. The third member was Ewald B. Nyquist, at that time assistant commissioner and later Commissioner for Higher Education for New York State. He was also chairman of the Commission on Institutions of Higher Education of the Middle States Association of Colleges and Secondary Schools. As one of the nationally recognized leaders in the field of accreditation, his presence on the Council's commission was of enormous benefit, especially as he took a special interest in social work and remained on the commission for an extended period of time.

A NEW ACCREDITATION CRISIS

With the commission appointed and work already underway on standards and a manual of procedures, the Council was ready in December 1952 to undertake its now clearly defined accrediting responsibilities. The promising plans of action were suddenly but only temporarily derailed by the National Commission on Accreditation. A "Program Note" issued late in 1952 asserted that the seven regional associations constituting the membership of the National Commission would, after January 1954, assume full responsibility for all accreditation of institutions of higher learning.

The unhappiness of college and university presidents with the multiplicity of accrediting bodies has already been noted in connection with the NASSA–AASSW controversy in the 1940s. In 1950, it was reported that "more than 200 agencies were in a position to impose their demands upon institutions of higher learning, and, in many instances, were competing with each other for the privilege of controlling and policing certain phases of higher education."[2] When the various associations of those colleges and universities came together within the National Commission, one of the main objectives was to terminate or curtail the accrediting activities of outside groups. Another was to cut down on the costs and disruption caused by too

many on-site visits. The "Program Note," sent to CSWE and other accrediting bodies, set forth a nine-point program, with a number of requirements
that would effectively transfer the regulatory authority from a professional
association to the regional bodies.

John C. Kidneigh, chairman of the Council's Commission on Accreditation, lost no time in writing to the president of the National Commission
on Accreditation. He expressed "appreciation of the difficulties faced by a
given university in dealing with a wide variety of accrediting authorities,"
and "expressed a willingness to enter into discussions with [the] Commission to find plans which would help reduce or eliminate these difficulties."[3]
He pointed out the legal and other widely accepted responsibilities discharged by the Council as an accrediting agency and asked for clarification
of specific points. He ended with an assurance of sympathy with the laudable objectives of the National Commission and expressed a desire to cooperate with the regional associations in appropriate ways. The Commission
was aware of the clear advantages as well as the difficulties of cooperative
work with a regional association because Kendall, at the invitation of the
Middle States Association, had already participated, as executive secretary
of the AASSW, in several all-university reviews.

The flurry of concern among the professions that greeted the 1952
"Program Note" was soon dissipated. Because the regional associations
were each at a different stage of readiness to take on an enlarged responsibility and with the established professional associations strongly objecting to
the proposal, the January 1954 deadline for the unification of all accrediting quietly disappeared. Nyquist suggested, in a talk to the Council membership in 1954, that the National Commission had been less than diplomatic in the presentation of its program. He lauded the overall objectives of
the National Commission on Accreditation, but added that initially it was
imperfect in its approach. He referred to its "undiplomatic pronouncements" to professional accrediting agencies and confusing and sometimes
unrealistic communications.[4] What emerged from the truncated crisis was a
new plan whereby recognized professional accrediting associations, such as

the Council, would enter into formal agreements with the six regional associations to establish defined cooperative relationships.

Reporting to the membership in 1954 on the agreements that had been reached, Kidneigh noted with satisfaction the progress made with the new approach, but also made clear that "only social work is competent to determine standards by which social work is to be measured." He continued with a statement on the social work position:

> While we are willing to co-operate fully with the regional associations in the accrediting process, we enter the co-operative process as equals and cannot abdicate the responsibility we have to the public, the field of social work, and the profession. Likewise, while we fully recognize that the evaluation process springs primarily from an institution's own aims and objectives, no profession can fulfill its obligation to society without reserving the right to determine the objectives of education for the given profession.[5]

The Council continued to participate with the Middle States Association in all-university reviews whenever accreditation schedules could be synchronized.[6] The commission conducted its own reviews while also joining all-university teams when invited to do so by the institution to be accredited or when evaluation schedules coincided. In addition to the Middle States, this happened most often in the Western and Northwestern regions, where agreements had been reached with the respective associations. Continuing discussions on agreements were also held with the remaining regional associations.

The experiment, as it was called, was never formally discontinued, but simply faded away. In the few years it was in effect, there were decided benefits to social work. They included equal treatment in the evaluation process with other professions and departments along with an opportunity to obtain greater recognition for the contribution a school of social work makes to the university as a whole. The experience of working as part of an all-university team and becoming involved with the overall aspects of university management broadened the sights of social work reviewers. While concentrating on the evaluation of the school of social work, they could assess more clearly the place and reputation of the school within the university structure and become aware of the ways in which it interacted or failed to interact with other disciplines and academic departments.

STANDARDS AND PROCEDURES

The responsibilities discharged by the Commission on Accreditation may be summarized as follows:[7]

Continuous review, formulation, and reformulation of accrediting standards for professional schools of social work. As already noted, professional education in this period meant graduate education. The responsibility of the commission was limited to the formulation and implementation of standards governing only those programs in the United States and Canada leading to the master's degree. As noted in Chapter 12, other means were developed to promote quality in undergraduate and doctoral programs. The commission had sole responsibility for the formulation of standards. Until 1958, the standards were forwarded for adoption to the Council of Delegates, bypassing the Board of Directors. Problems created by this provision were resolved in the revision of the by-laws, and from 1958 onward, the Board had the power to adopt but not to change or amend the standards. If positive action could not be taken, the standards were referred back to the commission for reconsideration.

Review and evaluation of programs of professional education applying for accredited status. The *Manual of Accrediting Standards*, completed and published in 1953, set forth the accrediting philosophy and procedures to guide the commission in its evaluation of educational programs. The following six goals summed up its approach to the task:

1. To assist schools toward sound educational goals;
2. To help schools achieve high standards rather than standardization of educational programs;
3. To encourage well-advised and planned experimentation in social work education;
4. To foster continuing self-analysis and self-improvement of schools

so as to encourage imaginative educational development;

5. To assist the school and the university of which it is a part to function in constructive and co-operative activities aimed at the realization of common educational objectives; and

6. To relate social work educational programs to the needs of the social work field.[8]

Through self-studies submitted by applicant programs, on-site visits by experienced educators, and review of the findings, the commission hoped to achieve the goals as outlined in the *Manual of Accrediting Standards*.

Review and evaluation of specialized sequences of schools applying for approval of specializations. With the formation of the Council, all accrediting in social work became the responsibility of its Commission on Accreditation. The authority to approve specialties in medical and psychiatric social work, previously the responsibility of their respective professional associations, was transferred to the Council. The practitioner groups in school social work and group work, specialties also subject to approval, had previously lodged the accrediting responsibility with the AASSW. The adoption of the 1952 curriculum policy statement, with its emphasis on a generic approach to social work education, initially posed problems about the role of specializations within the revised educational framework. In 1959, agreement was reached to terminate the approval of specialized sequences and schools were accredited on the basis of a unified two-year program.

Periodic review and evaluation of accredited programs at stated intervals to determine whether standards are being maintained. Initially, newly accredited schools were reevaluated within a three-year period to determine the extent to which commission recommendations were being carried out. Beginning in 1960, primarily as a result of the termination of approved specialized sequences, all schools became subject to a period review at 10-year intervals. This requirement became particularly important after the first anti-discrimination standard was adopted in 1962 and amplified in 1965 to spell out in greater detail the application of the standard to all aspects of the program and administration of a school of social work.

Maintaining standards while encouraging innovation and change. The Council, in its accrediting function, faced a continuing challenge of how to balance freedom and accountability and encourage experimentation and change while ensuring the integrity of the educational programs. Despite evidence of considerable care by the commission to avoid standardization in the development and implementation of standards, it could not escape criticism as a restraining rather than a liberating force with respect to experimentation. The commission and the Board sought to counteract such criticism by adopting a policy to stimulate experimentation and to provide for study, evaluation, and dissemination of the results. Throughout the 1960s, the commission approved a considerable number of applications from schools interested in initiating an experimental approach outside of curriculum policy and accreditation standards. A wide range of proposals included experiments on, for example, the training of volunteers, modification of curriculum policy to permit research specialization in the master's program, establishment of branch programs, innovations in field learning and teaching, and acceleration of the time needed to earn a master's degree.

Ten years after Nyquist addressed the Council membership on relations with the Middle States Association, he spoke again in the light of his experience as a continuing member of the commission from its conception. He set forth what he called "six vigorous assertions":

1. Accreditation in social work has passed through a first, long phase of development.

2. This first phase has placed emphasis more on the letter than the full spirit of qualitative standards and has concerned itself largely with the maintenance of minimal standards and the establishment of an accredited list.

3. In accord with a well-known principle that developments in accrediting are evolutionary not revolutionary, the accrediting function in social work is ready to enter a second stage. Indeed, it is part way into it.

4. Making the transition from the first stage to the second stage is not without pain and effort.

5. Part of the pain in making the transition may be a low level of expectations, an occupational hazard of social work, a lack of familiarity with the real function of accrediting, or a combination thereof.

6. The second stage must consist of a deliberate, aggressive program to work primarily for institutional improvement and the development of professional education in social work.[9]

He went on to proclaim as a deep-seated conviction that the single function of the Council's Commission on Accreditation must be to help improve the quality of social work in the United States. Accreditation was a means to that end. He said, "it [accreditation] is not important in itself, but only as a stimulus to institutional and professional improvement and as a recognition of sound achievement by those who are in the best position to assess it—mature, experienced, disinterested colleagues (and I mean by 'colleagues' those in our higher institutions, not practitioners)."[10]

Early in his talk, he commented on the altruism and dedication of professional social workers and wondered whether that dedication was not being exploited by the universities in which the schools of social work were located. In conclusion, he lauded the hard work and dedication of the Commission on Accreditation.

THE PRIMACY OF CURRICULUM POLICY

The goals and nature of social work education have been captured and delineated through the years in official curriculum policy statements that have served as the central instrument in the accreditation of schools of social work.[11] AASSW by-laws specified the requirement that "a currently acceptable interpretation of curriculum policy" be presented from time to time by the Board of Directors. The official statement of curriculum policy was attached to the by-laws as the main standard against which schools of social work were evaluated. The Council on Social Work Education made no mention of a curriculum statement in its by-laws, but its centrality in the accrediting process continued.

Historical Highlights

The first attempt at accreditation came in 1932 when AASSW (then called the Association of Training Schools for Professional Social Work) adopted and required a "minimum curriculum" as a condition of membership. Prescribed for one year only, the curriculum described 13 subjects classified into four groups as desirable. In addition to core subjects of casework, medical information, and psychiatric information, students were required to take something from each of the four groups. The curriculum policy statement became an attachment to the by-laws that, in time, also included other requirements for accreditation

The minimum curriculum did bring some measure of similarity in what was being taught. It remained the yardstick for determining eligibility for AASSW membership until 1944, although the association and many of its member schools had progressed far beyond it. The new demands made upon social work in the Depression era and the new opportunities opened up by the social legislation of the 1930s called for a vision and mandate for social work education far beyond that portrayed in the 1932 statement.

In 1944, after six years of preparatory work, a new curriculum policy statement was adopted by the member schools of AASSW. Popularly known as the "basic eight," it outlined eight areas of study that were described as the generic foundation of all social work practice. The subject areas included social casework, social group work, community organization, public welfare, social administration, social research, medical information, and psychiatric information. It was recommended that the subject areas should be covered, to the extent possible, in the first year of professional education.

The statement clearly stated that the eight subjects were areas of knowledge, but in practice, they were taken too literally as a listing of courses. While this had the effect of more nearly achieving the earlier desired goal of a measure of similarity, and made for easy transfer of credits from one school to another, it was criticized as lacking in imagination and productive of compart-mentalized learning. Sue Spencer, reporting in 1951 as executive secretary of AASSW, made this assessment of the "basic eight" statement:

> Although of great value at the time this report [the policy state-ment] was submitted, in crystallizing and solidifying a broad base for the training of professional social workers, the areas are not mu-tually exclusive; and, in addition, by the very effort to classify mate-rial into compartments, there has been a resulting effect on the school curricula, at least for a time, of compartmentalizing material along artificial lines. It is important to know that the thinking of the schools has not remained compartmentalized; and particularly dur-ing the period 1946 to 1950, there has been a constant redesigning of curriculum within schools to develop a curriculum structure of vitality and dynamic quality.[12]

A dormant Curriculum Committee was reactivated in 1950 to review and rewrite the 1944 curriculum policy statement. The statement, in the committee's judgment, did not represent current practice or reflect trends within the graduate schools and required complete reformulation. With AASSW on the verge of becoming part of CSWE, the committee was highly motivated to turn over to the new organization an updated and more accu-rate view of social work education. Following a year of intensive activity by the committee and a drafting subcommittee, a fifth draft of a proposed statement was accepted by the Board and circulated to all member schools. As one of its last official acts, AASSW adopted the sixth draft at a final membership meeting held in connection with the National Conference of Social Work in May 1952.

At the first business meeting of the new CSWE Board of Directors, also held at the same time as the National Conference, the following actions were taken to ensure the legality as well as to provide continuity of accred-iting activity:

1. That the Council take over the list of accredited schools of social work as of July 1, 1952, as currently maintained by the

AASSW until such time as its own list is available.

2. That the statements, policies and procedures established by the AASSW for accrediting be used by the Council until such time as it has established its own policies and procedures

3. That arrangements either transitional or permanent, be worked out as soon as possible to take care of pending applications for approval of specialized curricula, and for handling applications from those schools that are ready to request membership or change in their membership status.[13]

The Generic Curriculum—1952[14]

The 1952 policy statement ushered in a distinctively new approach to curriculum organization directed towards a generic two-year program of professional education for social work. The essential unity of the curriculum was emphasized, with the first year making provision for the acquisition of knowledge and skill in three broad areas of learning and the second year providing for the extension of knowledge and the further development of skill in those same areas. The three learning areas deemed basic for all students were classified as:

1. Knowledge and understanding of the social services.

2. Knowledge and understanding of human behavior.

3. Knowledge and understanding of social work practice.

This definite break from the past launched what has become, with slight changes in wording and the addition of research and field practicum, the traditional way of classifying the professional foundation areas of content. What is outlined under each classification, however, has differed markedly through the years.

The 1952 statement portrayed the curriculum as a cohesive whole, designed to produce graduates equipped with a substantial body of knowledge, with attitudes rooted in the philosophy, ethics, and obligations of the profession, and with the skills for beginning competence as a professionally qualified social worker in a wide variety of agencies, programs, and services.

It was expected that the curriculum as a whole would assist the student to grow and develop with the profession. Responsibility for determining and organizing the appropriate combinations of courses to meet the requirements of the policy statement was left to the individual schools, with the proviso that the curriculum must ensure balance of subject matter and progression in learning.

The idea of a unified curriculum did not suddenly spring full-grown from the AASSW Curriculum Committee. As far back as the 1920s, Edith Abbott anticipated the generic approach when she said:

> Perhaps we are not yet agreed as to what the mental furnishings of a good social worker should be; but if we add together what we think a good so-called family caseworker, a good children's worker, a good medical or psychiatric social worker, a good visiting teacher, a good social investigator, a good community organizer or chest executive should know, if we put those things all together, we should have a reasonably solid curriculum in social work and one that would compare not unfavorably with the curricula of the good schools of the older professions.[15]

Other leading educators and practitioners through the years voiced similar sentiments. The problems in the break from the past in the organization of the curriculum lay not in the philosophy of the statement but in its implementation.

Of the three subject areas, the one on social services presented the greatest difficulty. The term itself, which was used to convey the idea of a range of services broader than public welfare, was not immediately understood. The content to be conveyed also appeared rather daunting to schools that had limited their offerings to a course in public welfare with perhaps an additional course in public assistance or child welfare.

Study of the range, variety, and interrelationships of current social welfare programs was expected to impart knowledge of social needs and social organization; to communicate a broad historical perspective; and to help students develop a capacity not only for coping constructively with social change, but also to develop a potential for leadership in the formulation and execution of progressive social policies. It was assumed that students to some degree would bring from their undergraduate education a basic understanding of the cultural, political, social, and economic forces that affect the lives of people. How to organize a sequentially arranged series of courses through the two years of the master's program became the subject of many articles and workshops. While all the questions that arose were never fully answered, the section on the social services gave needed prominence and a new look to the "social" in the social work curriculum.

The second learning area, which soon became known as Human Growth and Behavior, bore almost no resemblance to the courses on psychiatric and medical information and psychopathology that flourished under previous statements. The policy now required attention to normal physical, mental, and emotional growth considered with due regard to social, cultural, and spiritual influences upon the development of the individual. Study of stages of development was to include the interaction of the individual with his or her environment. Students were also expected to acquire basic knowledge and understanding of group behavior and group relationships. Attention to deviations from the normal were summed up in one sentence. This break from the past stimulated considerable experimentation in the organization of sequentially arranged courses through the two years along with the assumption of teaching responsibility by social work educators rather than physicians or psychiatrists.

The policy prescription for social work practice consisted of a two-year class and field concentration in casework or group work. This rather narrow approach was mitigated by other requirements designed to produce social workers who would possess a core of professional knowledge and skill common to all social work practice. The statement required the student in casework to have a group experience and the student in group work to have an opportunity to work with an individual. It was required further that students be introduced to the common objectives, principles, and methods as well as the unique elements of the various social work methods, which listed administration, community organization, and research as well as casework and group work. This was usually interpreted to mean discrete courses in stated methods.

Although field experience was related primarily to the two-year case-work and group work sequences, it was also expected to help the student integrate learning from all the subject areas. Students with demonstrated competence in casework or group work were provided with opportunities, in their second year, for field experience in administration or community organization or research. This was the only reference to what might have been regarded as specialization. Although the statement made no mention of specializations, the sequences in psychiatric, medical, and school social work and in group work continued to be accredited. As the Council now carried responsibility for all accrediting, it accommodated the specialty practitioner interests by including their representatives as members of the Commission on Accreditation. The emphasis on basic content for all students, as postulated in the 1952 statement, was generally accepted, but it took until 1959 to phase out the accredited sequences.

The process of reaching agreement on a complete change to a generic curriculum with no specialized sequences involved a number of task forces that, over a period of several years, produced descriptions of practice statements for use in constructing the various sequences and in preparing teaching materials. Practitioners joined with educators to factor out desirable content for inclusion in the curriculum from the following nine fields: child welfare, community welfare planning, corrections, family social work, group services, medical social work, public assistance, psychiatric social work, and school social work. When specializations were officially discontinued in 1959, it was understood that a plan for periodic re-accreditation of schools of social work would be developed to judge the use and results of the policy. The Commission on Accreditation responded with a requirement that all schools of social work would be evaluated at 10-year intervals.

The content available from the analysis of the nine fields of practice was one of the factors prompting re-examination of curriculum policy. Recommendations for changes in the structure and organization of educational programs, stemming from the 13-volume curriculum study published in 1959, demanded careful analysis. The individual volumes also provided a rich lode of content for use in curriculum building.[16] The methodology of the study demonstrated the value and use in curriculum construction of teaching and learning theory, as interpreted by Ralph Tyler.[17] In addition to these pressing influences, the newly amended by-laws, in making organizational changes, eliminated the Commission on Educational Services and authorized the Board of Directors to appoint a standing Curriculum Committee. This was the Council's first committee for the important purpose of formulating curriculum policy for adoption by the Board and use by the Commission on Accreditation in the formulation of educational standards.

The committee appointed in November 1958 immediately began work on what became a task of almost Herculean proportions. The findings and policy implications of the completed Curriculum Study, along with the suggested curriculum content in the 13 volumes, had to be studied. In addition, a committee-sponsored survey of curriculum trends, issues, and concerns, as expressed by the undergraduate departments and graduate schools, brought in an impressive amount of material. The reports of the task forces on the nine fields of practice, together with substantial material from the NASW Commission on Social Work Practice, were added to the collection of data for review. The committee had to deal with the problem of a greatly expanded body of knowledge for inclusion in the generic curriculum and how to meet the growing interest of social work faculties in the application of teaching and learning theories in the construction of an educational program.

From the multitude of documents collected or prepared for use by the committee, it became clear that a statement for undergraduate education had to be given priority over a revised policy statement for the graduate schools. A guide to suggested content, learning experiences, and organization of undergraduate programs successfully came through a series of drafts and was adopted by the Board of Directors in October 1961.[18]

Expanding the Generic Concept—1962[19]

The 1962 curriculum policy statement, the first to be produced under the auspices of the Council, was the product of two years of work by a committee and subcommittees representative of the total membership. All elements of the constituency participated in a well-coordinated process of review of the voluminous materials. The process involved study of a succession of drafts by the House of Delegates, the Commission on Schools and Departments, the Commission on Accreditation, and the Board of Directors.

The new policy re-emphasized the concept of the curriculum as a unified whole, thus supporting the position of the previous statement while departing from it in several significant directions. A major difference was immediately apparent in the way in which the policy was presented. In 1952, the required content appeared in brief descriptive statements of what should be taught. In 1962, the objectives of each area of content are listed along with what the student was expected to learn. The principles of continuity, sequence, and integration in the construction of the curriculum are made explicit in a section on learning experiences. Those changes clearly reflected the use of the Tyler method of curriculum building, current at the time, and had the salutary effect of bringing the suggested content into sharper focus than would have a narrative description. The committee referred to the presentation as a middle level of abstraction, general enough to allow considerable leeway in curriculum building but specific enough to identify the knowledge, attitudes, and skills requisite to the achievement of the goals of social work education.

The broad areas of content remained the same, with the following changes in the titles: Social Welfare Policy and Services, Human Behavior and the Social Environment, and Methods of Social Work Practice. The most dramatic changes in content within these areas included the addition of group and community process and social structures to individual growth and behavior in Human Behavior and the Social Environment and community organization as a concentration in Methods of Social Work Practice.

Casework and group work in a two-year sequence of classroom and field instruction were recognized in 1952 as the appropriate routes to competence for beginning practice, although community organization, administration, and research were not entirely excluded. The 1962 policy retained the requirement of a concentration in a social work method, although not necessarily in a two-year sequence in the same method, as the best way to qualify as a professional practitioner. A major difference, welcomed by many schools, was the addition of community organization as a method in which a concentration could be organized. Administration and research remained possible as concentrations only in special circumstances, but explicit objectives for both gave them more prominence in the curriculum. Most schools followed the curriculum model of two-year sequences in one of the three methods as concentrations, but some developed other models to produce multi-method competence. The centrality of field instruction in each of the two years was expected to provide the specifics of practice and, in that sense, to offer opportunities for specialization.

A curriculum made up of largely required courses in a tightly organized program was perhaps an unavoidable consequence of the two generic policy statements. There was little or no room for electives and the term "straitjacket" began to be applied to the policy requirements. The generic curriculum went a long way toward helping social work educators identify and communicate the central concepts, principles, and values basic to its practice as a professional discipline and to give students a broadly based foundation on which to build their careers. But the times were changing. New realities gave rise to new conceptions of social work practice, which led to new approaches to social work education. A new curriculum policy statement was adopted in November 1969, becoming effective as an accreditation standard in 1970.

Freedom with Responsibility—1970[20]

The revival of a Commission on Educational Services in the by-law revision of 1968 brought together committees concerned with curriculum, teaching materials, and faculty development. The need to re-examine the curriculum in a time of widespread social change led to the appointment of a new Curriculum Committee, now under the jurisdiction of the Commission on Educational Services. The generic approach, in which all students marched together through two years of similar educational experiences, no longer fit the spirit of the times. Openness and innovation in educational programs along with greater participation of students in what and how they were taught emerged as desirable goals. The response of the Curriculum Committee to the new social realities became clear in one of the introductory paragraphs to the policy statement it produced:

> The Curriculum Policy Statement deals with the kind of substantive knowledge to be included in the master's program but does not present an organizing theme, suggest sequences, or in any other way direct how that knowledge is to be organized and conveyed. Each school carries full responsibility for the specific organization and arrangement of courses and other learning experiences. Each school is also expected to establish procedures for self-study and continuing evaluation of the effectiveness of its educational program.[21]

The Council, in accord with the spirit of the 1970s, thus put its stamp of approval on a high degree of freedom in curriculum development. Concentrations remained an option, but were no longer defined in familiar terms. There was less emphasis on methods. Practice was described as conducted through particular roles that required acquisition of specialized learning and competence. Schools were encouraged to consider new or expanded roles as well as a variety of modes or dimensions of competence. Field instruction, referred to as a "practicum," was described not as a required two-year component of the curriculum but as a learning experience.

The three broad areas of knowledge survived under the same titles, but it was explicitly stated that they were not intended "to delineate the structure of the curriculum or the categorization of courses."[22] The previously outlined objectives for student learning under each of the knowledge areas was replaced by descriptive paragraphs outlining the content to be provided. Within the areas of knowledge, the content for social welfare policy and services was greatly expanded and much more specific in relation to social change.

Content pertaining to Human Behavior and the Social Environment departs significantly from the previous statement. A basic understanding of individual and collective dynamics is stipulated for all students. To achieve this objective, it is stated, with the following additional explanation, that theories and knowledge from the biological, psychological, and social sciences as well as from the humanities are needed:

> There is no generally accepted unified theory of human behavior, nor is there any single theory or formulation of relevant content which is sufficient for all social workers. Rather, there are many theories and systems of knowledge which hove been developed for a variety of purposes and within a wide range of perspectives. These theories and perspectives, as well as their interrelationships should be recognized and reflected as specifically as possible in the curriculum design and modes of instruction.[23]

Under the 1962 policy, schools were granted full responsibility for the organization of courses and field instruction. The freedom conceded in the new policy went much further. Schools were asked to define for themselves what they were trying to do and what they expected to achieve through their educational programs. The policy statement was not widely circulated or discussed in draft form, thus giving rise to a number of questions after its adoption. To the question as to whether the policy permitted too much freedom, one dean replied:

> Our view is that the new curriculum policy statement is admirably constructed to offer the precise amount of freedom necessary for each school to fulfill its unique function in respect to the social welfare manpower system.[24]

The Curriculum Committee clearly intended to encourage experimentation and innovation and it had that effect. A number of schools tested alternative models of practice. The "generalist" model of integrated methods, which had begun to take different forms under the 1962 policy, was developed further. Team teaching, particularly in combined casework–group work concentrations, became more widespread. The unveiling of a variety of theoretical frameworks for concentrations in casework and group work gave traditional models of direct service intervention a brand new look. A number of schools that continued to offer single method concentrations developed two tracks, one for "micro" direct service and the other for "macro" functions.

Community organization attracted an increasing number of students eager to participate in grassroots and community action programs. The emphasis in the statement on progressive change in social agencies and the role of the social worker in bringing this about encouraged new concentrations in program planning, administration, and policy analysis

With so much diversity, questions of coherence, unity, and accountability had to be addressed. The mere existence of a policy for curriculum development and its centrality in the accrediting process meant that the freedom to experiment carried with it the responsibility to meet established standards. No matter how broad the perspective on the social goals and functions of social work, how open the curriculum, or how wide-ranging the options for individual students, the professional school of social work retained the familiar obligation to prepare men and women who would be recognizable and accountable to society as professional social workers.

The new statement was a fitting conclusion to the end of the first 20 years in the life of the Council on Social Work Education. Beginning in 1932, five curriculum policy statements had guided the development of social work education. Each one reflected a particular stage in the evolution of the profession and each one responded both to professional concerns and social forces. Despite the many differences, there is a logical progression, with each statement outlining what was thought at the time to be essential preparation for the professional practice of social work.

In discussions of educational policy, too much is said about the dead hand of the past and not enough about how much has been gained through the years by the timely response of educators to new forces within and outside the profession and to the need for both continuity and change in the curriculum policies governing social work education.

Chapter Eleven
The Multifaceted Program

While accreditation and curriculum policy always occupied a central place in the CSWE program, many additional services were developed to meet the needs of the constituency and to provide educational leadership for the profession. Some activities remained constant throughout the 20-year period, while others waxed and waned in response to changing social forces, practice developments, educational priorities, and financial resources. The adoption of the 1952 curriculum policy statement, with its marked departure from the previous pattern, generated intense interest in what constituted generic content and how it should be organized and integrated into the two-year graduate program. Curriculum concerns became the focal point of consultation services, workshops and conferences, and a major study.

CURRICULUM BUILDING

Some of the leading graduate schools had already experimented with the generic pattern of curriculum organization mandated by the 1952 policy. For most schools, however, the task of converting from the "basic eight" format posed practical problems as well as the discomfort usually accompanying a major change. Many schools, including those philosophically committed to the generic approach, received substantial faculty and student support from NIMH grants for psychiatric social work. Medical social work was a highly respected specialty with outstanding leadership. The new policy was accepted, even welcomed, but how to conserve the values and the financial benefits of the specializations became a problem of implementation. The initiation of a consultation project helped enormously in that regard.

THE CONSULTATION PROJECT

The project, financed by NIMH, entitled every graduate school of social work to two consultation visits in the course of a five-year period to assist in bringing the school's educational programs into conformity with the new policy. The rationale for NIMH support of the generic curriculum rested on an expressed desire "to maintain a high quality of social work education, especially in those schools receiving grants for training in psychiatric social work."[1] Because the NIMH grant did not cover the Canadian schools, the Council made the consultation service available to them from general funds.

The consultation service gave impetus to fruitful use of the curriculum policy statement as a guide to appraisal and revision of educational programs. The visits were clearly separated from accrediting to avoid, to the greatest extent possible, any coloration of inspection or enforcement. Many schools were stimulated to embark on total revision of the curriculum as a result of the first consultation visit and used the second visit to examine and appraise the new curriculum plan.

When the project was initiated, there was considerable variation in the attention given to methods of curriculum building and evaluation. The faculties found particularly helpful the method of establishing objectives for the curriculum as a whole and for the individual sequences and identifying the learning experiences necessary for their achievement. They also discovered the value of coming together as a whole faculty. The luxury of devoting three to five days to appraise and develop plans to remake their educational programs also had its special attraction.

The consultation project had ramifications far beyond assistance in curriculum building. It provided a strong incentive to individual schools of social work to engage in self-study and revision of the curriculum through use of systematic approaches to curriculum building and evaluation. The service also helped immeasurably in opening wide the channels of communication between the graduate schools and the Council. Increased understanding of educational needs and problems on the part of the staff had a decided impact on the future direction of the overall program. The educational services that follow were a direct outcome of the consultation project.

The Tyler Workshop

The enthusiastic response of faculty members to the use of a systematic method of curriculum building led to the organization in 1960 of a week-long workshop on curriculum building under Ralph Tyler.[2] An NIMH grant made possible the participation of one faculty member from each graduate school in a concrete learning experience in how to develop and evaluate an integrated curriculum. Canadian schools, at their own expense, also participated in this intensive review of the Tyler method of curriculum construction. The purpose was to demonstrate how a faculty working together could translate curriculum organizational principles into operational terms and produce an integrated curriculum. Sharing by the participants of this experience with their faculty colleagues had special significance because of the requirements of the 1952 curriculum policy statement. The workshop report,[3] with its detailed account of the methodology, was in constant use by the graduate schools in the continuing effort to build a unified and integrated two-year program of social work education as basic preparation for responsible entry into social work practice.

FIELD INSTRUCTION PROJECT

The involvement of field instructors in the consultation project sessions on curriculum building revealed a need for clarification of the content and methods of field teaching and a strong desire on the part of field instructors for help in this area. A second consultation project with a specific focus on field instruction was proposed to NIMH as an outcome and continuation of the completed curriculum project. It was approved and financed for another five-year period.

The pattern of consultation visits to schools continued, supplemented by organized workshops and institutes for field instructors, agency executives, and members of agency boards. Discussion centered on examination of field instruction objectives and learning experiences to clarify their relationship to classroom work in a generic program. Although field experience was primarily related to casework or group work sequences, there was an expectation that students should be helped to integrate learning from all subject areas. In addition, the elimination of specializations in the curriculum placed greater responsibility on the field instructors to underline the specifics or what was "special" in particular fields of practice.

These greater demands, along with the widespread interest in the field and in the classroom in how and what to teach, led to an enthusiastic response to the project. A number of the schools initiated or cooperated with the Council on pilot projects or demonstration of innovations or experiments in field teaching and learning.[4] Experiments included the supplementation of traditional methods of individual supervision with group teaching, multidiscipline collaboration, written work beyond case or group recording, and other ways of promoting learning.

The pivotal nature of the school–agency relationship in field instruction prompted exploration of the partnership. It seemed desirable to involve in project activities not only field instructors but also agency executives and agency board members. The Council in the early years worked closely with national agency members on activities, such as recruitment, scholarships, and the like, but not directly on curriculum concerns. A conference held in New York in 1964 marked the first full-scale participation of national agency members in consideration of the crucial curriculum issue. The 32 national agency representatives attending the conference were joined by representatives of 17 local agencies and 8 representatives of the Council's Board and key committees.[5]

Presenting a perception of field instruction with emphasis on the supervisor as teacher and the student as learner created problems as well as interesting new opportunities in the education–practice relationship. The agencies supported the field practicum as an educational experience, but it was recognized on both sides that staff shortages, agency pressures, and inadequate resources for the service functions could play havoc with the strongest commitment. How to go beyond a direct service to provide a broad range of learning experiences made a new and not fully understood demand on many agency field instructors.

Questions on how a supervisor becomes a teacher underlined the obligation of schools to listen to the voice of practice and to find better ways to communicate the many dimensions of the teaching function. Exploration of such questions did not yield definitive answers, but the discussions produced a large measure of shared understanding of the problems and possibilities in the education–practice relationship. Strengthening that relationship was seen and accepted as a joint responsibility in the preparation of well-qualified social workers. As a sequel to the conference, individual schools began to involve agency executives and agency board members in their workshops on field instruction.

MATERIALS FOR TEACHING AND LEARNING

The preparation and publication of teaching records was a significant function taken over by the Council from the AASSW. Continuing this activity involved a Teaching Materials Committee with five subcommittees, all of which included practitioners in addition to educators. The committees were charged with locating and selecting teaching records for use in the graduate schools, undergraduate departments, and agency staff development programs. In the early years, casework records predominated. They were edited, disguised, and published with teaching notes prepared by committee members. The records, much in demand, accounted for a small but steady source of income.

With the intensive activity of the 1950s and 1960s involving curriculum development to give greater emphasis to generic concepts and principles, teaching methodology took precedence over teaching materials. The committee underwent a marked change in both function and title. The change in name to Teaching Methodology and Materials was accompanied by an expanded charge. New materials of a different nature were produced. They included illustrations of conceptual approaches to teaching; sourcebooks covering a variety of materials for specific content areas; annotated bibliographies on teaching and learning; materials from fiction, biography, and autobiography; audio-visual aids; tape recordings; and an all-purpose compilation of teaching aids titled "The Teacher's Compendium." As a regular feature in the newsletter, "Teaching Materials News Notes" changed its name several times, ending up as "Teaching and Learning."

The Ford Foundation was especially generous in funding teaching aids. In the late 1960s, grants made possible an important extension of this activity. In addition to underwriting staff service and the production of a variety of teaching materials, Ford projects supported the establishment of a facility within the Council office to demonstrate learning and teaching aids. Beginning in 1968, in specially arranged quarters at Annual Program Meetings as well as at CSWE headquarters, many new types of aids were available for review and testing. The range of materials displayed and demonstrated included videotapes, audiotapes, overhead projection transparencies, felt board kits, slides, filmstrips, albums, microfiche, and any new "state-of-the-art" teaching aid available during that time period.

SIGNIFICANT NEW DIRECTIONS

Agencies, foundations, and organizations concerned with a particular social problem or staffing an underserved field of practice often turned to the Council for assistance in promoting their area of interest. This often led to grants for special projects of one kind or another. The different approaches included workshops to factor out content for introduction into established courses or organization into separate courses, teaching materials to introduce the new content, surveys of what was already being done, and studies to chart what should be done. This had the effect of keeping the curriculum current and hopefully relevant to new developments. Not all new directions came from outside. The 1962 curriculum policy statement, in recognizing community organization as a concentration, opened up new opportunities for strengthening the curriculum on the side of social action and social change.

The Community Organization Concentration

Classroom and field instruction in community organization, when offered, had traditionally focused on inter-agency coordination, fund-raising, community planning, and involvement of lay leadership. Community funds and councils worked with a select group of schools to encourage this type of professional preparation. The community action programs of the 1960s, however, introduced an entirely new context for community organization, education, and practice. The President's Committee on Juvenile Delinquency in HEW had a special interest in programs for urban renewal, grassroots organization, and delinquency prevention. Those programs and the war on poverty required skills for community action. This called into question traditional teaching of community organization as a social work method and a number of federal grants were forthcoming to ensure a broader approach in the new concentration.

One of the major projects undertaken by the Council in this period involved a study to review all aspects of the community organization curriculum and to develop recommendations and teaching materials.[6] The study, funded by the President's Committee on Juvenile Delinquency, was conducted by faculty members of the Heller School of Advanced Studies in Social Welfare under subcontract with Brandeis University. The broad scope of the study covered three areas or contexts of practice: (1) grassroots organization of population groups; (2) program development, planning, and implementation; and (3) social planning cutting across a number of agencies or fields involving problems of policy determination, resource allocation, and coordination. The findings and recommendations published in 1972[7] made a significant contribution to the professional literature.

Advocates for grassroots organization and advocacy also influenced the way in which the community organization concentration developed.[8] The federal projects funding community organization practice were located in such non-traditional fields as urban renewal, involving the poor, minorities, and welfare clients in planning and implementation. This created completely new contexts. The knowledge base required much more sophistication than before on the part of the teacher in selecting and integrating chosen social science concepts. The social worker as "advocate" or "broker" needed multi-method versatility of the kind seen in community development practice in third world countries. Educators faced formidable problems in providing an educational experience in such situations. A parallel movement to place students with trade unions, civil rights organizations, and offices of elected officials posed similar problems. To make field instruction an educational experience, the arrangements usually required the assignment and special training of school faculty members as supervisors.

Corrections

Midway through the 1950s and throughout the 1960s, the field of corrections was a focal point for a variety of educational services. Much of the interest was stimulated by a report on the subject in one of the volumes of the Curriculum Study.[9] An ad hoc committee on corrections established in 1955 also sparked a number of activities, including a casebook, but the significant breakthrough for this field came as a result of a Ford Foundation grant. A five-year project to foster and improve social work training of correctional personnel funded by the Ford Foundation was launched in 1960 with the importation from the United Kingdom of Eileen L. Younghusband, an internationally renowned social work educator and magistrate, to make an exploratory survey and suggest guidelines for the new activity. Her report, published as a supplement to the Council's newsletter, made a substantial contribution to the project through an analysis of obstacles and opportunities, the general and specific in curriculum content, the need for interdisciplinary collaboration and communication, and much more.[10]

Within the five-year period of the corrections project, CSWE consultants, experienced in both social work and corrections, pursued the difficult goal of professionalizing correctional staff through social work education. Social work educators and correctional administrators were brought together at the local level to open up channels of communication and develop resources for professional training. Paucity of field placements emerged as a major block to progress. Priorities were revised to place emphasis on the involvement of correctional policymakers and administrators in developing field resources and opportunities. This brought new partners and resources to bear on project activities.

With additional financial support from the President's Committee on Juvenile Delinquency, the first of a series of regional institutes was organized in March 1964 for the Rocky Mountain states. In planning this institute, Charles Prigmore, the CSWE consultant, worked closely with the Western Interstate Commission for Higher Education (the western regional accrediting body), the National Council for Crime and Delinquency, and the American Correctional Association. Governors of the seven states involved in the institute then became actively involved in activities to implement the recommendations for action.

The success of the western institute led to a conference at Arden House in June 1964 for all national organizations concerned with correctional manpower and training. The American Sociology Association joined with the Council and the organizations noted above in sponsoring the event, which was attended by 90 delegates representing national and regional organizations. With a Supreme Court Justice as the keynote speaker, followed by eminent speakers from Congress, federal agencies, and other professions in addition to social work, the actions taken carried great weight. A major outcome was an agreement by the delegates to establish a Joint Commission on Correctional Manpower and Training to forge a national plan for action. In 1965, the commission was constituted as a separate inter-professional and inter-organizational entity, with the Council as one of the sponsoring groups and Prigmore as its director.

Publications of the proceedings[11] marked the culmination of the project as a Council activity. The final report recorded a substantial increase in the number of students, field placements, and faculty members identified with corrections as a result of the work accomplished. All but three graduate schools had developed field placements and NIMH reported corrections as the second fastest growing of its stipend programs, exceeded only by psychiatric social work.[12]

In the same time period, the Council undertook a related project for the production of correctional teaching materials. This activity, also funded by the President's Committee on Juvenile Delinquency, was staffed by Elliot Studt, the author of the Curriculum Study volume on corrections. As a faculty member, Studt had demonstrated in two experimental programs a conceptual framework for teaching that showed great promise. The purpose of the project included the testing in the classroom of materials deriving from the experiments and the production of a casebook.[13] The conceptual structure for social work intervention outlined in the teaching units and records offered a framework not only for the field of corrections but also for all areas of the graduate curriculum.

Despite the intensive and highly successful activity to promote social work education as professional preparation for corrections, the long-range impact on the curriculum was less than anticipated. How to inject new blocks of content into an overcrowded generic curriculum, particularly when a number of fields compete for attention, remained an almost insuperable obstacle. With respect to corrections, there was also the perception, whether justified or not, that social work practice principles were not altogether compatible with the necessary elements of authority in this field.

Other Fields of Practice

Agencies facing a shortage of qualified social workers offered stipends and used field placements to recruit staff, but they also sought to penetrate the curriculum with content about their particular field of practice or area of interest. Project funds became available to underwrite workshops, conferences, and teaching materials for aging and public health. Teaching materials, developed for slighted areas such as mental retardation, alcohol and drug addiction, physical disabilities, and inter-group relations, were publicized in "The Teaching Material News Notes" in the Council newsletter and often became topics for discussion in workshops at the Annual Program Meeting.

Aging was the field most heavily subsidized in this group, primarily as a result of the White House Conference on that subject held in 1961. The

Council received a five-year grant in 1962 from the Ford Foundation to finance the preparation and distribution of case studies and other teaching materials related to aging for use in undergraduate and graduate education and in-service training. Major emphasis was placed on a wide range of materials designed to offer content across the entire curriculum. The source books, bibliographies, pamphlets, and other materials were supplemented by seminars or workshops to demonstrate the integration of content on aging in a generic program.

Public health was also explored as a source of valuable content for social work education in a significant conference held at Princeton University in 1962. Funding under a contract with the U.S. Public Health Service covered staff service, an advisory committee, and the participation at the conference of one faculty member from every school of social work in the United States and Canada. The conference was also attended by officials from each of the divisions of the Public Health Service, including the National Institutes of Health. The program, carefully planned by a CSWE consultant working with a committee representative of social work and public health, covered general information about public health along with specific content for inclusion in the curriculum. The social work participants found in the concepts of prevention and planning and the epidemiological approach a particularly interesting blend of the new and familiar. The proceedings, issued as a hard cover publication, contained 14 major papers, a compendium of workshop discussions, an evaluative summary, and a comprehensive annotated bibliography.[14]

RESEARCH AND EXPERIMENTATION

Research, or perhaps the need for more and better research, figured prominently in program plans. The first Commission on Research was unclear as to its function, whether it should be concerned with the teaching of research in the curriculum or with the promotion of research or whether it should undertake research. Some of that confusion continued, but it is obvious in a review of Council activities through the years that all three elements were present. There was constant exploration of how best to help students develop a sense of commitment to scientific inquiry along with an ability to read, evaluate, and use research findings. The master's thesis, a traditional requirement, gave way in many schools to a variety of learning experiences that ranged widely from library investigations to different types of individual or group projects with written reports.

Many of the special projects undertaken within the Council or on subcontracts with faculty members required the collection and analysis of data. Surveys were needed and used by the Council to obtain information for administrative or program purposes. Because the sheer bulk and variety of these activities defy easy summarization, this account touches briefly on experimentation in field instruction and deals in greater detail with the 13-volume Curriculum Study, the Council's major research effort in the 20-year period under review.

The greater demands made on field instruction to represent the total curriculum and widespread interest in the use of teaching and learning principles in the field as well as in the classroom gave rise to a surprising number of new approaches. Experiments or innovations included the supplementation of traditional methods of individual supervision with group teaching, multi-discipline collaboration, written work beyond case or group recording, and other ways of promoting learning. Some schools departed from the usual pattern of different placements for the first and second years to assign students to the same agency under a defined educational plan for both years. An important innovation created teaching centers, as distinct from traditional student units, where a major objective was teaching to reflect the whole curriculum. Group teaching and peer learning emerged as significant aspects of this type of field instruction.

The Curriculum Study

The profession had barely recovered from the impact of the Hollis-Taylor report on *Social Work Education in the United States* before the Council embarked in 1955 on another study of education. The earlier study, to the disappointment of many educators, admittedly did not deal with the curriculum content. The formation of the Council settled, at least for the time being, the question of professional education as graduate education, but did not solve the problem of the relationship of undergraduate education to graduate education. The change-over from the "basic eight" to the generic curriculum and questions issuing from the Council's consultation project revealed a need and readiness for a study that would deal specifically with curriculum content and organization.

The study addressed three questions: (1) What are the desirable educational objectives for social work education? (2) Into what curriculum areas should they be organized? And (3) what should be their distribution over the undergraduate–graduate continuum?[15] As a frame of reference for the study of those questions, statements were produced on the nature of social work as a profession and the nature of learning in social work education.

Werner W. Boehm, director and coordinator of the study, worked with a highly qualified full-time and part-time staff, a prestigious technical advisory panel, and a series of expert panels for specific curriculum areas. The study was published in 1959 in a series of 13 volumes numbered in alphabetical order by study area except for Volume I, which contained the comprehensive final report, and Volume II, an equally comprehensive report on undergraduate education. Although published separately, the various study projects were interdependent and used the same master design.

The study recommended that professional social work education should consist of three stages of learning spread over two undergraduate years and two graduate years. The first stage, beginning in the junior year, would include an introduction to related disciplines followed by the selection of concepts from those disciplines pertinent to individual behavior, group behavior, and society and focused on social welfare policy and services, human growth and behavior, and the values of social work. The second stage, described as the methods component, continued in undergraduate education. It would enable students to learn concepts from the foundation component and acquire knowledge of professional activities applicable to all methods. The third stage, in the first year of graduate education, consisted of two parts. The first part in an academic setting would enable the student to acquire knowledge of all the methods of social work and begin to develop skills in one of them in a combination of class and field instruction. In the second part, the student would spend a second year in a paid practicum experience in a selected teaching agency to further develop skills in practice. This would be followed by a summer session consisting of three integrative seminars. A master's degree would be awarded upon completion of the three stages of preparation.

The eagerly awaited findings and recommendations of the study gave rise to passionate discussion within faculties, at the Annual Program Meeting, and among colleagues in every branch of the CSWE constituency. The independence of the study and the responsibility of the study staff for its outcome was underlined by the Board of Directors. Ernest Witte declared in his annual report to the membership in 1959 that the Council staff would now join everyone else in the constituency in studying the recommendations.[16]

The newly established Curriculum Committee, charged with the production of a new curriculum policy statement, was asked by the Board to begin its work by analyzing the content, findings, and recommendations of the 13 volumes. The committee, with subcommittees and liaison members, embarked on a monumental task. Individual members were assigned volumes for analysis and submission of a full report to the committee. Requests for general comments and reactions to specific recommendations brought in an accumulation of responses from the graduate schools and undergraduate departments, the national employing agencies, the National Association of Social Workers, the House of Delegates, and the Board of Directors.[17]

The overwhelming response from the constituency pointed to a consensus around certain issues and content. The analysis of the nature of social work and the delineation of educational objectives were well-received. The content in a number of the volumes was found to be very useful and enriching. The rationale for the recommendations on the structure and

organization of the curriculum and their practicality, however, were questioned. Review and discussion of this wealth of material by the Curriculum
Committee and its subcommittees, including an active subcommittee on
undergraduate education, led to further deliberation and action on three
issues that had emerged as highly controversial: (1) the undergraduate–
graduate continuum; (2) the practicum; and (3) the separation of foundation knowledge from instruction in social work methods.

Unanimous agreement was reached on the following actions, here
summarized:

1. The continuum was not accepted.

2. Other solutions for educational problems in the undergradu-
    ate–graduate relationship required urgent attention.

3. Experiments in the distribution of undergraduate and graduate
    content in preparation for social work were highly recommended.

4. The practicum, as proposed in the study, was described as incon-
    sistent with the committee's rejection of the continuum and
    affirmation of the two-year graduate program of social work
    education.

5. Foundation knowledge should not be restricted and sepa-
    rated from subsequent class and field instruction in social
    work methods.

6. The assumption of direct service responsibility and related class-
    room instruction in a method of social work should begin in
    the first year of graduate education.

7. The results of experiments in the distribution of foundation knowl-
    edge and methods content should be so planned that results would
    be cumulative and definite. A proposal that such results should be
    reported only to the Curriculum Committee was amended by the
    Board of Directors to place responsibility on the Commission of
    Accreditation for evaluation of experiments.[18]

The Board accepted the conclusions of the Curriculum Committee when
it adopted the 1962 curriculum policy statement. The three contentious

recommendations did not disappear, but they were no longer issues to be resolved. The proposal of a practicum did not long survive, but the profession continues to seek an answer to the question of a continuum in undergraduate–graduate education. There were immediate outcomes, however, that led to significant developments. The comments received by the Curriculum Committee clearly indicated the need for priority attention to undergraduate education. The subcommittee appointed to work on the question produced a guide that, as already indicated, was approved by the Board of Directors in 1961 and published in 1962.[19] Another important outcome focused attention on submitting new ideas to examination through experimentation. This resulted in early action by the Commission on Accreditation for approval of experiments outside of curriculum policy.[20] It remained the responsibility of the Curriculum Committee to look at the results of experimentation within curriculum policy or for utilization in policy development.

Policy on Experimentation

The Commission on Accreditation, in its policy on experimentation and innovation, established three guiding principles in its evaluation of experimental or innovative projects outside of curriculum policy: (1) promise of contributing to social work education; (2) establishment of a specified time limit for the conduct and evaluation of results; and (3) provision for responsible evaluation, recording, and reporting of the results, and adequate resources for faculty and finances.[21] The last principle also included the need for evidence that possible adverse consequences for students or the public served were taken into consideration. With the door opened to planned change, a number of schools took advantage of the new policy. Discussion of experimental projects, within and outside of curriculum policy, may be found in articles in proceedings of the Annual Program Meetings and news notes and papers in the *Social Work Education Reporter*.

PROGRAM SERVICES

The domination of educational services in the Council program in the first 20 years was probably the result of the continuing emphasis on quality and quantity as priority concerns. This chapter closes with a brief account of other services that were perhaps equally valued by the constituency.

The Annual Program Meeting

Once a year, usually in January or February, the coming together of educators, practitioners, organizations, and lay leaders interested in social work education expressed in action the underlying philosophy of the Council. This was the time that the representatives from every constituency interacted, making visible the idea that preparation for social work was too important to the profession and society at large to be seen as the sole responsibility of the educators.

The meetings were sponsored by local schools and departments of social work and the communities in which they were held. On two occasions, the Board of Directors cancelled planned Annual Program Meetings. The meeting scheduled for Chicago in 1970 was cancelled in response to the brutal treatment of demonstrators at the Democratic National Convention. In 1972, the meeting scheduled for Detroit was cancelled because the Council and the schools were facing severe financial difficulties because of cuts in federal funding. The required annual business meetings of the House of Delegates were arranged for another time and place. Because of the nature of the problems to be discussed, the 1979 meeting of the House of Delegates in Williamsburg was expanded to include other participants by invitation.

The Annual Program Meeting was the place where committees met and business was conducted. But most important was the opportunity for exploration and exchange of ideas and experiences in forums and workshops. Whatever was current on the minds of Council members and staff appeared on the program. Keynote speakers, with one notable exception, more often than not came from academia. The exception was Eleanor Roosevelt who spoke at the 1954 Annual Program Meeting held in Washington, D.C. She endeared herself to her already admiring audience when she made this remark to refute the criticism that well-trained social workers lose their humanity:

> I think the really well-trained social worker understands economic
> conditions, understands human beings, their frailties, their strengths,
> and, as a rule, can do a tremendous amount to create the right kind
> of thinking in the community in which they work.[22]

Council staff worked with the Program Committees to make full use of opportunities at the Annual Program Meetings for discussion on issues, new ideas, and important developments affecting Council activities. Annual reports by the executive director described those activities along with problems requiring help from the membership for their solution. The published proceedings reveal the seriousness of purpose and the high quality of the work accomplished at the Annual Program Meetings.

But not everything at Annual Program Meetings promoted serious thought. Throughout much of the 1960s, some of the major issues facing the profession were subjected to examination from a satirical viewpoint. This trend began when Leo Perlis, a CSWE Board member representing the AFL-CIO, was quoted in the *New York Times* as saying that bartenders saw more people in trouble than anyone else and should be trained in social work. This struck Kendall as too interesting an idea to be discarded. A skit was produced which sent deans and directors with great vocal talents in pursuit of recruits through barroom research, placed federal luminaries as bar flies pouring out their troubles to a well-known dean as a bartender, and involved Milton Wittman of NIMH with a bagful of scholarships. The outcome after one year of professional education left the recruit unfit as a bartender but did not yet qualify him as a social worker, thus reflecting the position of the generic policy statements that you have to stay with it for two years. The skit, using parodies of well-known songs, offered gentle satire of recruitment, curriculum policy, NIMH largess, and more. For a few years the skits became a tradition at Annual Program Meetings with reruns at the National Conference of Social Work. Needless to say, scores of talented people worked happily on this unscheduled activity, creating dialogue, writing songs, singing lustily, and performing as players and musicians.

Unfortunately, a song in one of the skits, taken out of context, has been misinterpreted. In several undergraduate histories, the parodied "NASSA's (substituted for Massa's) in the Cold Ground" has been construed by some as indicative of the Council's rejection of undergraduate education. In the interest of equal treatment, it is only fair that this history should introduce the song from one of the skits that, to the tune of a well-known ditty from "The Mikado," did abolish every single graduate school of social work. The first lines tell the story:

> We have a little list, a pretty little list
> Of accredited schools of social work
> That never will be missed,
> That never will be missed

Each school on the CSWE list was then finished off. No offense was taken at any of the skits that were produced, perhaps because in the end social work always emerged triumphant and a little levity was appreciated.

Admissions and Student Selection

The Council inherited from the AASSW a Committee on Admissions that had already conducted an important study of the admissions process funded by NIMH. An analysis of almost 5,000 applications revealed that schools tended to agree generally on what made an applicant appear suitable for admission, but not on what made an applicant unsuitable. The variations in judgments appeared to be related to the nature and interpretation of the evidence used in the assessment of the applicant. With the formation of the Council, the activity was continued, leading to many years of productive work by a succession of Committees on Admission. The initial work was to a large extent encouraged by and financed with the help of Marian Kenworthy and Sidney Berengarten of the New York School of Social Work who were engaged in a pilot study of pre-admission interviews to assess personal suitability. Throughout the 1950s and into the 1960s, a series of funded and non-funded workshops sought and suggested answers to the following basic questions:

- What are the personality characteristics a candidate should bring to professional education and to practice in social work?
- How can the school, through its admission process, determine whether the applicant has the qualifications deemed necessary for successful practice?
- How can the school improve its admissions process?
- How can we validate the results of our assessment of the individual applicant and our predictions regarding his or her reaction to the educational experience?

Suggestions were put forward for obtaining information, in a more or less uniform manner, in the application and autobiographical forms submitted by candidates. But what captured the interest and continued involvement of the committee in the 1950s was study and use of the dynamic pre-admissions interview in the selection process. Stimulated by the New York School pilot study and under the leadership of Berengarten, national workshops with follow-up workshops at Annual Program Meetings were organized to gain understanding of the suitability of candidates through dynamically oriented interviewing. The special training in interviewing and in personality assessment given in various workshops led to the establishment by the Council of a National Roster of Interviewers. The purpose was to make available to all schools wishing to use the service a list of social workers in education and practice with special skill in this particular type of interviewing. Considerable use was made of the roster in the 1950s, but it disappeared in the 1960s as interest waned in the use of the analytically oriented interview in the selection of students.

The committee also sponsored an unduplicated count study of applications for admission in the 1961–1962 fall term. This proved extremely useful in providing information on the characteristics and backgrounds of the applicants. The study also made available information on the way in which applications were handled by the schools. Admissions predictions for the performance of each enrolled student and assessment at different levels of performance were of special interest. This committee and its mission attracted the high degree of commitment and dedicated volunteer activity that made possible continuing productive work on a particular subject area. Many other committees followed the same pattern of unremitting service, which explains how it was possible for the Council to undertake the multitude of activities described in this account.

The International Dimension

The by-laws amendment of 1964 to specify an international role for the Council simply affirmed what had been true for many years. From its inception, the Council actively supported an international perspective as an essential ingredient of professionalism in social work. International activities were promoted through committee work, consultation at home and abroad, and a special relationship with the International Association of Schools of Social Work. Specific activities carried out by the predecessor AASSW included active engagement with the U.S. Department of State, the United Nations, and UNICEF on advisory services, international exchange of faculty and students, and technical assistance to schools of social work in other countries. These activities were carried over and expanded.

India and Africa Projects. Under contractual arrangements already noted in the discussion of finances, the Council from 1956 to 1961 administered a project involving advisory service and student exchange with schools of social work in India and Africa. Individual staff members were also frequently called upon by the Department of State, the United Nations, UNICEF, the Pan-American Health Organization, and the Organization of American States to provide consultation in other countries and leadership for regional and international seminars, expert working groups, and conferences on social work education. Much of this activity was conducted by staff members on their vacation time.

CSWE-Sponsored Conferences. With funding from the Agency for International Development, Council staff planned and directed the first seminar for schools of social work in Central America in 1962 and an international conference on social work education and family planning at the East-

West Center in Hawaii in 1970. Other international meetings sponsored or cosponsored by the Council included three significant inter-professional conferences, one in 1959 on the training of technical assistance personnel, another in 1961 on the professional education of foreign students, and a third in 1967 on universals and differences in social work values and practice across cultures. The reports of these several conferences continue to offer a guide to the development of an international dimension in social work education.

International Committee. Through the 1950s and 1960s, and continuing into the early 1970s, an active international committee chalked up a noteworthy record of achievement through policy statements, workshops and seminars, pamphlets and publications, student and faculty international exchange programs, and the distribution of *Inter-Ed*, an occasional newsletter. In addition, the committee served as a resource for U.S. Government agencies and the United Nations on projects and preparation of materials related to social work training and education.

IASSW Secretariat. Upon the election in 1954 of Kendall as secretary of the International Association of Schools of Social Work (IASSW), the Council office served in effect as a volunteer secretariat, but with no commitment of funds for that purpose. As a non-governmental organization in consultative status with the Economic and Social Council of the United Nations, the IASSW was deeply involved with the United Nations in high-priority programs dealing with social work training and social welfare advisory services. The international interests of both the Council and the IASSW were well served through cooperative work on student and faculty exchange programs and in activities involving technical assistance to the emerging nations in the third world.

Throughout these 20 years, the Council, as a national association member of the IASSW, was represented on its Executive Board. In cooperation with the IASSW, it sponsored the thirteenth International Congress of Schools of Social Work held in 1966 in Washington D.C. An exhibit of all schools of social work in existence for 50 years or longer proved to be a major attraction at this congress. The pictures and documents contributed by the participating schools highlighted the history and evolution of social work education around the world.

Recognizing international work as a key function, the Council, as already noted, established in 1967 a Division of International Education to be staffed by a full-time director and secretary as one of the new program entities created in a structural reorganization. To carry out the work of the division, the Council converted the International Committee into a Commission on International Education, which projected an ambitious program. With the failure of Congress to appropriate funds for spending for social work education, continuing support for international education as a central function could not be justified. When the Director of International Education left the Council to serve the IASSW as its Secretary-General in a newly established secretariat, the International Division was discontinued. CSWE did, however, continue an interest in the Fulbright fellowship program as well as its relationship with the IASSW as a national member association with representation on the Board of Directors.

Publications

From its inception, the Council has produced an impressive list of publications. Those taken over from the AASSW and continued as serials included the annual report on *Statistics on Social Work Education*, the list of accredited schools of social work, an annual compilation of *Social Work Fellowships and Scholarships in the United States and Canada*, and a newsletter.

Beginning in 1929 as a mimeographed reprint by AASSW, known then as the Association of Schools of Professional Social Work, the annual publication on statistics has remained an invaluable source of data on social work education. Statistics on undergraduate programs approved by CSWE were included for the first time in 1974.

A directory of member schools and departments, issued periodically, has also taken many forms. In the beginning, CSWE issued a list of accredited graduate schools of social work. This was followed by a separate list of undergraduate departments as constituent members. Following the decision to develop criteria and standards for beginning-level practice at the undergraduate level, the Council issued an approved list of undergraduate programs in 1971, 1972, and 1973. With full-scale accreditation in place, a list of accredited baccalaureate programs was issued in 1974.

From the beginning, the Council has provided some form of newsletter as a membership benefit. Issued first in 1953 as *Social Work Education*, the name was changed in 1965 to *Social Work Education Reporter* to avoid confusion with the newly authorized journal. Now classified in the archives by the revised name, the original newsletter is a veritable cornucopia of historical information. News Notes covered people, committee activities, national, regional, and international events of interest, and happenings in schools and agencies. The newsletter also carried annual lists of dissertations, faculty changes and promotions, and committees and board members. Special issues, particularly for recruitment, contained detailed reports of what was being done throughout the country. Each issue provided articles about current subjects of significance to the entire constituency. From 1953 onward, the newsletter files are a rich source of historical information on all aspects of the organization and work of the Council.

Proceedings of Annual Program Meetings were published separately until 1965 when the Board authorized the production of a journal in which significant papers from each APM as well as other articles would be published. Beginning with two issues annually as the *Journal of Education for Social Work*, it was expanded to three issues in 1971. As a refereed journal, it has had as its central purpose through the years a "creative exchange on trends, new developments, innovations, and problems relevant to professional social work education at the undergraduate, master's and postgraduate levels."

Publications in the early years included a steady flow of educational materials on curriculum building, under-represented areas of content such as aging, public health, corrections, etc., teaching methodology and materials, field instruction, international education, undergraduate guides and syllabi, and much more.

The emphasis on recruitment in the 1950s and 1960s produced a cascade of career materials. The list of scholarships and fellowships and the special recruitment issues of the newsletter served as invaluable tools in nationwide recruitment efforts.

The 13-volume Curriculum Study reports remain the single most significant hardcover publications issued by the Council, but a number of other hardcover volumes have given valuable support to research and curriculum development at both levels of social work education. Whether in hardcover or paperback, the published reports of workshops, seminars, institutes, special projects, committee activities, and studies offered the membership an enduring source of practical help and professional nourishment.

Chapter Twelve

Educating Downward, Sideways, and Upward

The Council's mission to promote sound programs of social work education extended to all levels of study within its domain but not all received equal treatment. During the 1950s and into the 1960s, graduate education at the master's level occupied center stage with some attention given to doctoral programs and very little to undergraduate education. The priority concerns of recruitment, accreditation, and curriculum revision, along with the usual services to a membership group, completely occupied the small core staff of a director and three consultants. The additional staff that became available through special projects in the 1950s were engaged, with one exception, in activities related to graduate education. That one exception, on which many hopes were built, was a project in the CSWE Curriculum Study to produce a report and recommendations on undergraduate education. As we shall see in the account that follows, the marked changes that took place in the 1960s put undergraduate education at the forefront of Council concerns.

UNDERGRADUATE EDUCATION

The decision by AASSW to require graduate education as preparation for social work went into effect in 1939, with the consequences spelled out in Part 1 of this historical account. In affirming that decision, the Hollis-Taylor report also granted the possibility of terminal programs at the undergraduate level, but with the following proviso and caution:

> semiprofessional programs should be undertaken only after a survey
> of social work practice has identified and distinguished between
> professional and semi-professional functions in social work. Unless
> there is an adequate supply of professionally qualified social work-

ers, those with only semiprofessional and technical qualifications are too likely to be promoted to fill the vacuum.[1]

Views differ on the nature and quality of the initial relationship between undergraduate educators and their colleagues. The views expressed here reflect the personal experience of a Council staff member closely allied in committees and other activities with former members of NASSA.

Harmony and Benign Neglect

Acceptance of the findings of the Hollis-Taylor report and the coming together of NASSA and AASSW to establish the Council ushered in a period of relative harmony and amity, but did not solve the problem of the undergraduate–graduate relationship in the preparation of social workers. In the first years after the merger, the leaders in NASSA became involved in establishing graduate programs. Ernest Harper and Harold Wetzel, previous NASSA presidents, also became active leaders in general Council activities and management, identifying with the broader constituency while still remaining active within the undergraduate division of the Commission of Schools and Departments.

The hopes expressed at the outset for immediate cooperative work in thinking through conceptually what should be taught at the undergraduate level were not realized. The major undergraduate departments were too busy becoming graduate schools, the graduate schools were too occupied in implementing the generic curriculum policy statement, and the Council staff were too busy with an overload of priority activities to provide leadership. Recognizing the variation in what was being offered by the undergraduate members of the Council, the Undergraduate Division pressed the need for a study of curriculum content. The Board and staff, in complete agreement, placed the request high on the list of activities to be undertaken as soon as funds became available.

Meanwhile, a research project sponsored by Syracuse University, in cooperation with other educational institutions in New York State, promised to provide some guidance on the preparation needed by college graduates entering social welfare employment. Plans for the comprehensive Curriculum Study accorded top priority to undergraduate education and, as already noted, the published report as Volume II was given top billing with Volume I, the final report. Most but not all constituent members of the Council, including the undergraduate contingent, agreed with the judgment of the Curriculum Committee and the Board of Directors not to accept the recommendations of the Study for a new organizational pattern for professional education. The questions raised by the study and the continuing need for guidance in developing undergraduate social welfare programs led to a significant new approach to the subject. The period of benign neglect was coming to an end, but slowly. To understand the complicated undergraduate–graduate relationship, it is instructive to look at the prevailing view of that relationship in the early years of the Council.

Prevailing Attitudes

Until 1970 there was a consistent choice to keep the master's degree as the recognized qualification for the professional practice of social work. The position accepted at the time not only by the graduate schools but also by the membership as a whole, including the undergraduate departments, could be summarized in the following terms:

1. Undergraduate study of the arts and sciences leading to a bachelor's degree is basic to a career in social work.
2. Education for professional responsibility as a social worker should consist of an orderly progression from the final two years of undergraduate work through two years of professional study.
3. A proper concern of the undergraduate program in relation to social work is academic education designed to impart knowledge of man and society and understanding of social welfare as a social institution.
4. Undergraduate programs have a dual purpose: provision of content on the theoretical foundations of social work for students interested in professional study and provision of social welfare content for all students as preparation for responsible citizenship.

What was meant by liberal education and what should be included in the social sciences appear as persistent and somewhat baffling questions for social work educators. The AASSW worked hard on those questions in formulating a position on preprofessional education. A report identifying desirable undergraduate content accepted by the association in 1941 made this unequivocal statement:

> There can no longer be any debate over the primacy of the social sciences as preprofessional subjects for social work. Economics, political science, psychology and sociology are recognized by all social workers and by all members of faculties of schools of social work as basically related to the profession of social work.[2]

From that point forward, it has been a general practice, perhaps more often honored in theory than in reality, for graduate schools to require for admission all or some combination of the subjects noted above, always specified as within a liberal arts framework. Students without the social science background were not generally required to make up any deficiency. It was assumed that other desirable subjects, such as English, biology, and philosophy, would be covered within general education.

To clarify the place of liberal arts in the undergraduate–graduate relationship, a study was launched for the Council by the Institute of Higher Education of Columbia University, with a grant from the Carnegie Foundation. The Institute had already completed similar studies in a number of fields, including nursing, business administration, engineering, home economics, and others.[3] The study was conducted by Earl J. McGrath, executive officer of the Institute, and Gordon J. Aldridge, director of the School of Social Work at Michigan State University, the university that figured prominently in the NASSA chronicle. The study concentrated on facts, attitudes, and expectations about undergraduate liberal education as preparation for graduate social work education. As such, it served as a barometer of prevailing attitudes, as noted here:

> Insofar as the main issue in the present study is concerned, it can be said that from the earliest days of systematic university education for

the practice of social work the vast majority of the leading spokes-
men for the profession have favored a sound grounding in the liberal arts subjects. There have in the past been strong advocates of an
undergraduate professional course of study and a few still hold to
the view that the needs of society, the interests of the student, and
the expense in time and money involved in a strictly graduate preparation demand an earlier beginning of professional social work courses.
The findings of this study, however, show that this is not the prevailing view.[4]

What that liberal arts background should offer or include defied a ready
answer. It was found that students with a minimum of prior instruction in
the social sciences seemed to do just as well as those with a strong concentration. It was found, also, that students in physics or philosophy maintained just as good records as majors in psychology or sociology. Against
those conclusions, a contrary result was found in a study undertaken by
Sidney Berengarten in connection with the work of the admissions committee. He found that undergraduate majors in social welfare and English out-
performed all others in schools of social work.[5] The Aldridge-McGrath
study concluded that a positive relationship between high grades in undergraduate courses and graduate study was the best measure of performance.
There was also the strong inference that provision of a breadth of view, and
a capacity to think, to analyze, and to continue learning constitutes the
contribution from liberal education.

That was the situation in the 1950s. The change in attitude in the 1960s
to consider the possibility of professional education at the undergraduate
level came slowly but inevitably in the light of new considerations. The
many factors influencing attitudes included more serious attention to the
continued severe shortage of qualified social workers, the manpower studies that pointed to the need for downward expansion of training facilities,
and the participation of college graduates in the Peace Corps and Vista
programs as an indication of the greater maturity of this generation and
their readiness to assume professional responsibility. Comments by leading

educators illustrate in graphic terms the evolving nature of the change. Charles Brink, a well-known dean, said this in reviewing the need for expansion of training facilities:

> Not too many years ago anyone who mentioned undergraduate education was thought to be indecent and excommunication was a possibility. Today, even nice people are considering extending social work education to the undergraduate level.[6]

Speaking in 1967, Ernest Witte, former executive director of the Council, noted the growing change in attitude. He said that he now found at the CSWE Annual Program Meeting a greater willingness to reconsider the traditional stand taken by many social work educators. He stated further that failure to take the lead in making possible a contribution of undergraduate education in meeting social welfare manpower needs would plunge the field into a renewal of what he called a fruitless struggle.[7]

Turning of the Tide

As already noted, the preoccupation in the beginning years of the Council with graduate education and its curriculum concerns, plus limitations in funds and staff, delayed action on activities in undergraduate education. The tide began to turn in 1960 when the Curriculum Committee gave priority to the formulation of a guiding statement for undergraduate education related to social work and appointed a subcommittee to produce it as quickly as possible. Drafts were prepared and discussed in the Division of Undergraduate Departments, comments were obtained from the undergraduate members, and the statement finally underwent review by the Curriculum Committee and the Board. The reactions ranged widely. Mereb Mossman, chair of the subcommittee, said in a report at the Annual Program Meeting:

> Some feared that the Guide placed too much emphasis on preparation for employment immediately after the undergraduate years, while others felt it didn't place enough; some felt that those who came through the proposed undergraduate program should be given

preferential admission to graduate professional social work education, while others felt there should be no special consideration for
those who have had a carefully planned sequence in social welfare.[8]

The third draft of the guide was highly commended and approved by
the Curriculum Committee in June 1961, by the Board of Directors in
October 1961, and published as *Social Welfare Content in Undergraduate
Education* in 1962.[9] The guide almost immediately became a bestseller. At
the recommendation of the Curriculum Committee, the Board, at the same
meeting, also appointed its first Committee on Undergraduate Education.

The Guide—1961 and 1967

The guide specified five educational objectives to be achieved within the
framework of liberal education:

1. Knowledge of man and insight into human growth and behavior;
2. Knowledge of society and social interaction;
3. Appreciation of the philosophical values underlying social welfare activities;
4. Problem-solving and communication abilities; and
5. Understanding of social welfare as a social institution and social work
   as a profession.

Concepts and areas of content relevant to social welfare and social work
were outlined under each of those headings. The development of content
for the areas of social welfare as a social institution and social work as a
profession soon became the subject of numerous workshops, institutes, and
demonstrations. Field observation and experience, carefully distinguished
from field practice at the graduate level, was put forward as a means of
relating social welfare content to the practice and settings of social work. A
variety of models of structured social welfare programs were introduced at
meetings and workshops. It was not expected that all students enrolling in
the undergraduate programs would be interested in social work as a career.
The sequences were thus planned to enrich the education of all liberal arts
students who wished to enroll as well as to provide a foundation for graduate study or entry into some form of human service employment.

The guide was revised in 1967 in response to changes and developments within the field of social welfare and within the Council. Efforts within government circles to develop two career lines in social welfare employment and general questions within the profession of differential use of social work personnel became more and more insistent. Acceptance within the Council in 1966 of a broader educational policy designed to meet all social welfare staffing needs paved the way for new approaches to undergraduate education.

The availability of an official document made possible the marshaling of new resources to assist in the development of the undergraduate social welfare sequence. The newly appointed Committee on Undergraduate Education worked on clarification of the objectives and content suggested by the guide. More and more information about undergraduate education appeared in the *Social Work Education Reporter*. Teaching materials were developed and widely circulated. *Social Welfare as a Social Institution*, a booklet of syllabi for what became the basic course in the sequence was published in 1963 and reprinted in later editions.[10] A second syllabus in the series, *Social Work: A Helping Profession in Social Welfare*, appeared in 1966 as a guide to teaching in the second major area in the social work sequence.[11] Field experience was examined.[12] Papers presented at Annual Program Meetings were compiled and published as pamphlets. Institutes were sponsored by the Southern Regional Education Board and the Western Interstate Commission on Higher Education. Graduate schools in various combinations across the country organized conferences and workshops. The Silberman Fund made the production of a basic text on social welfare as a social institution the object of its first grant to the Council. *Social Welfare: Charity to Justice as a Social Institution*, a text written by John M. Romanyshyn, was a helpful addition to the steadily increasing list of source material.[13]

All of this production was tied together by the Committee on Undergraduate Education appointed by the Board of Directors and with the assistance of a full-time consultant, a combination made possible by a grant from the Field Foundation. The committee was expected to:

1. Develop the undergraduate education project;

2. Encourage sound development of undergraduate social welfare programs;

3. Identify, with the Curriculum Committee, the curriculum objectives, content, and organization in undergraduate social welfare education; and

4. Study the relationship of this education to professional education for social work and to social work practice in positions not now requiring professional education.

The committee followed the pattern of all Council units in drawing representation from the total constituency. Chaired initially by Mossman, the leading exponent of undergraduate education in the early years, the committee was later led by Witte. Under both leaders and with the tireless assistance of consultant Cordelia Cox, the committee fully redeemed its charge, as indicated by the many initiatives leading to a steady stream of educational materials.

The greatly increased service to undergraduate educators was also facilitated by a survey in 1965–1966, which for the first time provided comprehensive data on undergraduate programs, students, and faculty members.[14] Funded by a grant from the Welfare Administration of the U.S. Department of Health, Education and Welfare (HEW), the survey was not limited to CSWE members but covered all bachelor's degree programs in the United States. With a response rate of more than 70 percent, it was discovered that 529 colleges and universities reported some form of instruction in social welfare or social work at the undergraduate level.

The findings of the survey put a spotlight on the 232 undergraduate programs in Council membership and gave rise to questions about the quality of some of the programs. The consultation service also revealed wide variation and unequal quality in what was being offered. The undergraduate committee, recognizing the need for some form of quality control, developed new membership criteria specifying the requirements to be met by all new programs and, within three years, all current members.[15] The requirements, which were adopted by the Board of Directors in November 1967,[16] paved the way for the next step in the direction of official recognition as professional social work training programs. That step was pushed forward when NASW in 1968 recognized graduates of baccalaureate programs and admitted them to membership as BSW social workers. The Council began immediately to initiate an accrediting process.

Recognition Achieved

To extend its accrediting authority to undergraduate education the Council had to apply to the Council on Post-Secondary Accreditation (the national accrediting body) for permission. Preliminary to the accreditation of undergraduate members, the Council in 1970 adopted standards for "approval" of the programs. In summation, the requirements specified, in addition to the criteria adopted in 1967: (1) a primary objective of preparation for practice; (2) educationally directed field instruction; (3) a full-time faculty administrator; (4) inclusion in the faculty of an MSW-qualified social worker; and (5) content on social work practice to be taught by an MSW-qualified social worker.[17] The standards became effective on July 1, 1971. A pamphlet was issued almost immediately containing guidelines for curriculum development, faculty recruitment and responsibilities, agency relationships, library resources, student recruitment and admissions, and administrative organization.[18] Of the 200-plus members applying for approval, 151 met the new requirements. Baccalaureate education for social work became fully professionalized in 1974 when the national accrediting body granted the Council authority to accredit undergraduate programs. What happened then and what came afterwards fall outside the orbit of this historical account and must await another chronicler.[19]

Social Work Technicians

Witte, serving as chair of the Committee on Undergraduate Education, emerged as the leading exponent of preparation below the level of graduate education for social welfare employment. In the early 1960s he had floated a trial balloon for the training of sub-professionals in associate degree programs. The idea was not rejected, but it became buried in the rapidly developing plans for greater recognition of baccalaureate programs. He also saw a role for social work technicians, which was favorably regarded by many at HEW. Preoccupation, particularly in HEW, with staff shortages in the social welfare field gave rise to numerous ideas on how to solve the problem. They included analysis of tasks, classification of jobs, and development of a two-track occupational system with a career ladder. Within this context, the possibility of training technicians at the associate degree level emerged as a subject for exploration. The newsletter carried articles, and discussions were held at Annual Program Meetings. Several projects were developed and financed to consider the content and administration of associate degree programs but none left a permanent mark. Instead, the Council, in addition to continuing work on undergraduate education, directed its attention to the expansion of facilities for master's degree programs and to continuing education.

EXPANDING GRADUATE EDUCATION

The success of the recruitment program, combined with new demands arising from the anti-poverty programs and other Great Society initiatives, thrust expansion of educational facilities into a high priority position. The existing schools were filled to capacity, efforts were made to expand faculties and field placements, and branch programs were developed, but good candidates continued to be lost to the field. The Board of Directors in 1965 recognized that its emphasis on quantity and quality as inseparable concerns required the allocation of resources to the creation of additional graduate schools of social work. An Advisory Committee was appointed in October 1965 to develop with the staff a master plan for a new schools project. With a grant from the National Institute of Mental Health (NIMH), a special project was launched in July 1966.

Eight action proposals were designed to stimulate the establishment of new schools and to provide the consultation and assistance needed for newly established programs to achieve high standards of preparation. They were stated, as follows:

1. Development of a master plan for the location of new schools of social work.

2. Stimulation of interest (at the regional, state, and local levels) in the development of new schools of social work.

3. Development of a corps of social work educators who are qualified to make the intensive study of community and university resources essential for the development of a new school.

4. Provision, on a regular basis, of intensive consultation services from the Council on Social Work Education to universities and communities during the planning period and pre-accreditation phase of a new school.

5. Planning and provision of opportunities for the development of administrative leadership for new schools.

6. Development and provision of opportunities for help with curriculum building and faculty development in the critical first years in the life of a new school.

7. Preparation and publication of written materials relative to the expansion of social work education through the development of new schools of social work.

8. Evaluation of the project in terms of new patterns for social work education and future educational needs and possibilities.[20]

The response to the project exceeded initial expectations. Eighteen of the 25 universities receiving consultation service in the first year had themselves initiated the request. The remaining five were encouraged to apply for service by NASW chapters and local welfare councils. Feasibility studies were used to measure whether there was enough interest and capability on the part of the university and the community to warrant the establishment of a graduate school of social work. The findings of these reports suggested that interest usually arose from one or more of the following factors: (1) the evolution of a college into a university; (2) recognition of community service as a university function; (3) community pressures; and (4) special needs associated with a region or special ethnic group.[21]

A review of project activities by its Advisory Committee in 1969 revealed the long process from an initial expression of interest to the accredi-

tation of a new graduate program of social work education. Adequate financing not only for the support of the school but also for the support of
students in need of economic help frequently posed problems for interested
universities. For quality programs, well-qualified faculty, always in short
supply, were needed and hard to find. Nevertheless, by 1970 5 new schools
had been accredited, 15 universities were involved in the process of opening
a new school or had a new program working toward accreditation, and 42
were in an early stage of exploration or already engaged in a feasibility
study. The project continued into the 1970s with positive gains for the
profession.

CONTINUING EDUCATION

Work on continuing education was another of the far-reaching effects
of the decision reached by the Council in 1965 to extend the range of its
concerns to embrace greater responsibility for education and training at
levels below or different from graduate education. NIMH, with special interest in this activity because of its own newly established Continuing Education Branch in 1966, again appears as a motivating agent. In 1968, it
funded a special project to enable the Council to provide leadership and
service in this area for its membership.

Under the direction of a staff consultant, the activities undertaken included a survey of the programs offered by schools of social work, workshops, institutes, and circulation of information on available offerings.[22]
The survey, conducted in 1968, found that a majority of the graduate schools
considered continuing education an important ongoing part of their educational function. A highly diversified group of practitioners participated in
the programs offered by the schools in the summer months and throughout
the academic year. Practitioners of various educational levels, ranging from
MSW graduates and graduates of baccalaureate programs to the completely
untrained, were enrolled in the different offerings. Community leaders, po-
lice officers, board members, juvenile court judges, house parents, foster parents, and clerical workers also took advantage of the educational opportunities.

Social work methods, including administration and supervision, predominated in the listing of subject matters. Fields of practice ran a close second to methods. Child welfare was easily the most popular subject in this group, followed by corrections, medical social work, mental retardation, rehabilitation, and programs for the aging. Social welfare policy, planning, and current issues, such as inner-city concerns, poverty, race, and the urban crisis, accounted for offerings other than those dealing with methods and fields of practice. Many of these subjects were covered in short-term offerings of a few days or a few weeks. Casework, group work, child welfare, and human behavior and the social environment were more likely to be offered as part-time courses for a full semester.

As the continuing education project moved into the 1970s, plans were developed and successfully carried out for faculty seminars, workshops, publication of articles, and an annual listing of summer offerings with details on the subject areas, prerequisites for admission, fees, and other information of interest as a guide to professional development. Continuing education, like undergraduate education, was reaching new levels of recognition as a significant area of concern.

THE ADVANCED CURRICULUM

Like the Council, post-master's degree education was a brave new venture in 1952. Until the late 1940s, doctoral education had been centered for many years on only two schools of social work, the Graduate School of Social Work and Social Research at Bryn Mawr College and the School of Social Service Administration at the University of Chicago. The newly established NIMH sought qualified social work personnel for advanced clinical, administrative, supervisory, and research positions in the burgeoning mental health field. Scholarships and faculty grants became available in the 1950s to schools of social work for advanced education in third-year and doctoral programs. The Council inherited from the AASSW an NIMH-financed Committee made up of leading social work educators representing the 12 schools that offered advanced education subsidized to some extent by NIMH.

Despite much discussion of the need for some kind of quality control over advanced education, it was not possible then or later to use the accrediting process for that purpose. The Committee, however, took responsibility for establishing principles to guide the development of programs of advanced education. Published in 1953 in the first of a series of pamphlets on post-master's degree education, the principles outlined "the nature of advanced study, the resources required, and the qualifications students should have to meet the requirements for the degree."[23]

Although no attempt was made to standardize these programs, a restricted report of a series of consultation visits by the Council consultant assigned to work with the Committee revealed a marked unity of purpose in the statements of objectives formulated by the schools engaged in doctoral and third-year education. In almost every case, the objectives envisaged a broad professional competence and perspective, as well as deepened knowledge and skill in a particular subject matter or area of practice. In keeping with the traditions of doctoral education, all the schools stressed the research orientation of their programs and voiced the expectation that doctoral students, through a dissertation, would make a contribution to knowledge and demonstrate a capacity for continuing productive scholarship. Some schools placed greater emphasis than others on acquisition of knowledge from related fields, but a desired breadth of education implicit in all the objectives did seem to require interdisciplinary teaching and learning. Teaching, research, and administration were the activities most often mentioned as the professional activities for which the schools wished to prepare students.[24]

The guiding principles specified advanced study curriculum content that (1) broadens knowledge of the field of social work as a whole; (2) deepens knowledge and furthers skill in an area of specialization; (3) draws upon knowledge from other disciplines; and (4) develops research competence. While there were differences in the selection and organization of the content to be covered under the several rubrics, there was general agreement on what should be offered except in respect to field work, on which there was a sharp division of opinion. About half of the schools held that field work is central to social work education, no matter what the level of instruction. Another group of schools agreed with the general statement but argued that field work should be a discretionary and not an absolute requirement. Several schools saw no place for field work unless it was a research placement, arguing that what the profession needed most at that stage in its development were scholars and researchers. The committee encouraged further study and experimentation in this area, which was later carried out through a special project, again financed by NIMH.

Another knotty question arose with respect to the place of the social sciences in the doctoral programs. There was considerable conviction that knowledge of and from the social sciences was an essential component of a doctoral program, but beyond that point there was little agreement. The method used by most of the schools involved sending students to enroll in courses in other departments. This posed a variety of problems. Advanced courses in the social sciences required previous knowledge that few doctoral students in social work possessed. One school sought to answer the social science question by appointing a social scientist to the faculty. Experiments with joint teaching and interdepartmental seminars were seen as other possible solutions.

Research competence was expected of all doctoral students, but again there were problems in how to achieve that objective. The schools had to cope with inadequacies in the previous research preparation of many of the doctoral students and few of the faculty were themselves engaged in research endeavors of their own. School-sponsored research, in which faculty and doctoral students participated, appeared to be an appropriate and even necessary solution to those particular problems. Questions also arose as to how much statistical competence a student should acquire, particularly as this was the area in which many of the students were deficient.

All of the questions involved in fashioning doctoral programs of high quality were thoroughly studied by the Committee on Advanced Education. Educating at this level was a new venture for most of the schools represented, which tended to place emphasis on problems to be solved rather on the accomplishments achieved in the few years of experience. Third-year programs also offered problems but they were of a different order and more amenable to solution.

The objectives for third-year programs focused on extending and deepening knowledge and skill in an area of professional practice. The types of activity for which the programs hoped to prepare were, in general, supervision, teaching, administration, and advanced practice. The students who entered the third-year programs were usually experienced social workers who wanted a period of formal study to advance from one level of practice to another or from one type of professional activity to another. A deepening of skills and improvement of their practice, most often in psychiatric social work, was what usually motivated them to apply for the scholarships available from NIMH. There were fewer curriculum dilemmas in the third-year programs because casework was the specialization most often favored.

There was one problem, however, that occupied the committee throughout the 20-year period. This had to do with the relation of the third-year program to the doctoral program. Did it stand alone or was it the first year in what could become a doctoral program, if the student so desired? Proponents for a clinical doctorate saw no problem in a student continuing from the third-year to the doctorate, while research-oriented schools questioned making a highly specialized third year the core of a doctoral program. This question continued to be examined from all angles throughout the 20 years of this historical account.

The professional degree, Doctor of Social Work or Doctor of Social Welfare, was chosen by eight of the 12 schools as the appropriate qualification for completion of doctoral study. The remaining four schools, by choice or because of university regulations or both, conferred the degree of Doctor of Philosophy. Completion of a third-year program led to the award of a certificate. In 1951–52, 62 students were enrolled in the 12 schools of social work for doctoral study and 8 doctorates were awarded. In 1971–72,

565 full-time students were enrolled in post-master's programs in 23 schools of social work and 114 degrees were awarded. With years of experience, greater sophistication in all aspects of social work education, and faculties qualified by doctoral study, the 66 schools currently offering doctoral education perhaps have found satisfactory answers to the questions tackled by the 12 pioneer schools.[25]

Epilogue

A Personal Statement

This journey through the two decades before and two decades following the formation of the Council on Social Work Education has persuaded me to end this chronicle on a personal note. Digging deeply into the events of the first two decades became a rewarding voyage of discovery. At the beginning, I knew only what I had read or been told about the antecedents. Although I was engaged in an educational activity, my only connection with the struggle between NASSA and AASSW happened when I was at the United Nations preparing its first international survey of social work training. The report listed in the appendix all the social work programs in existence around the world in the late 1940s, and for the United States I had included the membership of both associations. I had been advised that the NASSA programs, while not recognized as professional schools, provided social work training that made them eligible for inclusion. So, we have an interesting historical fact that before the two associations came together within the Council and while they were still at arms length, their programs were listed together in *Training for Social Work: An International Survey,* published by the United Nations in 1950.

My interpretation of the controversy differs somewhat from the accounts most often cited. This is understandable in view of the complexity underneath what on the surface may have seemed like a fairly straightforward struggle for domination. With the differences in roots, evolution, and immediate and long-range aims of the two organizations, various interpretations are certainly possible and none can claim to be absolute truth. Working with the records of the conflict often reminded me of the story of the blind men touching the elephant, with each one arriving at a different conclusion as to what it was. Contrary to the widely held opinion that the NASSA members lost out because of weakness, I have come, in working with the same material, to a different conclusion. I do not see them as weak and oppressed. Their cause did not get a proper hearing, but they were strong enough to overturn the educational establishment and to bring together the total profession to examine and reorganize social work education. I agree with Hattie Cal Maxted, a loyal and tireless member of NASSA, when she said at the end of the struggle

> It does not appear to be bragging if we claim that NASSA should be given credit for providing the motivating force for the formation of the Council. It seems fantastic what a small group with no prestige and no money to speak of has accomplished.[1]

As we have seen, the original hopes for clear connections between the last two years of undergraduate education and two years of graduate study were only partially realized. The evolution of undergraduate education into what finally emerged in the final chapters of this history was beset by attitudinal and financial problems. The Council tried hard to meet the needs of all components of its broad membership, but circumstances and funding made graduate education its major concern, which led to the neglect of undergraduate education. Waiting for an answer to the question of what should be taught to future social workers in the last two years of undergraduate study also delayed the positive action that might otherwise have been taken to build a strong baccalaureate foundation for graduate professional education. When a suggested answer came in the Council's Curriculum Study, it was judged unacceptable by all except a small contingent of members. The question was finally answered officially in a series of policy statements, but a continuing uneasiness in the undergraduate–graduate relationship suggests that this is a sphere of unfinished business for the profession and the Council.

If the production of part one was a voyage of discovery, the preparation of part two was a nostalgic journey through 20 of the most rewarding and challenging years of my career. What a privilege it was to help launch an organization newly established by the total profession and with the backing of graduate schools, undergraduate departments, professional associations, public and private employing agencies, and concerned citizens. It is no wonder that the core staff for many years of Ernest Witte, Betty Neely, Mildred Sikkema, and myself felt a driving sense of mission. Fortunately, all of us shared the same faults and virtues of unsparing effort to accomplish the tasks assigned to us. Witte once remarked in an annual report that the staff felt frustrated by the demands coming from every membership category of the Council to give attention, without regard to staff and financial implications, to a wide variety and ever-increasing number of educational concerns and fields of operation. He was told to stop complaining and begin to worry when the membership stopped turning to the Council for leadership and help in solving problems.

With the passage of time and accumulation of special projects, the staff was enlarged to include additional permanent members in the Headquarters Office, along with temporary faculty members on contracts to carry out Council tasks from their university base. In the beginning, the small staff performed like a family enterprise, with close personal relationships and cooperation on all that transpired. With additional staff and more formal structure the atmosphere became more like that of a faculty, loosely organized. By the end of the 20-year period, with its very large staff the Council had all the earmarks of a departmentalized company.

Throughout the 20 years, the Council was fortunate in the quality of its staff. Leading educators were recruited as consultants, and foremost researchers took on temporary appointments to conduct special studies. Faculty members were invited to use their sabbatical leaves of absence to undertake Council assignments, with some interesting results. A prominent educator and former Council president decided, upon retiring as a dean, to spend three days a week of her sabbatical as a volunteer staff member at the Council office. This was a significant contribution as it involved travel from a neighboring city and rental of an apartment in New York. The same spirit of dedication pervaded the Board and committee structure.

The work that was accomplished could not have been done without the constant help of volunteers from the membership giving time and effort along with exerting influence in the quest for money to keep the Council afloat. One of the great joys of a new beginning like the establishment of the Council comes, as I perceived it, from the almost universal desire to fulfill the promise it offers. In my nostalgic journey through the articles, news items, and documentary records of those years, I revisited exciting professional events, relived successes and failures, and relished again the gratifying partnership in work with scores of colleagues, who also became close friends.

There is much more that could be written and said about the multitudinous activities described in this historical account. For me, the deepest pleasure came in work on all aspects of the curriculum. The generic curriculum policy statements, which were right for their time, sorted out and put into effect for graduate education a constellation of knowledge areas and learning experiences that was recognized as the basic professional equipment of qualified social workers. The changeover for the schools from providing a curriculum of specified courses ("the basic eight") to an integrated educational program with stated objectives and identified learning experiences organized for sequence and progression in learning was a challenging task. It would be hard to match, for professional satisfaction and excitement, the experience of the consultation service provided by the Council, the workshops on curriculum building, the seminars on teaching and learning, and the gratification of faculties as they worked successfully with this new approach to the performance of an old traditional task.

There was excitement, too, in working on the consequences for undergraduate education when the organizational recommendations of the Curriculum Study were not accepted. It was clear there could no longer be any excuse for not providing guidance on the content of a social welfare major or sequence at the undergraduate level. What should be included and how the content should be organized became something of a struggle for the committee assigned to produce a document. That was the point at which Ernest Witte turned over to me a batch of material and told me to put it together and soon. There was only one problem. I was about to go off on vacation. Usually my vacations were taken up by overseas assignments related to the International Association of Schools of Social Work. This particular year, 1960, was the first time since my arrival at the Council that I had planned a vacation with no work. A month in a comfortable house in the upper peninsula of Michigan promised relaxation and rejuvenation. But the sentiment in our office that work came first could not be denied. The mornings of my vacation were spent on the assignment and the rest of the day on fun and games. At the end of the period, a document emerged that almost immediately became *A Guide to Social Welfare Content in Under-graduate Education*, published in 1961.

The generic curriculum served well for the period in which it was in effect, but its fading relevance became apparent toward the end of the 1960s. The Council's quantity-quality mantra had now become quantity-quality-diversity. Social work involvement in the civil rights movement and anti-poverty programs had a profound impact on professional education. A fascinating complication was introduced into planning for the future of social work education by the emergence of the service-minded young people headed for the Peace Corps, the fighters for social justice on all fronts, the leaders of underserved minorities, indigenous leaders in anti-poverty programs, and the students on campus who were making their views known by demonstrating, sitting-in, and standing up for radical changes in society and education. Where did all these elements and workers for a more just society fit into the world of social work education? The generic program did not answer that question with sufficient clarity nor did it meet emerging and future needs with sufficient power. It was gracefully retired. It should not be forgotten, however, that the curriculum policy statements of 1952 and 1962 brought to the fore the broad areas of knowledge still used in describing the general areas of content to be covered in both undergraduate and graduate education for social work.

The chronicle ends in a period of tremendous change within the Council, in both its structure and its educational policy and practices. The decision to cover the first 20 years for this account was taken because that was the period of my association as a staff member. As it has turned out, the 20 years represent a distinct cycle of development that came to an end in 1972. With changes in the by-laws and a change in the status of undergraduate education, the Council entered a new period of development.

Readers looking back from today at these events of another era may have difficulty with some of the terminology (such as manpower, which was a word in constant use), with the views that prevailed at the time on certain questions (such as the role of undergraduate education), and with the apparent simplicity of curriculum policy. That was then, and today is today. It is my ardent hope that what has been recorded will be viewed not from current perspectives but from what was needed and achieved in the 1950s and 1960s. There are problems identified then that remain to be solved, and much can be learned from the services provided and the unified approach in that period to promoting sound programs of social work education. Because the lessons of history are notoriously overlooked, there is no better way to end this very personal statement than by repeating the following, cited in 1966 in *Contemporary Education in the United States*:

> A profession develops out of a past and into a future; it has a history
> and a destiny. Action is responsible when the challenges of the here
> and now are illuminated by a historical perspective and responded
> to with a sense of destiny.[2]

Notes

CHAPTER ONE. SETTING THE STAGE

[1] For detailed information on the beginnings of social work education, see Katherine A. Kendall, *Social Work Education: Its Origins in Europe* (Alexandria, VA: Council on Social Work Education, 2000) and Leslie Leighninger, *Creating a New Profession: The Beginnings of Social Work Education in the United States* (Alexandria, VA: Council on Social Work Education, 2000).

[2] AASSW, *Education for the Public Social Services*, Report of the Study Committee (Chapel Hill: North Carolina University Press, 1942), 6.

[3] Ben Youngdahl, "Shall We Face It?" in *Professional Education*, Five Papers Delivered at 29th Annual Meeting of the AASSW, Minneapolis, MN, January 21, 1948 (New York: AASSW, 1948), 32.

[4] Karl de Schweinitz, "Social Work in the Public Services," *Social Work Journal* 29, no. 3 (July 1955): 88.

[5] Grace Browning, "The Responsibility of the Schools of Social Work for Training for the Public Welfare Services," in *Proceedings of the National Conference of Social Work*, Cleveland, Ohio, 1944 (New York: Columbia University Press, 1944), 353.

[6] Edith Abbott, "Some Basic Principles," in *Education for Social Welfare* (Chicago: University of Chicago Press, 1931), 80.

[7] NASSA Constitution and By-Laws, Adopted April 22, 1944, Maxted Papers, Box 1, Social Welfare History Archives, University of Minnesota.

[8] Hattie Cal Maxted, "The Need for Undergraduate Trained Social Workers in Arkansas," 1945, Maxted Papers, Box 1.

[9] E. J. Urwick, "A School of Sociology," in *Methods of Social Advance*, ed. C. S. Loch (London: Macmillan, 1894), 81.

[10] Amos G. Warner, "Philanthropology in Educational Institutions," in *Sociology in Institutions of Learning*, ed. A. G. Warner, International Congress of Charities, Correction and Philanthropy, Chicago, 1893 (Baltimore, MD: Johns Hopkins Press, 1894), 81.

[11] James E. Hagerty, *The Training of Social Workers* (New York: McGraw Hill Book Company, 1931), 56.

[12] Abbott, 71.

[13] Ibid, 72.

[14] Warner, *passim.*

[15] Jeffrey R. Brackett, "Instruction in Educational Institutions," in *Supervision and Education on Charity* (New York: Macmillan, 1903), 158.

[16] Ibid, *passim.*

CHAPTER TWO. THE BONES OF CONTENTION

[1] Ernest B. Harper, "Accomplishments and Aims of the National Association of Schools of Social Administration," Annual Proceedings, NASSA, in *Social Welfare* (Fayetteville, AR: University of Arkansas: 1945), 15.

[2] Minutes of Interim Committee on Professional Education, Buffalo, NY, May 29, 1946, CSWE Records, Box 15, Social Welfare History Archives, University of Minnesota.

[3] Bradford W. Sheafor and Barbara W. Shank, *Undergraduate Social Work Education: A Survivor in a Changing Profession* (Austin: University of Texas–Austin, 1986), 7–8.

[4] Hagerty.

[5] Ibid, 79.

[6] Unsigned answer to questions on "Social Work Education," April 10, 1951, Maxted Papers, Box 1.

[7] Abraham Flexner, "Is Social Work a Profession?" in *Proceedings of National Conference of Charities and Corrections, 1915* (Chicago: Hildmann Printing Company, 1915), 580.

[8] Sue Spencer, "Major Issues in Social Work Education," in *Proceedings of National Conference of Social Work,* San Francisco, 1947 (New York: Columbia University Press, 1948), 441.

[9] de Schweinitz, 92.

[10] Abbott, 80.

[11] Leighninger, 87.

[12] Maurice J. Karpf, "Progress and Problems in Social Work Education During the Depression," Presidential Report, Annual Meeting, AASSW, 1933, CSWE Master Files, Alexandria, VA.

[13] Gordon Hamilton, "Education for Social Work," in *Social Work Yearbook,* 1945 (New York: Russell Sage Foundation, 1945), 144.

[14] Ibid, 146.

[15] AASSW History of the Advisory Committee, Minutes of Meeting of the

Advisory Committee on Training and Personnel, October 26, 1940, CSWE Records, Box 2.

[16] Ibid, 6.

[17] AASSW, *Education for the Public Social Services*, 11.

[18] Ibid, 14.

[19] Ibid, 15.

[20] AASSW, "Prerequisites for Admission to Schools of Social Work: A Report of the Curriculum Committee of the American Association of Schools of Social Work," *Social Service Review* 11, no. 3 (September 1937): 466.

[21] Mary Sydney Branch, "Consultation on Preprofessional Social Work Education," *The Compass* 32, no. 2 (January 1946): 13.

[22] Marian Hathway, "Twenty-Five Years of Professional Education for Social Work—and a Look Ahead," *The Compass* 27, no. 5 (June 1946): 15.

[23] Letter from Ernest Harper to President R. G. Gustafson, October 30, 1947, Maxted Papers, Box 7. Harper and Maxted, in an exchange of letters, also referred to it as a "master stroke" on the part of AASSW.

[24] Mildred Fairchild, "Preprofessional Education for Social Work," *The Family (Journal of Social Case Work)* 26, no. 3 (May 1945): 97–100.

[25] Anne F. Fenlason, "The Present Status of Education for Social Work in Institutions of Higher Education in the United States," *American Sociological Review* 10, no. 5 (October 1945): 689.

[26] Ibid, 97–98.

[27] Ibid.

[28] Report of NASSA Committee on NASSA Functions, Maxted Papers, Box 1, 4.

[29] Letter from Ernest B. Harper to Dean Theodore Blagen, Graduate School, University of Minnesota, November 20, 1947, Maxted Papers, Box 1.

[30] Harper, "Accomplishments and Aims of NASSA," 18–20.

CHAPTER THREE. IN PURSUIT OF STANDARDS

[1] Stanley P. Davis, "Working Toward One Professional Standard—Public and Private," in *Proceedings of the National Conference of Social Work* (Chicago: University of Chicago Press, 1933), 434, 438.

[2] Kenneth L. M. Pray, "Analysis and Appraisal of Changes in Social Work Practice Function during the War Years," *The Compass* 27, no. 3 (1946): 3.

[3] Sue Spencer, "Education for Social Work," in *Social Work Yearbook*, ed. R. Kurtz (New York: Russell Sage Foundation, 1949), 173.

[4] Spencer, "Major Issues in Social Work Education," 437–438.

[5] Stanley P. Davis, "The Professional Influence in Social Work," *The Compass* 15, no. 9 (June 1934): 7.

[6] "Standards of Professional Education," *The Compass* 16, no. 1 (September 1934): 7.

[7] Hagerty, 170.

[8] "Defining 'Approved' Technical Social Work Courses," *The Compass* 15, no. 4 (December 1933): 7–8.

[9] Ibid.

[10] AASSW History and Objectives, 1938, CSWE Records, Box 15, 5–6.

[11] AASSW, *Education for the Public Social Services,* 12.

[12] Youngdahl, 65.

[13] Letter from Hattie Cal Maxted to Ernest B. Harper, April 14, 1947, Maxted Papers, Box 1.

[14] Letter from Ernest B. Harper to Hattie Cal Maxted, April 14, 1947, Maxted Papers, Box 1.

[15] Earl J. McGrath, "Education and Social Work," in *Social Welfare Forum, 1949* (New York: Columbia University Press, 1950).

[16] Sheafor and Shank, 9. The analysis was attributed to Esther Brown of the Russell Sage Foundation, who chaired a Joint Committee of NASSA and AASSW in 1945.

[17] Leighninger, 133–134.

[18] AASSW History and Objectives, 1938, CSWE Records, Box 15.

[19] Sydnor J. Walker, *Social Work and the Training of Social Workers* (Chapel Hill: North Carolina Press, 1928), 162–163.

[20] Ibid.

[21] Ibid, 175.

[22] AASSW History and Objectives, 3.

[23] Ibid, 6.

[24] Ibid, 9.

[25] Leighninger, 132.

[26] Letter from Ernest B. Harper to President E. G. Gustavson, Chairman of the Joint Committee on Accrediting, October 30, 1947, Maxted Papers, Box 1.

[27] Report of the Joint Accrediting Committee, National Association of State Universities, April 26–27, 1946, Maxted Papers, Box 1.

[28] Memorandum from T. W. Cape, President, to NASSA Member Schools, November 24, 1947, Maxted Papers, Box 1.

[29] Minutes of the Meeting of the Joint Committee on Social Work Education AASSW–NASSA, November 1–2, 1945, CSWE Records, Box 15, 5.

[30] Ibid, 6.

[31] Recommendations by the Joint Accrediting Committee, Washington, DC, November 11, 1947, Maxted Papers, Box 1.

[32] Letter from Hattie Cal Maxted to Ernest B. Harper, November 17, 1947, Maxted Papers, Box 1.

[33] Letter from Hattie Cal Maxted to T. W. Cape, August 9, 1947, Maxted Papers, Box 1.

CHAPTER FOUR. THE CONVOLUTED PATH TO COOPERATION

[1] AASSW Background of Committee's Assignment, Interim Committee on Professional Education, May 29, 1946, CSWE Records, Box 15, 1.

[2] Leighninger, 134–135.

[3] AASSW Background of Interim Committee's Assignment," Interim Committee on Professional Education, Exhibit 1, CSWE Records, Box 15.

[4] AASSW Minutes of the Joint Committee on Social Work Education, April 28–29, 1945, CSWE Records, Box 15, 1.

[5] Ibid, 13.

[6] AASSW Minutes of the Meeting of the Joint Committee on Social Work Education, December 1–2, 1945, CSWE Records, Box 15, 1.

[7] Ibid, 2.

[8] Ibid, 8.

[9] Ibid.

[10] The summarized material in this account is based on the following sources and will not be further identified except in direct quotation: Minutes of Meetings of the AASSW Board of Directors, Pittsburgh, PA, January 23, 24, 25, and 28, 1946, Document #682, CSWE Master Files, and Minutes of the Annual Business Meeting of the AASSW, January 24, 25, 26, 1946, Document #689, CSWE Master Files.

[11] Minutes of Meeting of AASSW Board of Directors, January 23, 1946, CSWE Master Files, 21.

[12] Ibid, 21–22.

[13] Minutes of Annual Business Meeting of AASSW, January 24, 1946, CSWE Master Files, 9.

[14] Ibid, 10.

[15] Ibid, 22–23.

[16] Recommendations—Schools of Social Work, Report of the Joint Committee on Accrediting, National Association of State Universities, Chicago, April 26–27, 1946, Maxted Papers, Box 1.

[17] Letter from Hattie Cal Maxted to Mrs. Whooten, Department of Sociology, North Texas State Teacher's College, December 13, 1945, Maxted Papers, Box 1.

[18] Letter from Benjamin E. Youngdahl to T. W. Cape, November 19, 1947, Maxted Papers, Box 1.

[19] NASSA Report of Action Taken on the Recommendations of the Joint Committee on Education for Social Work, CSWE Records, Box 15.

[20] Letter from Ernest Harper to Joseph Anderson, February 8, 1946, Maxted Papers, Box 1.

[21] Letter from Hattie Cal Maxted to Ernest Harper, June 1, 1945, Maxted Papers, Box 1.

[22] Letter from Ernest Harper to Hattie Cal Maxted, June 23, 1945, Maxted Papers, Box 1.

CHAPTER FIVE. THE CURTAIN FALLS ON AASSW AND NASSA

[1] At this time, specialized sequences in medical social work and psychiatric social work in the graduate schools were accredited, respectively, by the American Association of Medical Social Workers (AAMSW) and the American Association of Psychiatric Social Workers (AAPSW). The National Association of School Social Workers (NASSW) and the American Association of Group Workers (AAGW) had assigned responsibility for approval of their specialties to the AASSW. The Social Work Research Group (SWRG) and the Association for the Study of Community Organization (ASCO) did not function as accrediting bodies.

[2] Minutes of Interim Committee of Education for Social Work, May 22, 1946, CSWE Records, Box 15.

[3] NCSWE Certificate of Incorporation, 1947, Document #1166, CSWE Records, Box 19.

[4] NCSWE Proposal for a Comprehensive Study of Social Work Education, March 1947, CSWE Records, Box 19.

[5] Alice Taylor Davis, *Making of a Teacher—50 Years in Social Work* (Silver Spring, MD: NASW, 1988), 134.

[6] Ibid.

[7] The report carries her name as Alice Taylor. At its publication in late 1951, she celebrated another event with her marriage to Michael Davis. Later references to her participation usually carry her married name.

[8] Davis, *Making of a Teacher*, 135.

[9] Kenneth L. M. Pray, "The Plan for a Study of Social Work Education," *The Compass* 28, no. 3 (March 1947): 10.

[10] Davis, *Making of a Teacher*, 131.

[11] Ibid, 142–143.

[12] Ibid, 142.

[13] Ibid, 139.

[14] Ibid, 150.

[15] Ernest Hollis, "Position Statement on Role of the Undergraduate College in Social Work Education," Document #2015, CSWE Records.

[16] Letter from Ernest Harper to H. C. Wetzel, April 17, 1949, Maxted Papers, Box 2.

[17] Ernest V. Hollis and Alice L. Taylor, *Social Work Education in the United States* (New York: Columbia University Press, 1951), 30.

[18] Ibid, 182.

[19] Ibid.

[20] Ibid, 183.

[21] Arlien Johnson, "The Hollis-Taylor Report as Seen From the Viewpoint of a Social Work Educator," *Social Work Journal* 33, no. 3 (July 1952): 136.

[22] Helen R. Wright, "The Professional Curriculum of the Future," *Social Service Review* 25, no. 4 (December 1951): 466.

[23] Ibid, 475–476.

[24] Ernest Harper, "The Study of Social Work Education: Its Significance for the Undergraduate Educational Institutions," *Social Work Journal* 32, no. 4 (October 1951): 182, 183.

[25] Hollis-Taylor, xi–xii.

[26] Ibid, 234.

[27] Ibid, 228.

[28] Ibid, 225.

[29] Grace L. Coyle, "Mutuality—The Foundation Principle of the Council on Social Work Education," in *Education for Social Work*, Proceedings of the Annual Program Meeting, 1960 (New York: Council on Social Work Education, 1960), 85.

[30] Hollis-Taylor, 231.

[31] Ibid, 243.

[32] Ibid.

[33] NCSWE Report of Special Committee on Structure, Document #32, CSWE Records, Box 19, 1.

[34] Helen R. Wright, "The Years Ahead," *Social Work Journal* 33, no. 2 (April 1952): 85.

[35] Hattie Cal Maxted, "President's Report," Annual Business Meeting, NASSA, May 29, 1952, Maxted Papers, Box 1.

[36] Ibid.

[37] Harper, "The Study of Social Work Education," 197.

[38] Letter from Ernest Harper to Hattie Cal Maxted, March 17, 1952, Maxted Papers, Box 3.

[39] Letter from Hattie Cal Maxted to Ernest Harper, March 11, 1952, Maxted Papers, Box 3.

[40] AASW Minutes, Meeting of the Executive Committee, November 1949, quoted in Walter Kindelsperger, "Towards the Mature Profession—Current Responsibilities and Concerns of NASW" (Unpublished Manuscript, 1963).

[41] See Chapter 9, pp. 129-134 for further details on AASW financial support of the Council on Social Work Education.

[42] NCSWE Minutes of Meeting, December 8–9, 1950, Document #39, CSWE Records, Box 19, 4.

[43] Harriet M. Bartlett, "The Significance of the Study of Social Work Education," in *The Social Welfare Forum 1951*, Proceedings of the 78th National Conference of Social Work (New York: Columbia University Press, 1951), 70.

CHAPTER SIX. NEW BEGINNINGS

[1] NCSWE Report of Special Committee on Structure for a Social Work Education Organization, March 1950, Document #32, CSWE Records, Box 19.

[2] Quoted in Katherine A. Kendall, "Excellence Revisited—A Tribute to Ernest F. Witte" (Paper Presented at the Council on Social Work Education, Annual Program Meeting, 1987).

[3] Helen R. Wright, "O Pioneers," in *Education for Social Work*, Proceedings of Annual Program Meeting, 1953 (New York: Council on Social Work Education, 1953), 29–30.

[4] Ibid, 31.

[5] For details on the commissions, see Chapter 7.

[6] CSWE Report of the Commission on Schools and Departments of Social Work at the First Corporate Meeting of the Council of Delegates, Cleveland, Ohio, June 4, 1953, Document #3-26-1, CSWE Master Files, 14–15.

[7] Ibid.

[8] Harold E. Wetzel, "Educational Priorities as Seen by the Undergraduate Department," in *Education for Social Work*, Proceedings of the Annual Program Meeting, 1953 (New York: Council on Social Work Education, 1953), 60–61.

[9] Statement presented by Nathan Cohen to CSWE Board of Directors, Minutes of Meeting, January 24, 1955, Document #5-16-M, CSWE Master Files.

[10] Wright, "O Pioneers," 33–34.

[11] Maurice O. Hunt, "Educational Priorities—As Seen by a Public Welfare Agency," in *Education for Social Work*, Proceedings of the Annual Program Meeting, 1953 (New York: Council on Social Work Education, 1953), 44.

[12] Jeanette Regensburg, "Educational Priorities—As Seen by a Voluntary Agency," in *Education for Social Work*, Proceedings of the Annual Program Meeting, 1953 (New York: Council on Social Work Education, 1953), 42.

[13] Chester L. Bower, "Educational Priorities—As Seen by a Community Chest and Council," in *Education for Social Work*, Proceedings of the Annual Program Meeting, 1953 (New York: Council on Social Work Education, 1953), 46, *passim*.

[14] Hollis–Taylor, 422.

[15] Elinor K. Bernheim, "Social Work Education and the Board Member," *Social Work Journal* 34, no. 4 (October 1953): 155.

[16] Minutes of Meeting of Committee on Personnel and Finance, Chicago, July 10, 1952, Document #200, CSWE Master Files.

[17] Kindelsperger includes a detailed account of the early history of AASW–AASSW relationships. The story told in this account is taken largely from a working draft of the unpublished manuscript in the personal files of the author and will not be further identified except in direct quotations.

[18] Kindelsperger, 40–41.

[19] AASSW Report of the Executive Secretary, Annual Business Meeting, January 30, 1952, Document #2204, CSWE Records, Box 15.

[20] Elizabeth S. L. Govan, "The Canadian Study of Social Work Education—A Mutual Project of Schools and Agencies," in *Education for Social Work*, Annual Program Meeting, 1955 (New York: Council on Social Work Education, 1955), 57–63.

[21] CSWE Membership, July 1, 1952, Document #118, CSWE Master Files.

[22] Ernest F. Witte, "CSWE 1961–1962," Report of the Executive Director, in *Education for Social Work*, Annaul Program Meeting, 1962 (New York: Council on Social Work Education, 1962), 26.

CHAPTER SEVEN. TRIAL AND ERROR IN GOVERNING

[1] Hereinafter in this chapter referred to as CSWE to distinguish it from the Council of Delegates.

[2] By-Laws Approved at Constitutional Convention held on January 28, 1952, CSWE Master Files.

[3] Memorandum to Dean Newstetter from Dean Arthur Larson, November 30, 1953, CSWE Master Files.

[4] First Report of the Committee to Study the Function and Purpose of the Council of Delegates, Document #4-18-9A, CSWE Master Files. This item is undated but the context indicates November or December 1954.

[5] Ibid.

[6] Staff Proposals for Reorganization of the Structure of the Council on Social Work Education, December 15, 1955, Document #5-16-9R, CSWE Master Files, 1.

[7] By-Laws Approved by Action of the Council of Delegates, January 28, 1958, February 20, 1958, Document #8-49-1, CSWE Master Files. This version of the by-laws served as the frame of reference for all changes in the first 20 years.

[8] Staff Proposals for Reorganization of the Structure of CSWE, 6.

[9] By-Laws Approved by Action of the House of Delegates, January 23, 1968, Article 2, Document #68-816-1, CSWE Master Files.

[10] Katherine A. Kendall, "Time for Decision," CSWE Work Program 1965–1966, Document #65-16-26R, CSWE Master Files, 1.

[11] See Chapter 8.

[12] By-Laws Approved by Action of the House of Delegates, January 23, 1968, Article IV, CSWE Master Files.

[13] Committee of Students Meeting, December 18–19, 1967, CSWE Master Files.

[14] "NFSSW Joins CSWE as Constituent Member," *Social Work Education Reporter* 17, no. 1 (March 1969): 10.

[15] Recommendations of Committee on Students, Background Document #63-350-47CC for Board of Directors Meeting, November 21–22, 1968, and Recommendation from Committee on Students on Ethnic Minority Students, Document #368-350-18-CC, March 13, 1968, CSWE Master Files.

[16] By-Laws Approved by Action of the House of Delegates, January 23, 1970, Article II, Document #70-S16-1800, CSWE Master Files. For the full text of the new purpose, see Chapter 9.

[17] See Chapter 8.

[18] CSWE By-Laws, May 15, 1972, Document #72-816-1, CSWE Master Files. Due to the cancellation by the Board of Directors of the Annual Program Meeting scheduled for Chicago in January 1972, the Annual Business Meeting of the House of Delegates was held in Atlantic City, NJ, in connection with the National Conference of Social Work.

CHAPTER EIGHT. PURPOSE, FUNCTIONS, AND PRIORITIES

[1] By-Laws Approved at Constitutional Convention held on January 28, 1952, CSWE Master Files.

[2] See Chapter 7.

[3] By-Laws change adopted by the House of Delegates, January 23, 1970, Document #816-2BOD, CSWE Master Files.

[4] Werner W. Boehm, "Education for Social Work," in *Encyclopedia of Social Work, Vol. 1, 1971* (New York: NASW, 1971), 270.

[5] Current and Proposed Council Work Program 1956–57 and Report of Progress 1955–56, Document #6-16-24, CSWE Master Files.

[6] The full statement is reproduced in Letter from the President, May 1964, No. 35, Appendix II, Document #64-16-13R, April 9, 1964, CSWE Master Files.

[7] Katherine A. Kendall, "Time for Decision."

[8] The text that follows comes from a summary of the discussions of "Time for Decision" within the staff and the Board written by Kendall, Executive Director, and reported to the House of Delegates, January 25, 1966, under the title: "Meeting Social Welfare Needs: Educational Opportunities, Choices, and Questions at Issue," Document #66-26-1, January 5, 1965, CSWE Master Files.

[9] Minutes, Meeting of the Board of Directors, Document #66-26-1, October 29-31, 1965, CSWE Master Files. See also "Board Makes Program and Budget Decisions," *Social Work Education* 13, no. 4 (December 1965), 11.

[10] Ibid, 2.

[11] Ibid, 4. In this connection, it may interest current readers that "one delegate stated definitely that accreditation was, in his opinion, neither possible nor desirable for the next 40 or 50 years. His major reasons were the large number of programs and the need for flexibility."

[12] Report of Discussion on Agenda Item VI: Meeting Social Welfare Manpower Needs—Opportunities, Issues and Educational Choices, Meeting of House of Delegates, January 25, 1966, Document #66-26-5, February 4, 1966, CSWE Master Files, 3.

[13] For the complete text of the report of the Special Committee, see "Future Program and Structure of the Council on Social Work Education," *Social Work Education Reporter* 14, no. 2 (June 1966): 18–20.

[14] For a detailed description of the new priorities, see Arnulf M. Pins, "Challenge and Change in Social Work Education," *Social Work Education Reporter* 17, no. 1 (March 1969): Special Supplement: 34A–34D.

CHAPTER NINE. FINANCES—THE DOLLAR CHASE

[1] Witte, 22.

[2] Proposed Budget for 1962–63, Document #61-4-4 (10/6/61), CSWE Master Files.

[3] See Chapter 6.

[4] Minutes, Finance Committee Meeting, CSWE, Document #3-4-M, October 28, 1953, CSWE Master Files.

[5] CSWE Financial Report, Fiscal Year 1964, Document #64-4-2, CSWE Master Files.

[6] Minutes, Meeting of the Board of Directors, CSWE, October 1960, Document #60-16-15M, CSWE Master Files, 46–47.

[7] The material that follows is taken from two documents in the CSWE Master Files: "Statement of Issues and Problems Affecting Organizational Relationships in Social Work Education," CSWE Document #63-26-9, December 30, 1963 (Presented to the CSWE House of Delegates, January 29, 1964) and "Final Report, Ad Hoc CSWE–NASW Joint Board Committee," CSWE Document #64-16-15, March 18, 1964. These documents were written by Katherine A. Kendall, CSWE Executive Director, and signed also by Joseph P. Anderson, NASW Executive Director.

[8] Kendall, "Statement of Issues and Problems."

[9] Minutes, Meeting of the Board of Directors, CSWE, April 1970, Document #70/30M, CSWE Master Files, 13.

[10] Letter from Chauncey A. Alexander, Executive Director, NASW, to Arnulf M. Pins, Executive Director, CSWE, July 7, 1970, CSWE Master Files.

[11] Minutes of the Meeting of the House of Delegates, CSWE, April 17–18, 1972, Document #72-813-16, CSWE Master Files, 2–3.

[12] U.S. Department of Health, Education, and Welfare (HEW), *Closing the Gap in Social Work Manpower*, Report of the Departmental Task Force in Social Work Education and Manpower (Washington, DC: U.S. Government Printing Office, November 1965).

[13] For news stories underscoring the significance of Johnson's remarks and the consequent legislation, see CSWE, *Social Work Education Reporter* 15, no. 1 (March 1967); 15, no. 3 (September 1967); and 15, no. 4 (December 1967).

[14] CSWE Financial Report, July 1, 1962, through June 30, 1963, "Letter from the President," No. 33, November 1963, CSWE Master Files, 9–10.

[15] Reproduced in CSWE, "Letter from the President," No. 17, June 1958, CSWE Master Files, 3.

[16] CSWE, "CSWE Income More than Doubled in Five-Year Period," *Social Work Education Reporter* 14, no. 4 (December 1966): 11.

[17] CSWE, "Henry N. Sachs Provides Leadership," *Social Work Education Reporter* 9, no. 1 (February 1961): 3.

CHAPTER TEN. THE PATH TO EXCELLENCE

[1] By-Laws Approved at Constitutional Convention held on January 28, 1952, Document #110-29-52, CSWE Master Files.

[2] Albert N. Jorgensen, "Current Developments in Accreditation," in *Education for Social Work*, Proceedings of Second Annual Program Meeting, Washington, DC, 1954 (New York: Council on Social Work Education, 1954), 23. Jorgensen was president of the University of Connecticut and a member of the National Commission on Accreditation. This article is also the main source of additional information on this subject.

[3] Letter from John C. Kidneigh to Reuben G. Gustavson, President, National Commission on Accreditation, December 9, 1952, CSWE Master Files, 1.

[4] Ewald B. Nyquist, "Regional Developments in Co-operative Evaluation and Accrediting Activity," in *Education for Social Work,* Proceedings of Second Annual Program Meeting, Washington, DC, 1954 (New York: Council on Social Work Education, 1954), 32.

[5] John C. Kidneigh, "Accrediting of Professional Schools of Social Work," in *Education for Social Work*, Proceedings of Second Annual Program Meeting, Washington, DC, 1954 (New York: Council on Social Work Education, 1954), 47.

[6] For details on the nature and content of cooperative agreements with the Middle States Association, see Nyquist, "Regional Developments."

[7] The responsibilities are classified under the headings used by Council staff in describing accrediting activities in the Annual Work Program presented to the Board of Directors at its fall meeting for approval.

[8] CSWE, *Manual of Accrediting Standards* (New York: Council on Social Work Education, 1953).

[9] Ewald B. Nyquist, "The Wing Wherewith We Fly to Heaven or the Real Function of Accreditation," in *Education for Social Work*, Proceedings of the Twelfth Annual Program Meeting, Toronto, Canada, 1964 (New York: Council on Social Work Education, 1964), 107–108.

[10] Ibid, 110.

[11] Unless otherwise noted, the material and much of the text in the section on curriculum policy is taken from the following documents and articles written by the author: "Education Got Social Work," in *Social Work Yearbook, 1954*, ed. R. Kurtz (New York: American Association of Social Workers, 1954); "Curriculum

Policy and Educational Practice," *Social Service Review* 29, no. 2 (June 1955); "The Social Work Curriculum" (1964), unpublished manuscript prepared as a background document for seminars and conferences conducted or co-sponsored by the Council on Social Work Education; "Curriculum Policy: 1952 and 1962," Document #62-91-2, Presented at the Annual Meeting of the House of Delegates, January, 1962, CSWE Master Files; and "The Curriculum of the Sixties in the Undergraduate and Graduate Education—Introductory Remarks," in *Education for Social Work*, Proceedings of the Eleventh Annual Program Meeting, 1963 (New York: Council on Social Work Education, 1963), 35–37, 46.

[12] Sue Spencer, "Gaps and Lacks of Current Policy Materials on the Social Work Professional Curriculum—January 17, 1951," quoted in AASSW, "A Report of the Curriculum Committee, January 1952 to July 1952," Document #120, CSWE Master Files, 3.

[13] Minutes of the Meeting of the Board of Directors, CSWE, May 27, 1952, Document #114, CSWE Master Files, 3.

[14] Official Statement of Curriculum Policy for the Master's Degree Program in Graduate Schools of Social Work, CSWE, Document #120a, CSWE Master Files.

[15] Edith Abbott, *Social Welfare and Professional Education* (Chicago: University of Chicago Press, 1931).

[16] See Chapter 11 for an account of the production and outcome of the curriculum study.

[17] See Chapter 11 for examples of the Tyler influence on curriculum development in the 1950s and 1960s.

[18] See Chapter 11 for details on the production of the guide and Chapter 12 for its use by the undergraduate departments.

[19] Official Statement of Curriculum Policy for the Master's Degree Program in Graduate Schools of Social Work, CSWE, adopted at the meeting of the Board of Directors, October 18–20, 1962, Document #61-91-15R5, CSWE Master Files.

[20] Official Statement of Curriculum Policy for the Master's Degree Program in Graduate Schools of Social Work, CSWE, adopted at a meeting of the Board of Directors, November 20, 1969, Document #69-380-20, CSWE Master Files.

[21] Ibid, 1.

[22] Ibid, 2.

[23] Ibid.

[24] Arthur J. Katz, "New Curriculum Policy Statement: Freedom and/or Regulation," *Journal of Education for Social Work* 7, no. 3 (Spring 1971): 48.

CHAPTER ELEVEN. THE MULTIFACETED PROGRAM

[1] News Note on the Five-Year Consultation Project, *Social Work Education Reporter* 7, no. 7 (October 1959): 4. Much of the text that follows was taken from this summary, which was prepared but not signed by this author.

[2] At this time, Tyler was director of the Institute of Behavioral Sciences at Stanford University, and was serving as a special consultant to the Curriculum Study staff.

[3] CSWE, *Building the Social Work Curriculum*, Report of the National Curriculum Workshop (New York: Council on Social Work Education, 1961).

[4] See CSWE, *Contemporary Education for Social Work in the United States*, prepared for distribution at the Thirteenth International Congress of Schools of Social Work, Washington, DC, August 31–September 3, 1966, Document #66-63-05, CSWE Master Files, 23-26.

[5] Katherine A. Kendall, "The Crucial Role of the Agency in Social Work Education," *Social Work Education Reporter* 12, no. 4 (August–September 1964): 1, 10, 11.

[6] Arnold Gurin, "Community Organization Curriculum Development Project: A Progress Report," *Social Work Education Reporter* 14, no. 4 (December 1965): 58.

[7] Arnold Gurin and Robert Perlman, *Community Organization and Planning* (New York: John Wiley & Sons, 1972).

[8] Charles F. Grosser, "The Legacy of the Federal Comprehensive Projects for Community Organization," *Social Work Education Reporter* 15, no. 4 (December 1967): 46.

[9] Elliot Studt, *Education for Social Workers in the Correctional Field, Vol. 5, Social Work Curriculum Study* (New York: Council on Social Work Education, 1959).

[10] Eileen L. Younghusband, "Report on a Survey of Social Work in the Field of Corrections," *Social Work Education Reporter* 8, no. 4 (August 1960): Supplement 1-24.

[11] Charles Prigmore, *Manpower and Training for Corrections* (New York: Council on Social Work Education, 1964).

[12] CSWE, "CSWE Corrections Project Columinates with Publication of Book," *Social Work Education Reporter* 14, no. 2 (June 1966): 9.

[13] Elliot Studt, *A Conceptual Approach to Teaching Materials: Illustrations from the Field of Corrections* (New York: Council on Social Work Education, 1985).

[14] CSWE, *Public Health Concepts in Social Work Education* (New York: Council on Social Work Education, in cooperation with the Public Health Service, Department of Health, Education, and Welfare, 1962).

[15] Werner W. Boehm, *Objectives of the Social Work Curriculum of the Future, Vol. 1, Social Work Curriculum Study* (New York: Council on Social Work Education, 1959).

[16] Ernest F. Witte, "Annual Report of the Executive Director," in *Education for Social Work*, Proceedings of the Seventh Annual Program Meeting, Philadelphia, 1959 (New York: Council on Social Work Education, 1959), 1.

[17] The Curriculum Committee records in the CSWE Master Files, document series #59 and 60-91, reveal the prodigious amount of work involved in the analysis and review of the Curriculum Study reports.

[18] Minutes of the Meeting of the Board of Directors, October 6-8, 1960, Document #60-16-9M, CSWE Master Files.

[19] See Chapter 12 for details on the publication and use of the guide in undergraduate education.

[20] CSWE Commission on Accreditation, Policy on Curriculum Experimentation and Innovation, Document #61-12-27R1, CSWE Master Files.

[21] Ibid, 2–3. See also CSWE, "A Guide for the Preparation of Proposals for Innovation and Experimentation," *Social Work Education Reporter* 12, no. 3 (June–July 1964): 4.

[22] Eleanor Roosevelt, "Threats in Our Time," in *Education for Social Work*, Proceedings of Second Annual Program Meeting, Washington, DC, 1954 (New York: Council on Social Work Education, 1954), 1.

CHAPTER TWELVE. EDUCATING DOWNWARD, SIDEWAYS, AND UPWARD

[1] Hollis-Taylor, 387.

[2] AASSW, *A Compilation of Three Reports on Pre-Professional Education* (New York: American Association of Schools of Social Work, 1946), 2. This document contains valuable information, in three reports, a foreword, and a summary, on the content of undergraduate education as later developed by undergraduate constituent members of the Council on Social Work Education. The quotation is taken from a copy in the personal possession of the author; an archival copy is numbered AASSW 683.

[3] Gordon J. Aldridge and Earl J. McGrath, *Liberal Education and Social Work* (New York: Teachers College Press for the Institute of Higher Education, 1965).

[4] Ibid, 86.

5 Sidney Berengarten, *Admissions Prediction and Student Performance in Social Work Education* (New York: Council on Social Work Education, 1964), 39–44.

[6] Charles B. Brink, "Expansion of Education and Training Facilities," in *Education for Social Work*, Proceedings of the Twelfth Annual Program Meeting, 1964 (New York: Council on Social Work Education, 1964), 132.

[7] Ernest F. Witte, "Implications and Next Steps for Undergraduate Education," in *Continuities in Undergraduate Social Welfare Education* (New York: Council on Social Work Education, 1969), 62.

[8] Mereb B. Mossman, "Social Welfare Content in Undergraduate Education," in *Education for Social Work*, Proceedings of the Eleventh Annual Program Meeting, Boston, 1963 (New York: Council on Social Work Education, 1963), 39.

[9] CSWE, *Social Welfare Content in Undergraduate Education: A Guide to Suggested Content, Learning Experiences, and Organization* (New York: Council on Social Work Education, 1962).

[10] CSWE, *Social Welfare as a Social Institution—Illustrative Syllabi for the Basic Course in Undergraduate Social Welfare* (New York: Council on Social Work Education, 1963).

[11] Irving B. Tebor and Patricia Pickford, *Social Work: A Helping Profession in Social Welfare* (New York: Council on Social Work Education, 1966).

[12] Mereb B. Mossman, *Field Experience in Undergraduate Programs in Social Welfare* (New York: Council on Social Work Education, 1967).

[13] John Romanyshyn, *Social Welfare: Charity to Justice* (New York: Random House, 1971).

[14] Sherman Merle, *Survey of Undergraduate Programs in Social Welfare, Faculty, Students, and Programs* (New York: Council on Social Work Education, 1967).

[15] For a detailed listing of the criteria, see "New CSWE Undergraduate Membership Requirements," *Social Work Education Reporter* 15, no. 4 (December 1967): 15.

[16] Minutes of the meeting of the Board of Directors, November 2–3, 1967, Document #68-812-1, CSWE Master Files, 14.

[17] For a detailed description of the requirements and the events leading up to their adoption, see "Undergraduate Programs in Social Welfare," *Social Work Education Reporter* 18, no. 3 (September–October 1970): 15–16.

[18] CSWE, *Undergraduate Programs in Social Work: Guidelines to Curriculum, Content, Field Instruction, and Organization* (New York: Council on Social Work Education, 1971).

[19] For a brief summary of later events, see Sheafor and Shank, 20–27.

[20] CSWE, "Report on the New Schools Project," *Social Work Education Reporter* 15, no. 3 (September 1967): 13.

[21] CSWE, "New Schools Advisory Committee Reviews Activities and Perspectives," *Social Work Education Reporter* 18, no. 2 (June 1970): 11.

[22] Deborah Miller, "Continuing Education Programs of Schools of Social Work, 1969—Report of a Survey," Document #69-441-5, CSWE Master Files.

[23] CSWE, "Principles Adopted by the Committee on Advanced Education in Social Work," in *Social Work Education in the Post Master's Program: Number 1—Guiding Principles* (New York: Council on Social Work Education, 1953), 9.

[24] Katherine A. Kendall, "Problem Areas in Advanced Education for Social Work," a restricted report for use by the Committee on Advanced Education, 1954, Document #4-14-7, CSWE Master Files. Much of the text that follows this note comes from this report.

[25] CSWE, *Statistics in Graduate Schools of Social Work in the United States: 1972* (New York: Council on Social Work Education, 1973): Table 200, "Summary Enrollment of Full-Time Students Enrolled, 1952-72" and Table 201, "Summary of Degrees Granted."

EPILOGUE. A PERSONAL STATEMENT

[1] Hattie Cal Maxted, "President's Report," Annual Business Meeting, NASSA, May 29, 1952, Maxted Papers, Box 1.

[2] Dwayne Huebner, "Editor's Preface," *A Reassessment of the Curriculum* (New York: Teachers College, Columbia University, 1964), v. Cited in CSWE, *Contemporary Education for Social Work in the United States* (New York: Council on Social Work Education, 1966).

Bibliography

Abbott, Edith. *Social Welfare and Professional Education*. Chicago: University of Chicago Press, 1931.

———. "Some Basic Principles." In *Education for Social Welfare*. Chicago: University of Chicago Press, 1931.

Aldridge, Gordon J., and Earl J. McGrath. *Liberal Education and Social Work*. New York: Teachers College Press for the Institute of Higher Education, 1965.

American Association of Schools of Social Work (AASSW). *A Compilation of Three Reports on Pre-Professional Education*. New York: American Association of Schools of Social Work, 1946.

———. *Education for the Public Social Services*, Report of the Study Committee. Chapel Hill: North Carolina University Press, 1942.

———. "Prerequisites for Admission to Schools of Social Work: A Report of the Curriculum Committee of the American Association of Schools of Social Work." *Social Service Review* 11, no. 3 (September 1937).

Bartlett, Harriet M. "The Significance of the Study of Social Work Education." In *The Social Welfare Forum 1951*, Proceedings of the 78th National Conference of Social Work. New York: Columbia University Press, 1951.

Berengarten, Sidney. *Admissions Prediction and Student Performance in Social Work Education*. New York: Council on Social Work Education, 1964.

Bernheim, Elinor K. "Social Work Education and the Board Member." *Social Work Journal* 34, no. 4 (October 1953).

Boehm, Werner W. "Education for Social Work." In *Encyclopedia of Social Work, Vol. 1, 1971*. New York: National Association of Social Workers, 1971.

———. *Objectives of the Social Work Curriculum of the Future, Vol. 1, Social Work Curriculum Study*. New York: Council on Social Work Education, 1959.

"Board Makes Program and Budget Decisions." *Social Work Education* 13, no. 4 (December 1965).

Bower, Chester L. "Educational Priorities—As Seen by a Community Chest and Council." In *Education for Social Work*, Proceedings of the Annual

Program Meeting, 1953. New York: Council on Social Work Education, 1953.

Brackett, Jeffrey R. "Instruction in Educational Institutions." In *Supervision and Education on Charity*. New York: Macmillan, 1903.

Branch, Mary Sydney. "Consultation on Preprofessional Social Work Education." *The Compass* 32, no. 2 (January 1946).

Brink, Charles B. "Expansion of Education and Training Facilities." In *Education for Social Work*, Proceedings of the Twelfth Annual Program Meeting. New York: Council on Social Work Education, 1964.

Browning, Grace. "The Responsibility of the Schools of Social Work for Training for the Public Welfare Services." In *Proceedings of the National Conference of Social Work*, Cleveland, Ohio, 1944. New York: Columbia University Press, 1944.

Council on Social Work Education (CSWE). "A Guide for the Preparation of Proposals for Innovation and Experimentation." *Social Work Education Reporter* 12, no. 3 (June–July 1964).

———. *Building the Social Work Curriculum*, Report of the National Curriculum Workshop. New York: Council on Social Work Education, 1961.

———. *Contemporary Education for Social Work in the United States*. New York: Council on Social Work Education, 1966.

———. "CSWE Corrections Project Columinates with Publication of Book." *Social Work Education Reporter* 14, no. 2 (June 1966).

———. "CSWE Income More than Doubled in Five-Year Period." *Social Work Education Reporter* 14, no. 4 (December 1966).

———. "Henry N. Sachs Provides Leadership." *Social Work Education Reporter* 9, no. 1 (February 1961).

———. *Manual of Accrediting Standards*. New York: Council on Social Work Education, 1953.

———. "New Schools Advisory Committee Reviews Activities and Perspectives." *Social Work Education Reporter* 18, no. 2 (June 1970).

———. "Principles Adopted by the Committee on Advanced Education in Social Work." In *Social Work Education in the Post Master's Program: Number 1— Guiding Principles*. New York: Council on Social Work Education, 1953.

———. *Public Health Concepts in Social Work Education*. New York: Council on Social Work Education, in cooperation with the Public Health Service, Department of Health, Education, and Welfare, 1962.

———. "Report on the New Schools Project." *Social Work Education Reporter* 15, no. 3 (September 1967).

———. *Social Welfare as a Social Institution—Illustrative Syllabi for the Basic Course in Undergraduate Social Welfare.* New York: Council on Social Work Education, 1963.

———. *Social Welfare Content in Undergraduate Education: A Guide to Suggested Content, Learning Experiences, and Organization.* New York: Council on Social Work Education, 1962.

———. *Social Work Education Reporter* 15, no. 1 (March 1967).

———. *Social Work Education Reporter* 15, no. 3 (September 1967).

———. *Social Work Education Reporter* 15, no. 4 (December 1967).

———. *Statistics in Graduate Schools of Social Work in the United States: 1972.* New York: Council on Social Work Education, 1973.

———. *Undergraduate Programs in Social Work: Guidelines to Curriculum, Content, Field Instruction, and Organization.* New York: Council on Social Work Education, 1971.

Council on Social Work Education (CSWE) Master Files. Alexandria, Va.

Council on Social Work Education (CSWE) Records. Social Welfare History Archives. University of Minnesota, Minneapolis, MN.

Coyle, Grace L. "Mutuality—The Foundation Principle of the Council on Social Work Education." In *Education for Social Work*, Proceedings of the Annual Program Meeting, 1960. New York: Council on Social Work Education, 1960.

Davis, Alice Taylor. *Making of a Teacher—50 Years in Social Work.* Silver Spring, MD: NASW, 1988.

Davis, Stanley P. "The Professional Influence in Social Work." *The Compass* 15, no. 9 (June 1934).

———. "Working Toward One Professional Standard—Public and Private." In *Proceedings of the National Conference of Social Work.* Chicago: University of Chicago Press, 1933.

"Defining 'Approved' Technical Social Work Courses." *The Compass* 15, no. 4 (December 1933).

de Schweinitz, Karl. "Social Work in the Public Services." *Social Work Journal* 29, no. 3 (July 1955).

Fairchild, Mildred. "Preprofessional Education for Social Work." *The Family (Journal of Social Case Work)* 26, no. 3 (May 1945).

Fenlason, Anne F. "The Present Status of Education for Social Work in Institutions of Higher Education in the United States." *American Sociological Review* 10, no. 5 (October 1945).

Flexner, Abraham. "Is Social Work a Profession?" In *Proceedings of National*

Conference of Charities and Corrections, 1915. Chicago: Hildmann Printing Company, 1915.

"Future Program and Structure of the Council on Social Work Education." *Social Work Education Reporter* 14, no. 2 (June 1966).

Govan, Elizabeth S. L. "The Canadian Study of Social Work Education—A Mutual Project of Schools and Agencies." In *Education for Social Work*, Annual Program Meeting, 1955. New York: Council on Social Work Education, 1955.

Grosser, Charles F. "The Legacy of the Federal Comprehensive Projects for Community Organization." *Social Work Education Reporter* 15, no. 4 (December 1967).

"A Guide for the Preparation of Proposals for Innovation and Experimentation." *Social Work Education Reporter* 12, no. 3 (June–July 1964).

Gurin, Arnold. "Community Organization Curriculum Development Project: A Progress Report." *Social Work Education Reporter* 14, no. 4 (December 1965).

Gurin, Arnold, and Robert Perlman. *Community Organization and Planning.* New York: John Wiley & Sons, 1972.

Hagerty, James E. *The Training of Social Workers.* New York: McGraw Hill Book Company, 1931.

Hamilton, Gordon. "Education for Social Work." In *Social Work Yearbook, 1945.* New York: Russell Sage Foundation, 1945.

Harper, Ernest B. "Accomplishments and Aims of the National Association of Schools of Social Administration," Annual Proceedings, NASSA. In *Social Welfare.* Fayetteville, AR: University of Arkansas, 1945.

———. "The Study of Social Work Education: Its Significance for the Undergraduate Educational Institutions." *Social Work Journal* 32, no. 4 (October 1951).

Hathway, Marian. "Twenty-Five Years of Professional Education for Social Work—and a Look Ahead." *The Compass* 27, no. 5 (June 1946).

Hollis, Ernest V., and Alice L. Taylor. *Social Work Education in the United States.* New York: Columbia University Press, 1951.

Huebner, Dwayne. "Editor's Preface." In *A Reassessment of the Curriculum.* New York: Teachers College, Columbia University, 1964.

Hunt, Maurice O. "Educational Priorities—As Seen by a Public Welfare Agency." In *Education for Social Work*, Proceedings of the Annual Program Meeting, 1953. New York: Council on Social Work Education, 1953.

Johnson, Arlien. "The Hollis-Taylor Report as Seen From the Viewpoint of a
Social Work Educator." *Social Work Journal* 33, no. 3 (July 1952).

Jorgensen, Albert N. "Current Developments in Accreditation." In *Education
for Social Work*, Proceedings of Second Annual Program Meeting, Washington, DC, 1954. New York: Council on Social Work Education, 1954.

Katz, Arthur J. "New Curriculum Policy Statement: Freedom and/or Regulation." *Journal of Education for Social Work* 7, no. 3 (Spring 1971).

Kendall, Katherine A. "The Curriculum of the Sixties in the Undergraduate and
Graduate Education—Introductory Remarks." In *Education for Social
Work*, Proceedings of the Eleventh Annual Program Meeting, 1963. New
York: Council on Social Work Education, 1963.

———. "The Crucial Role of the Agency in Social Work Education." *Social
Work Education Reporter* 12, no. 4 (August–September 1964).

———. "Curriculum Policy and Educational Practice." *Social Service Review*
29, no. 2 (June 1955).

———. "Education Got Social Work." In *Social Work Yearbook, 1954*, ed. R.
Kurtz. New York: American Association of Social Workers, 1954.

———. "Excellence Revisited—A Tribute to Ernest F. Witte." Paper presented
at the Council on Social Work Education, Annual Program Meeting,
1987.

———. "The Social Work Curriculum," [unpublished manuscript] 1964.

———. *Social Work Education: Its Origins in Europe*. Alexandria, VA: Council
on Social Work Education, 2000.

Kidneigh, John C. "Accrediting of Professional Schools of Social Work." In
Education for Social Work, Proceedings of Second Annual Program
Meeting, Washington, DC, 1954. New York: Council on Social Work
Education, 1954.

Kindelsperger, Walter. "Towards the Mature Profession—Current Responsibilities and Concerns of NASW." [unpublished manuscript] 1963.

Leighninger, Leslie. *Creating a New Profession: The Beginnings of Social Work
Education in the United States*. Alexandria, VA: Council on Social Work
Education, 2000.

Maxted, Hattie Cal. Papers. Social Welfare History Archives. University of
Minnesota, Minneapolis, MN.

McGrath, Earl J. "Education and Social Work." In *Social Welfare Forum, 1949*.
New York: Columbia University Press, 1950.

Merle, Sherman. *Survey of Undergraduate Programs in Social Welfare, Faculty,
Students, and Programs*. New York: Council on Social Work Education, 1967.

Mossman, Mereb B. *Field Experience in Undergraduate Programs in Social Welfare.* New York: Council on Social Work Education, 1967.

———. "Social Welfare Content in Undergraduate Education." In *Education for Social Work,* Proceedings of the Eleventh Annual Program Meeting, Boston, 1963. New York: Council on Social Work Education, 1963.

"New CSWE Undergraduate Membership Requirements." *Social Work Education Reporter* 15, no. 4 (December 1967).

News Note on the Five-Year Consultation Project. *Social Work Education Reporter* 7, no. 7 (October 1959).

"NFSSW Joins CSWE as Constituent Member." *Social Work Education Reporter* 17, no. 1 (March 1969).

Nyquist, Ewald B. "Regional Developments in Co-operative Evaluation and Accrediting Activity." In *Education for Social Work,* Proceedings of Second Annual Program Meeting, Washington, DC, 1954. New York: Council on Social Work Education, 1954.

———. "The Wing Wherewith We Fly to Heaven or the Real Function of Accreditation." In *Education for Social Work,* Proceedings of the Twelfth Annual Program Meeting, Toronto, Canada, 1964. New York: Council on Social Work Education, 1964.

Pins, Arnulf M. "Challenge and Change in Social Work Education." *Social Work Education Reporter* 17, no. 1 (March 1969), Special Supplement.

Pray, Kenneth L. M. "The Plan for a Study of Social Work Education." *The Compass,* 28, no. 3 (March 1947).

———. "Analysis and Appraisal of Changes in Social Work Practice Function during the War Years." *The Compass* 27, no. 3 (1946): 3.

Prigmore, Charles. *Manpower and Training for Corrections.* New York: Council on Social Work Education, 1964.

Regensburg, Jeanette. "Educational Priorities—As Seen by a Voluntary Agency." In *Education for Social Work,* Proceedings of the Annual Program Meeting, 1953. New York: Council on Social Work Education, 1953.

Romanyshyn, John. *Social Welfare: Charity to Justice.* New York: Random House, 1971.

Roosevelt, Eleanor. "Threats in Our Time." In *Education for Social Work,* Proceedings of Second Annual Program Meeting, Washington, DC, 1954. New York: Council on Social Work Education, 1954.

Sheafor, Bradford W., and Barbara W. Shank. *Undergraduate Social Work Education: A Survivor in a Changing Profession.* Austin: University of Texas–Austin, 1986.

Spencer, Sue. "Major Issues in Social Work Education." In *Proceedings of National Conference of Social Work,* San Francisco, 1947. New York: Columbia University Press, 1948.

―――. "Education for Social Work." In *Social Work Yearbook, 1949,* ed. R. Kurtz. New York: Russell Sage Foundation, 1949.

"Standards of Professional Education." *The Compass* 16, no. 1 (September 1934).

Studt, Elliot. *A Conceptual Approach to Teaching Materials: Illustrations from the Field of Corrections.* New York: Council on Social Work Education, 1985.

―――. *Education for Social Workers in the Correctional Field, Vol. 5, Social Work Curriculum Study.* New York: Council on Social Work Education, 1959.

Tebor, Irving B., and Patricia Pickford. *Social Work: A Helping Profession in Social Welfare.* New York: Council on Social Work Education, 1966.

"Undergraduate Programs in Social Welfare." *Social Work Education Reporter* 18, no. 3 (September–October 1970).

Urwick, E. J. "A School of Sociology." In *Methods of Social Advance.* Edited by C. S. Loch. London: Macmillan, 1894.

U.S. Department of Health, Education, and Welfare (HEW). *Closing the Gap in Social Work Manpower.* Report of the Departmental Task Force in Social Work Education and Manpower. Washington, DC: U.S. Government Printing Office, November 1965.

Walker, Sydnor J. *Social Work and the Training of Social Workers.* Chapel Hill: North Carolina Press, 1928.

Warner, Amos G. "Philanthropology in Educational Institutions." In *Sociology in Institutions of Learning,* ed. A. G. Warner, International Congress of Charities, Correction and Philanthropy, Chicago, 1893. Baltimore, MD: Johns Hopkins Press, 1894.

Wetzel, Harold E. "Educational Priorities as Seen by the Undergraduate Department." In *Education for Social Work,* Proceedings of the Annual Program Meeting, 1953. New York: Council on Social Work Education, 1953.

Witte, Ernest F. "Annual Report of the Executive Director." In *Education for Social Work,* Proceedings of the Seventh Annual Program Meeting, Philadelphia, 1959. New York: Council on Social Work Education, 1959.

―――. "CSWE 1961-1962." Report of the Executive Director. In *Education for Social Work,* Proceedings of the Annual Program Meeting, 1962. New York: Council on Social Work Education, 1962.

———. "Implications and Next Steps for Undergraduate Education." In *Continuities in Undergraduate Social Welfare Education.* New York: Council on Social Work Education, 1969.

Wright, Helen R. "O Pioneers." In *Education for Social Work*, Proceedings of Annual Program Meeting, 1953. New York: Council on Social Work Education, 1953.

———. "The Professional Curriculum of the Future." *Social Service Review* 25, no. 4 (December 1951).

———. "The Years Ahead." *Social Work Journal* 33, no. 2 (April 1952).

Youngdahl, Ben. "Shall We Face It?" In *Professional Education.* Five Papers Delivered at 29th Annual Meeting of the AASSW, Minneapolis, MN, January 21, 1948. New York: AASSW, 1948.

Younghusband, Eileen L. "Report on a Survey of Social Work in the Field of Corrections." *Social Work Education Reporter* 8, no. 4 (August 1960).